The Balance of Terror

The Balance of Terror

A Guide to the Arms Race

by Edgar M. Bottome

Beacon Press   Boston

To Howard and Roz Zinn

I appeal as a human being to human beings: remember your humanity, and forget the rest. If you can do so, the way lies open to a new paradise: if you cannot, nothing lies before you but universal death.

BERTRAND RUSSELL

Contents

Preface   *xiii*

I · EARLY YEARS OF THE ARMS RACE (1945–1952) · 1

Postwar Disarmament   *1*

The B-36 and the H-Bomb   *6*

Korea and National Security Paper #68   *14*

II · THE EISENHOWER YEARS: MASSIVE RETALIATION AND COLLECTIVE SECURITY (1953–1957) · 18

Massive Retaliation   *18*

Tactical Nuclear Weapons and NATO   *25*

Collective Security   *31*

The Bomber Gap   *35*

III · THE MISSILE GAP: A STUDY IN MYTH CREATION (1957–1961) · 39

Soviet Strategy, American Intelligence, and the Missile Gap   *41*

Budgetary, Partisan, and Military Effects of the Missile Gap   *58*

The Impact of the Missile Gap Abroad   *69*

IV · *THE KENNEDY ADMINISTRATION: FLEXIBLE RE-SPONSE AND SECOND-STRIKE COUNTERFORCE (1961–1963)* · 74

Flexible Response   77

Second-Strike Counterforce   80

Vietnam, Berlin, and Cuba   86

The Test Ban Treaty   96

NATO   97

V · *JOHNSON-NIXON: LOGIC FULFILLED (1963–1970)* · 111

American Strategic Superiority   116

Soviet Attitudes   123

ABM and MIRV   125

The Soviet Reaction   131

Nixon and Laird   133

Epilogue   147

Appendix A   153

Appendix B   169

Glossary   171

Notes   187

Index   209

Graph for page 162

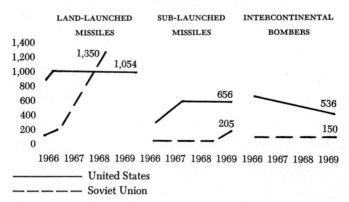

COMPARISON OF U.S. AND SOVIET STRATEGIC
NUCLEAR WEAPONS SYSTEMS[48]

OFFENSIVE

Graph for page 169

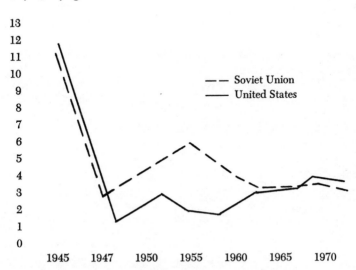

Total Manpower in the Armed Services of the United States
and the Soviet Union—1945–1970

Acknowledgments

I am indebted to a number of individuals who aided in the writing of this study, either directly or indirectly. A number of pioneering works done on the Cold War were invaluable and the author is indebted to men such as D. F. Fleming, David Horowitz, I. F. Stone, Gabriel Kolko, and Gar Alperovitz. In addition, invaluable technical expertise was gleaned from such defecting scientists as P. M. S. Blackett and Ralph Lapp. The author would like to thank Alan Cameron for his constructive criticisms of the manuscript. Valuable research assistance was provided by Terry Poe and John Barzman, with a special word of thanks due to the ability of Peter Irons. Miss Abigail Dunlop, Mrs. Valery Sorensen, and Mrs. Cynthia Stocking provided helpful editorial and typing assistance; and a particularly high debt of gratitude is due to Mrs. Ann Flink for her tireless efforts in editing the manuscript. I would also like to thank Fairleigh Dickinson University Press for permission to reprint parts of my book, *The Missile Gap: A Study of the Formulation of Military and Public Policy*. Finally, the author would like to thank Howard Zinn of Boston University and Arnold Tovell of Beacon Press for their unstinting encouragement and support of my efforts in writing this book.

Preface

This book is a critical study of the thermonuclear balance of terror and the accompanying arms race between the United States and the Soviet Union. At the outset, a brief word of explanation of the meaning of a balance of terror is needed. In its simplest form, a balance of terror exists when two nations can annihilate each other no matter which side attacks first. In this sense, in the thermonuclear age, power has become absolute in that mutual destruction is assured in the event of war between the superpowers. With over 50,000 megatons (equivalent to 50,000 million tons of TNT, or 15 tons of TNT for every man, woman, and child on this earth) stored and deliverable by diverse means, there is no way that either the United States or the Soviet Union can guarantee the security of the citizens of their countries. The simple fact of the balance of terror is that the modern nation-state is obsolete as a guarantor of the security of its people.

This incredible increase in the destructive power available to the modern nation-state has substantially changed the "rules of the game" in the conduct of a nation's foreign policy. For example, the move from the old balance of power concept to a balance of terror means that additional allies no longer immediately add to a nation's security. On the contrary, additional allies may actually decrease a nation's security. Also, whereas in the past the addition of a new weapons system would add to a nation's military position (e.g., a new gun or battleship), this no longer remains essentially true. The addition of a new missile system or bomber force may actually decrease the security of a nation faced with another thermonuclear power. (For example, the introduction of an antiballistic missile system may create a false sense of security among national leaders and lead to the kind of reckless act that could bring about a thermonuclear war.)

The exact date of the arrival of the balance of terror is open to some question, but it would appear that mutual annihilation was assured sometime around 1955–1956 with the introduction of the first Soviet long-range bombers capable of reaching the United States. Therefore, this study will be limited to an introductory chapter on the development of the arms race from 1945–1954. Then, a detailed analysis of American military strategy will be undertaken starting with the doctrine of massive retaliation and continuing to 1970.

A nation's military policy is only *one* of the major instruments used in the conduct of its foreign policy. Nonetheless, to understand the role of military strategy the total goals of the nation's foreign policy must be understood. Within this context, this writer would contend *that the basic goal of American foreign policy following World War II has been and remains the maintenance of the status quo throughout the noncommunist world.*

After World War II the economic power of the United States was greatly enhanced, whereas the economies of the remainder of the industrial world were seriously damaged. Militarily the United States emerged as sole possessor of the atomic bomb and the means to deliver it. American power had increased both absolutely and relatively in relation to the other world powers.

Not only was the American position in the world considered advantageous in 1945, but it was believed that this superiority would increase over the years rather than decrease. In order to assure this, the United States proceeded to develop a foreign military policy based on the fundamental premise that the maintenance of this status quo and the existing forms of dependent governments was essential for American economic and military needs. The perceived military requirements to attempt implementation of this strategy during the first twenty-five years of the Cold War can be divided into two rather distinct periods.

The first period (1945–1961) was characterized by the accumulation of allies into collective security pacts and the almost exclusive reliance on the American superiority in nuclear weapons and the means to deliver these weapons as the military instrument of diplomacy. This policy originated with Harry Truman's "atomic diplomacy" and culminated with John Foster Dulles' unsuccessful attempt to make massive retaliation a viable instrument of American diplomatic relations.

The second period, roughly 1961 to the present, has been based on the Kennedy-McNamara strategy of a decreased reliance on nuclear forces to maintain the status quo (except in Soviet-American relations this policy had failed) and a concomitant increase in the American ability to meet challenges to existing governments with more varied forms of military power. This strategy has been defined by the term "flexible response" doctrine, and its application can be found in such obvious efforts as Vietnam, the Dominican Republic (1965), and Cuba (Bay of Pigs invasion); and on a less obvious level, in such areas as Bolivia (Special Forces), Greece (arms shipments), or Laos (Central Intelligence Agency operations). This policy was pursued because the Kennedy administration recognized that the atomic bomb could not stop the potent indigenous forces represented by Castro in Cuba, Kassem in Iraq, or Ho Chi Minh in Vietnam. More military flexibility had to be added to the American arsenal if the status quo in the noncommunist world was to be maintained. And, of course, this is exactly what was done starting in 1961.*

It is my contention that with minor exceptions, the United States has led in the development of military technology and weapons production throughout the Cold War. This constant superiority in thermonuclear weapons and the means to deliver them has meant that throughout the postwar era only the United States has had the potential to initiate a surprise attack on its opponent. At no time during the past twenty-five years has the

---

* It should be indicated here that the United States has been willing to tolerate minor changes and "token reform" in certain areas that were threatened with more drastic upheavals so long as there appeared to be no challenge to basic American interests. When these interests were challenged a form of military power was used, e.g., Cuba and the Bay of Pigs or the Dominican Republic. Only when there appeared to be *no* chance of success by military intervention or when forces were not available did the United States fail to intervene, e.g., China.

United States had less than a 2–1 advantage in nuclear delivery vehicles over the Soviet Union, and most of the time it has been better than a 4–1 advantage. The Soviet Union has been placed in a position where all it could do was react to American initiatives in bomber or missile building programs. This American superiority, along with the highly ambitious nature of American foreign policy, has placed the United States in a position of being fundamentally responsible for every major escalation of the arms race.

In order to justify spending over $1,000 billion on defense, the forces that govern the United States have been constantly in the business of myth creation in the field of national security. This process began with the myth of American disarmament following World War II and continues to this day with the ABM-MIRV debate. It has been so successful that the American people have paid the bill for the defense establishment with only rare challenges. The magnitude of the success of this policy can only be truly appreciated when it is realized that at no time since World War II has the security of the United States been threatened by Soviet preparation for a surprise thermonuclear attack. Yet even into the 1970s the American people are being cajoled, manipulated, and frightened into believing that either the Soviet Union or China (or both) are preparing such an attack. The process continues after twenty-five years of success.

As the arms race continues into the 1970s it is the subject of increasing public interest. During 1970, Melvin Laird, Secretary of Defense, claimed that the Soviet Union was preparing for a surprise attack on the United States and that:

> The Soviets are continuing the rapid deployment of major strategic offensive weapons systems at a rate that could by the mid-1970s, place us in a second-rate strategic position with regard to the future security of the Free World.[*]

[*] U.S., Congress, Senate, *Authorization for Military Procurement, Research and Development, Fiscal Year 1971 and Reserve Strength*, 91st Cong., 2d sess., February 20, 1970, p. 8.

Secretary Laird was careful not to remind the American people of such earlier defense myths as the "bomber gap," the "missile gap," or Mr. Nixon's nonexistent "security gap" in 1968. Senator Edward Kennedy (Dem.-Mass.) pointed out that Secretary Laird had also conveniently ignored the fact that the United States had a "commanding lead" in nuclear armed submarines and bombers, and that the United States had begun to deploy MIRV weapons which the Soviet Union may not even have tested.*

But, as in the past, the period of maximum danger to the United States was claimed to be some time in the future. In the face of a 2–1 warhead delivery advantage over the Soviet Union in 1970, American leadership could not convince the American people of any imminent threat of surprise attack on the United States, but it was possible to claim maximum danger for 1974 when faced with alleged Soviet SS-9 missiles (with MIRV) or in 1975 when faced with 50 Chinese ICBMs. The fact that it would make no more sense for the Russians or Chinese to commit national suicide in the mid-1970s than it did in 1970 was also ignored.

This tendency to place the "period of maximum danger" at some time in the future has been a consistent characteristic of American defense planning throughout the Cold War. But what I hope to show is that in all instances of predicted Soviet superiority (such as the missile gap or bomber gap), the Soviet Union did not perform in the manner anticipated by the leaders of the United States. These leaders would not admit to themselves that the Soviet Union was not preparing for a surprise attack on the United States. Nor would they admit that the foreign policy of the Soviet Union was becoming progressively more conservative, to a point where it rivaled the conservatism

* *The Boston Globe*, July 31, 1970, news article by Richard H. Stuart. Senator Kennedy made these remarks on the Senate floor to refute the Nixon administration's demand for an expansion of the ABM system. It is worth noting that in 1969 Senator Kennedy did not vote for the Smith Amendment to cut all funds from the ABM system, but in 1970 he did vote for the Hughes Amendment that attempted to accomplish the same task.

of American foreign policy. Likewise, throughout the Cold War, the Soviet Union has been unable or unwilling to engage in the massive expenditures that would have been required in order to match the American military spending dollar for dollar. The failure of the United States to recognize the true nature of Soviet defense policy and military doctrine has been a costly one—both in terms of human lives and in dollars.

I would think that the past errors and faulty military estimates emanating from the United States government on Soviet programs and attitudes would lead many Americans to challenge the new allocations being made in 1970, but apparently this is not the case. Likewise, a government that has been so consistently incorrect in its assessment of the arms race might also be suspect in its military judgment on such situations as Vietnam, but this does not appear to be the case either.

Although it is a risky business, my purpose in writing this book is to explore the development and solidification of the balance of terror and attempt to assess the degree of responsibility of the individuals and the nations that led to our present state. This task is immensely complicated, and handicapped by the fact that much of the crucial documentation on military matters remains classified in Washington and Moscow. In addition, government officials in both the United States and the Soviet Union have a demonstrable capacity for lying when they feel national security is at stake. Yet, in spite of these handicaps, an incredible amount of "secret" information is made available to the determined researcher in the field of national security affairs.

The most valuable sources in this field are the numerous congressional hearings and investigations into American defense policy. In addition, memoirs and papers are invaluable sources of information and attitudes of those involved in the formulation of American military strategy.

Yet even with the aid of these sources, the study of military policy still resembles a large and complicated puzzle that must be put together piece by piece as information becomes available. This additional information comes from various segments of the mass media in the United States. The value and credibility of this nonofficial data is due to the following factors:

(1) The extreme interservice rivalry which leads a military service to "leak" to friendly news sources information favorable to its individual position.

(2) Certain representatives of the friendly journalist corps are actually used as unofficial leaks by the Pentagon as a whole.

(3) Political pressures and partisanship often lead to the official release of classified information to defend a political party or individual.

(4) Finally, solid research by concerned scholars and journalists often turns up a large amount of accurate information on a given weapons systems or military strategy.

It is my hope that this book will raise certain fundamental questions about United States defense policy that have been too long dormant. Dut to the nature of the arms race—its technology, its incredible jargon, and its secrecy—many questions can only be imperfectly answered. Yet it seems essential that the process of myth creation be analyzed and understood in order to have even the remotest chance of preventing an exact repetition of the first twenty-five years of the arms race in the years to come. As of 1970, new myths were being created and the United States was well on its way toward a repetition of its mistaken actions and policies of past years of the Cold War.

EMB

Boston, Mass.
September 1970

The Balance of Terror

I

Early Years of the Arms Race

(1945–1952)

The balance of terror between the United States and the Soviet
Union did not become a reality until 1955–1956 when the Soviet
Union developed its first operational intercontinental bomber
capable of reaching the United States. Once the Soviet Union
could deliver hydrogen weapons on the United States, the balance of terror between the two superpowers became the domi-
nant, underlying military-political factor in the conduct of great
power diplomacy. However, from 1945 to 1949 the United States
possessed a monopoly on nuclear weapons and then from 1949
to 1955 a monopoly on the means to deliver these weapons.
During this decade of American absolute superiority, the events
surrounding the arms race made the reality of the balance of
terror in the mid-1950's inevitable. Therefore, in order to understand the balance of terror and its origins, it is essential to sketch
briefly these early years of the arms race between the United
States and the Soviet Union.[1] This discussion will center around
three basic questions: 1) the nature of American and Soviet
disarmament following World War II; 2) the B-36 debate and
the decision to build the hydrogen bomb; and 3) National
Security Council Paper #68 and the Korean War.

POSTWAR DISARMAMENT?

There have been numerous estimates on the extent of Soviet and
American reductions of manpower immediately following World

1

War II; the fact that both drastically reduced their military manpower is not challenged, although many Americans still believe that the United States disarmed after World War II, while the Soviet Union maintained large numbers of men under arms in preparation for future aggression. In the atomic age the number of men under arms is only one indication of a nation's military strength, but it is an important one. Both P. M. S. Blackett and Raymond Garthoff have accepted the following figures: from 1945 to 1948 the Soviet Union reduced its military manpower 75 percent from 11,365,000 to 2,874,000; while the United States reduced its military manpower 87 percent from almost 12,000,000 to 1,500,000.[2] (See Appendix B.)

But manpower figures do not tell the entire story. At the end of the war, the Soviet Union had secured its borders from the threat of foreign invasion. In any calculation of national security, however, the Soviet Union still remained extremely vulnerable to attack due to the new developments in heavy long-range bombers and the existence of atomic weapons. In 1945 only the B-29 heavy bomber could carry the cumbersome early A-bombs, weighing about five tons, and only the United States had the B-29 bomber* *and* the air bases near enough to Soviet territory to deliver these weapons.[3]

At the end of the war the United States not only had well over 1,000 B-29 bombers, but also had foreign airfields well within range of *all* of the major cities of the Soviet Union. The United States had major airfields in Greenland, Iceland, Okinawa, Japan, and Alaska. In addition to these bases, the United States began to acquire additional airfields on the perimeter of the Soviet Union. Listed below are the countries that the United States approached for airbase leases and the dates of the initial discussions:

Spain—1945
Saudi Arabia—1945
Tunisia—1946

---

* The B-29 had a range of approximately 2,000 miles. That is, it had the capability to strike a target 1,000 miles from its base and return, or make a 2,000 mile one-way trip.

French Morocco—1951
Turkey—1946

The United States eventually built strategic military bases in all of these countries.[4]

But the existence of a large number of bombers and foreign bases near the Soviet Union obviously had to be accompanied by the atomic weapons to be delivered by this bomber force. Although the exact rate of American production of atomic bombs following the war is a well-guarded secret, there is substantial evidence to indicate that the United States proceeded with all possible speed to build a large atomic arsenal during the postwar period. At the end of the war Secretary of State Byrnes declared, ". . . we should continue the Manhattan Project [the secret project to build the atomic bomb] with full force."[5] The fact that this work continued at a rapid rate after the war was later confirmed at the Oppenheimer Hearings.[6] By 1949 the United States had between 500 and 800 B-29s stationed at overseas bases within range of the Soviet Union,[7] and estimates at that time placed the atomic bomb arsenal in the hundreds.[8]

On the other hand, the United States did not develop a large, effective ground force capable of what was to become known as a limited conventional war. The decision had been made by the United States government to rely on atomic weapons as the major military instrument of diplomacy. It was felt that this form of "atomic diplomacy" was the most effective way to protect American interests and contain what U.S. leaders perceived as an aggressive, hostile Soviet Union.

The existence of the growing American nuclear strength placed the Soviet Union in an extremely vulnerable position. Although the Soviet Union exploded its first atomic bomb in 1949, this still did not resolve the fundamental problems surrounding the security of Soviet territory. By 1947, the Soviet Union was beginning production of the Tupylov-4 (the TU-4, nicknamed "BULL" by the United States). This aircraft was a copy of the American B-29 and could not deliver atomic weapons on the United States without either foreign bases close to the United States or in-flight refueling. The Soviet Union had no such bases and did not develop in-flight refueling until 1957, or possibly not until as late as 1959.*

In its simplest terms, this means that the Soviet Union had no direct means of deterring an American atomic attack on its territory from 1945 to 1955. The only means available to the Soviet Union to prevent such an attack was to raise the strength of the Red Army to a level where it could not possibly be challenged on the Eurasian land mass. This is exactly what the leaders of the Soviet Union proceeded to do. The number of men under arms in the Soviet Union increased from approximately 2.8 million in 1948 to over 5.7 million by 1955 (See Appendix B.)† With this large number of fighting men under arms, the leaders of the Soviet Union could seriously threaten the security of Western Europe, even if attacked first by the United States.

By 1949 the first major stage of the arms race was completed. The United States increasingly relied on its growing monopoly in the means of delivering atomic weapons. On the other hand, the vulnerability of the Soviet Union to American air power led the Soviet Union to increase the size of the Red Army to a point where it could march across Europe in the event of an American attack on Soviet territory. In a very real sense, Western Europe had become a Soviet hostage in order to deter an American

---

* In-flight refueling is a method whereby an aircraft in the air can be refueled by a tanker aircraft and thus substantially increase its range. Evidence of the Soviet capacity for in-flight refueling is difficult to find. This information is extremely important in any determination of Soviet strategy and intentions during the period prior to the development of an intercontinental bomber force in 1955. After 1955, the importance of a Soviet in-flight refueling capability decreased due to the introduction of the intercontinental bomber, the Bison. The fact remains that from 1945 to somewhere around 1954–1955 the Soviet Union was incapable of delivering atomic weapons on the territory of the continental United States (see: H. S. Dinerstein, *War and the Soviet Union,* rev. ed., New York: Frederick Praeger, 1962, p. 230; and *The New York Times,* news article by Hanson Baldwin, March 25, 1959.

† It is interesting to note that once the Russians had an operational intercontinental bomber in 1955, Soviet force levels began to go down and were down to 3.6 million men under arms by 1960.

attack on Soviet territory until the Soviet Union could develop its own atomic arsenal and delivery system.

The United States did not disarm following World War II, but simply shifted its emphasis from a large army and navy to belief in the efficacy of the air force and the atomic bomb as the major military instruments of American foreign policy. In the case of the Soviet Union, this nation responded in the only manner possible in face of the American atomic monopoly; it increased the size of the Red Army.

In view of this American strategic superiority over the Soviet Union, what is most surprising about the development of American postwar attitudes and military policy was the lack of sustained, energetic debate on the assumptions made by American leadership and the policies these assumptions were producing. Some Americans raised their voices in protest, but in reality there was never a sustained public debate. The major voice of dissent during this early period of the cold war was Secretary of Commerce Henry Wallace: he lost his job for his efforts. Although the Wallace movement of later years was disowned by Wallace himself, the fundamental questions raised as early as 1946 by Mr. Wallace deserve careful consideration. If more Americans had sincerely asked these questions, there is a chance that the Cold War and the arms race might have both taken a very different course. Mr. Wallace asked:

How do American actions since V-J day appear to other nations? I mean by action concrete things like $13,000,000,000 for the War and Navy Departments, the Bikini tests of the atomic bomb and continued production of bombs, the plan to arm Latin America with our weapons, production of B-29s and planned production of B-36s, and the effort to secure air bases spread over half the globe from which the other half of the globe can be bombed. I cannot but feel that these actions must make us look to the rest of the world as if we were only paying lip service to peace at the conference table.

These facts make it appear either 1) that we are preparing ourselves to win the war which we regard as inevitable or 2) that we are trying to build up a predominance of force to intimidate the rest of mankind. How would it look to us if Russia had the atomic bomb and we did not, if Russia had 10,000 mile bombers and air bases within 1,000 miles of our coastline and we did not.[9]

However, these questions were evidently not considered debatable, for on September 20, 1946, Secretary Wallace was dismissed from the Truman Cabinet.

THE B-36 AND THE H-BOMB

When the debate over American military policy finally emerged publicly in the United States, it did not pertain to the nature of the challenge (this was accepted) as being an aggressive, hostile Soviet Union, but to the type of weapons systems that America needed to meet the challenge. That is, whether to build bombers or aircraft carriers, whether to develop the H-bomb or stay with the less powerful fission A-bomb, and whether to use Universal Military Training (UMT) or rely on a more limited draft system to meet the military manpower needs of the future. All three of the questions had been discussed as early as 1945, but it was in 1949—marked by the testing of the first Soviet atomic bomb, the Berlin blockade, and the victory of Mao's forces in China—that the debate emerged into a full-scale public discussion.

The major manifestations of this debate surrounded the question of whether or not to build the B-36 intercontinental bomber. The importance of this controversy was not the actual decision to build the B-36 because it became obsolete shortly after it went into production, but that it laid the foundation and established the methods and procedures that were to be followed in future debates on any given weapons system. Therefore, a rather detailed analysis of the B-36 controversy is an essential first step in order to understand the domestic forces that produced the arms race.

The debate offered an almost classical split of the military forces involved in American defense policy formulation. It is an excellent case study of the early stages of interservice rivalry and the conflict over strategic doctrines of American military policy that have characterized the entire postwar period. The

B-36 controversy centered on two questions: the nature and length of a future war; and the weapons systems needed to fight this war. The Army, Navy, and the Air Force along with their industrial, journalistic, and congressional friends lined up on opposite sides and the debate was on.

During this early controversy, a standard procedure was established for future conflicts among the military services for budgetary allocations. Under this procedure, each branch, along with its various industrial and political allies, would devise a military strategy to increase its appropriations. Then, each group would come before Congress and the nation and claim that its particular strategy and given weapons system had to be implemented or dire consequences for American national security would result. This recurrent effort literally to terrorize Congress and the American people continues to this day as each of the services raises the specter of an enemy prepared or preparing to fight its kind of war.*

The B-36 was strictly an Air Force weapon and, of course, the Air Force wanted it produced and deployed immediately in large numbers. At this time (1949) and to the present, the United States Air Force has claimed that any major war with the Soviet Union would be a relatively short one and that air power would be the decisive weapons system in this type of conflict.† The Air Force in 1949 was still enthralled with Douhet's theory of air power and its efficacy in winning wars by mass bombing.[10] This early strategy was based on an exag-

---

* Perhaps the best early example of this approach occurred in the immediate postwar period. In 1946, a specially equipped American B-29 had proven that trans-Arctic flights were, in fact, possible. At this time the UMT debate was taking place and advocates of this program and a large ground army immediately invoked the specter of an enemy using this route to drop "hordes of airborne troops" on the United States. The advocates of a large army further claimed that these airborne troops could not be overcome by a small army and therefore the size of the existing army should be increased. (*The New York Times*, October 7, 1946.) Needless to say, the fear of "hordes of airborne troops" descending on the United States was not the most realistic assessment of the situation in 1946.

† In 1949, the Air Force was probably wrong in its assessment. Today there is not much question that after a massive thermonuclear exchange the war

gerated belief in the destructive power of these early atomic weapons which it was thought would lead to a rapid Soviet surrender. Likewise, in the late 1940s, the Air Force believed atomic weapons were too scarce to be used on Soviet military forces and therefore they would have to be used on Russian cities. The result was that the Air Force saw the B-36 as a means of delivering atomic weapons on Soviet cities and not as a means of attacking Soviet military targets.

But if the Air Force was to get its B-36, the United States Navy was afraid that not only would it be denied its new "super carrier" but also that its actual aircraft carrier force would be reduced from fourteen to six.[11] The major spokesman for the Navy position was Admiral Arthur W. Radford; he argued against the Air Force "counter-city doctrine" on the following grounds:

(1) The next war would not be won quickly by atomic weapons.

(2) The morality of attacking Soviet cities was highly dubious.

(3) It was contended that all nations would lose the peace.

(4) And, finally, that the military need facing the United States was not for a means to attack Soviet cities, but for the capability to attack the enemy's atomic installations and the airfields of the Soviet's long-range bombers.[12] (They had none in 1949.)

It was further agreed that there was a definite need to meet limited aggression with ground forces, and the Army continued to push for UMT.[13]

The major spokesman for the Air Force point of view was the Secretary of the Air Force, Stuart Symington. Secretary Symington accused the Navy of grossly underestimating the potential air power. He continued by stating that it was not

---

would be over, and so probably would human life on this planet. This Air Force belief in the efficacy of the use of air power continued to re-appear throughout the arms race. The belief that air power could win the war in Vietnam is only the most recent example of this attitude.

true that the Air Force favors "mass atomic bombing of civilians." Yet Secretary Symington proceeded to advocate just that
when he stated that if the country's safety was at stake:

> I can't see the difference between trying to stop a man at a
> lathe building a bomber to attack us and trying to stop a soldier.[14]

No matter what the major spokesmen at the top were saying,
the fact remains that the B-36 was designed primarily to attack
cities. First, the B-36 was not designed to attack specific objects,
but "was primarily for area attacks on cities" due to its limited
accuracy at an altitude of 40,000 feet, from which it would be
forced to bomb due to Soviet air defense.[15] Second, in 1949
there was no Soviet delivery system for the B-36 to strike. The
Soviet Union did not have a delivery system capable of reaching
the United States and was not to have one until 1955. By that
time the increasing obsolescence of the B-36 led to its replacement by the B-47 medium-range bomber and eventually by
the B-52.*

In 1949, the Navy argued in humanitarian terms that were
rare in later years. One Navy admiral characterized strategic
bombing of the type advocated by the Air Force as "ruthless
and barbaric" and went on to say that the Air Force strategy
would mean the "random slaughter of men, women and children
in the enemy country."†

---

* The B-47 was built in large quantities by the United States (over 1,200
bombers). It had a range of 3,600 miles and could carry a nine-ton bomb
load. (Dinerstein, *War and the Soviet Union*, p. 23.) It was stationed primarily at American overseas bases in Greenland, Iceland, Britain, North
Africa, Saudi Arabia, the Philippines, Formosa, Okinawa, and Japan.
(Blackett, *Atomic Weapons*, pp. 51–56.) The B-47 had an in-flight refueling capacity. The B-52 was built in smaller quantities (around 500 were
operational at any given time) and could reach the Soviet Union from
United States SAC bases. The reader should keep in mind that the Soviet
Union has never had more than 300 operational bombers capable of reaching the United States. (See Appendix A.)

† *The New York Times*, quoting Admiral Ralph Ofstie, October 12, 1949.
It is interesting to note that this Navy argument against city strike weapons
never came from advocates of the Regulus and later the Polaris systems in
the late 1950s and early 1960s. These earlier submarine missile systems

Obviously the B-36 debate went far beyond humanitarian concerns. It was not only a debate over American strategic doctrine and the budget, for even at this early stage the Navy felt that it could conceivably be fighting for its very existence. After the Air Force was separated from the United States Army, a number of Navy men began to fear that the role of the Navy would be drastically reduced and permanently relegated to an inferior position behind the Army and the Air Force. Added to the Navy's suspicions was the fact that at this time a successful attempt was being made to reduce the air arm of the Navy, and plans for a large aircraft carrier had recently been scuttled.[16] Along with attacking the B-36 the Navy constantly called for increased appropriations for naval requirements throughout the world in order to avoid a long "siege war."[17]

The final results of the B-36 debate had a lasting impact on American military strategy. First, the B-36 was approved, put into mass production, and became the major SAC bomber until the B-47 and the B-52 came along. American willingness to mass produce this weapon and keep its navy and army at reduced levels indicated that the United States would continue to rely on atomic and then thermonuclear weapons to deter war and to gain its diplomatic objectives (the decision to build the H-bomb had been made at the same time as the B-36 decision had been made—see below). Second, the American decision to build the B-36 was a commitment on the part of the United States to a doctrine of massive retaliation or, more

---

were fairly inaccurate when compared to bombers or fixed-position ICBMs. Later, Polaris generations (A-2 and A-3) did achieve a degree of accuracy that could qualify this system for a counterforce strike. Also, the Navy's humane concern of 1949 did not seem to have been present in 1947 when the Navy Department ruled out long-range bombers as "insufficiently reliable," and in turn called for the delivery of atomic weapons from floating bases 500 miles off of the enemy's shore (presumably an aircraft carrier) or by short range missiles of the V-2 types. (*The New York Times,* April 10, 1947.) This Navy reaction was triggered by an earlier War Department study which concluded that the strategic bomber was the "single most important element of our military capabilities." (*The New York Times,* April 19, 1947.)

aptly, of threatening the Soviet Union with a massive city strike if war came. The United States was not capable of any other type of immediate response to a major Soviet challenge. American air power was to counterbalance the Red Army. Third, the initial fight over American strategic doctrine was won by the Air Force, and this pattern of Air Force preponderance continued until the Kennedy years. And, finally, the B-36 debate was the last major debate in which any of the military services would feel that its very existence or over-all importance was challenged. From this point on, debates would center increasingly, not on whether a weapons system should be built, but which of the military services should build any given system. Each of the military services felt confident that a certain percentage of the defense appropriation "belonged" to a given branch even if it did not get prime responsibility for a system.

The decision to produce the B-36 was not the only major American strategic decision in 1949. Under the stimulus of the rather surprising Soviet test of an A-bomb in August of that year, the United States had evidently decided by November 1949 to proceed with the development of the hydrogen bomb.[18]

It should be emphasized that the decision to build the H-bomb was an important one for all mankind as well as a revolutionary development for the future of delivery vehicle systems. The atomic bomb had proved its destructiveness; however, weapons in the kiloton range were relatively low in explosive and radiation yield when compared to the megaton range of thermonuclear weapons.* Atomic fission weapons did not appear to threaten the existence of mankind; thermonuclear fusion weapons did.

A single megaton warhead (the one used on the American Minuteman II) can cause severe blast damage to an area of 60 square miles and do moderate damage up to 110 square miles. Or, put another way, moderate damage would be suffered over an area with a radius of approximately 6 miles.[19] A ten

---

* One kiloton is the explosive equivalent of 1,000 tons of TNT, whereas one megaton is the equivalent of 1,000,000 tons of TNT.

megaton explosion (an American B-52 carries four of these) can destroy an area of roughly 400 square miles and cause serious damage within a radius of about 12 miles.[20] In other words, a ten megaton bomb exploded over London (the largest land area of the world's cities) would destroy most of London, or 3 one megaton explosions spread over the city of Boston would effectively destroy that city.

The exact effects of fall-out in the event of an all-out thermo-nuclear exchange of the 50,000 odd megatons possessed by the United States and the Soviet Union are not fully known. But there is a real possibility that the fall-out from these explosions would destroy human life; if it did not completely destroy it, it could very drastically alter the entire genetic make-up of what we now call human beings. Any attempted explanation of the possible effects of thermonuclear war is truly impossible. The destruction and horror not only stagger the imagination but go completely beyond it.[21]

Aside from the unbelievable power unleashed by the intro-duction of hydrogen weapons and the fact that they laid the foundation for a balance of terror which had not existed before, thermonuclear weapons also had a major impact on the stra-tegic thinking of American policy makers. The future strategies to be adopted by the United States relied directly upon the existence of these terror weapons and their threatened use (e.g., massive retaliation or second-strike counterforce).

Before long, each of the military services (and their allies) had developed strategies and weapons systems designed to maximize their role in the thermonuclear age. For the Air Force, hydrogen weapons strengthened their belief in the effi-cacy of the bomber that could now carry the equivalent of 40,000,000 tons of TNT. Likewise, thermonuclear weapons even-tually made the intercontinental ballistic missile system (ICBM) a "viable, economic" possibility for future Air Force systems. For the Navy, the argument was strengthened for the heavy aircraft carriers and, more important, the Navy began develop-ment of what was to be a number of generations of submarine-launched thermonuclear missiles—Regulus, Polaris, Poseidon. The Army also got a number of intermediate-range ballistic missiles—Redstone, Jupiter, "the atomic cannon," and, more important, it was assigned the air defense role which led to the antiballistic missile systems—Nike X, Sentinel, Safeguard. The military services believed they could not fail in devising a strategic doctrine to apply thermonuclear power in the conduct of the missions assigned to them. They did not fail.

The fact remains that the introduction of thermonuclear weapons assured the reality of a balance of terror between two powers if they would admit that it existed. The problem has been that the United States government has continually tried to convince the American people that some additional weapons system would add to a security that the government has not been able to guarantee since 1955 nor will be able to guarantee in the future (the B-1, MIRV, and Safeguard notwithstanding).

By the end of 1949 and on the eve of the Korean War, not only had the United States decided to build the B-36 bomber and the hydrogen bomb, but this country was also in the final stages of "enormous growth" of the Strategic Air Command (SAC), which had engaged in a crash program to reach maximum strength by January 1949. A peak in American atomic weapons production had also been announced by the Atomic Energy Commission on January 21, 1949. And in February of that year, the United States announced that an American B-50A bomber had flown around the world nonstop, demonstrating not only American advances in prop-jet aircraft, but also a substantial in-flight refueling capability.[22]

It should be noted that the decision on the B-36 and the H-bomb can claim to have been a direct result of the Soviet A-bomb test in August 1949, but under no circumstances can this reason be used for the strengthening of SAC or the increased production of atomic weapons earlier in the year.

By 1949 and early 1950, the United States represented a formidably armed nation for strategic, atomic warfare with the Soviet Union. There appears to be no question that the United States could have inflicted an extremely severe blow on the Soviet Union. If the United States had attacked with over 500 atomic weapons, it could have done more damage in twelve hours than that done by the Nazis in four years of war. It also appears that by this time the American people approved of this massive armaments effort, and specifically approved of the preponderant effort being given to the Air Force over the other two services.[23]

KOREA AND NATIONAL SECURITY PAPER #68

The commonly accepted belief that the United States disarmed following World War II was one more in a rather long list of postwar myths that surrounded American military policy. Another of these myths is the continued belief that the United States decided to increase its arms expenditures drastically in response to the war in Korea and that it was this conflict which led to the tremendous increase in the military budget for 1951. Yet, a close scrutiny of the facts surrounding this budget increase indicates that the *decision* to increase the military budget threefold was made almost four months *before* the Korean War started.

Prior to the fiscal 1951 military budget, American military spending had ranged from $11 to $14 billion a year (roughly 10 percent of the Gross National Product, a figure that has remained remarkably constant over the years). A combination of conservative economic forces in the United States and a degree of confidence in American military security had led to the belief that this amount of spending was the minimum necessary for the security of the United States.

The decision to build the H-bomb and the B-36 were, in part, responses to perceived challenges, but even with the decision to build these two weapons systems, the United States still had not defined its over-all military doctrine. The attempt to do so was National Security Council Paper #68 (NSC #68).

This document was drawn up in February 1950 and was accepted by President Truman in April 1950. It was considered "the first comprehensive statement of national strategy."[24] NSC #68 represented a major assessment of American defense policy. It is interesting that the original authors of the ideas of NSC #68 were civilians from the State Department and not military from the Pentagon. And, although NSC #68 was later accepted by the military, it was the civilian sector that came to the conclusion that the American military response to the Soviet challenge was not adequate. It was believed that the Western powers lacked a conventional capability in Europe and were critically weak in this area. Furthermore, it was estimated that by 1954 "the Soviet Union would have the nuclear *capability* [emphasis added] to launch a devastating attack on the United States."[25] The paper rejected the choices of doing nothing, launching a preventive war, or withdrawing to "fortress America"; instead, the paper advocated

. . . an immediate and large-scale build-up in our military and general strength and that of our allies with the intention of *righting the power balance* [emphasis added] and in the hope that through means other than all-out war we could induce a change in the nature of the Soviet system.[26]

It was estimated that the implementation of the policies and programs recommended by NSC #68 would cost approximately $35 billion. This represented a threefold increase in American defense spending over that originally planned for Fiscal Year 1951.[27]

An analysis of NSC #68 reveals not only some of the basic thinking on national security problems in early 1950, but also some of the basic assumptions that have dominated postwar national security policy. Three recurrent fallacies appear in the assumptions behind NSC #68:

(1) The tendency to base policy exclusively on the maximum Soviet capability rather than on a mixture of Soviet potential and a realistic assessment of Soviet intent.

(2) The American belief that as they approached the thermonuclear balance of terror they were still working within the framework of the balance of power.

(3) The assumption that ". . . we could induce change in the nature of the Soviet system" by American military programs.

These three assumptions (along with others) furnished recurrent themes in military policy of the 1950s and 1960s. When

NSC #68 defined the period of maximum danger of Soviet attack as 1954, it established a precedent that is still followed, that is, an estimate based on Soviet capability and possible future threats to American security. For example, the belief in 1950 that the Soviet Union would have the capability to launch a devastating attack in 1954 proved to be false. Yet this did not prevent advocates of the "bomber gap" from making the same threat in 1955 about a Soviet attack in 1957, nor proponents of the missile gap from predicting in 1958 the same fate for the United States in 1961. In 1970, the same predictions were being made with regard to the devastating surprise attack that the Soviet Union could launch in 1975 with the SS-9 missile. At some point in the propagation of these dire but unfulfilled predictions one would think that the credibility of those making such predictions would be challenged. There is a possibility of this happening in the 1970s, but for years this type of projection of Soviet capability went almost completely unchallenged.

Before NSC #68 could be implemented, the Korean War started in June 1950. From the outset, one fact of American military planning became obvious. The United States had prepared for the wrong war, in the wrong place, and at the wrong time, and was involved in a type of war that it was least prepared to fight. Post-World War II military planning had been based on the belief that the United States could use its monopoly on the atomic bomb and the means to deliver it as a deterrent to any type of war initiated by the Soviet Union. This policy may have been correct if aggressive intent on the part of the Soviet Union is accepted, but the United States had not foreseen or planned for participation in a war such as Korea—a war in which the Soviet Union was not directly involved and which may have started without Soviet control and direction.

Thus, in June 1950, the United States found itself with an extremely limited conventional capability—only ten understrength divisions, eleven regimental combat teams, and two understrength Marine divisions.* At the same time, the United States had 48 aircraft wings including 18 SAC wings (at 45 planes

---

* An American division has approximately 15,000 men.

each for a total of 810 bombers).[28] As General James Gavin later pointed out, the United States had placed its complete reliance on air power, and therefore:

. . . the greatest industrial nation of the world could do no better than to airlift two rifle companies and a battery of artillery to meet six aggressor divisions in the initial stages of the [Korean] war.[29]

In order to correct this critical manpower shortage in conventional forces, the United States mobilized over 650,000 reservists and National Guard troops and inducted another 585,000 men into the armed forces during the first year of the Korean War.[30]* The United States eventually placed 253,250 American troops in Korea by June 30, 1951; by June 30, 1952, there were 265,864; and by July 31, 1953, the total United States manpower in Korea was 302,483 men.[31] At the end of the Korean War, 33,629 Americans had died in combat; 20,617 were listed as dead from other causes; and 103,284 men had been wounded.[32] As the casualties increased and the war continued, the frustration and anger of the American people also increased to the point where Truman's heir-apparent, Adlai Stevenson, was easily defeated by Dwight Eisenhower in the 1952 election.

* Total American military strength went from 1.7 million men in 1948 to a total of 2.8 million men in 1951. Huntington, *The Common Defense*, p. 54.

II

The Eisenhower Years: Massive Retaliation and Collective Security

(1953–1957)

MASSIVE RETALIATION

The Korean War and the election of Dwight Eisenhower signaled the end of an era in American defense policy. From 1945 to 1953 American military policy had not been clearly articulated. Despite the discussions within the Truman administration of NSC #68, the public had been content to drift along, secure in the belief that the American atomic monopoly and means of delivery guaranteed American and Western European security. The first stirrings of an attempted policy definition had occurred periodically in the past, but these discussions did not lead to an explicit statement of American strategy. The Korean War cut these discussions short as the United States mobilized to fight this confusing and frustrating conflict. Therefore, when Eisenhower came to the White House in 1953, there was no clearly defined policy toward the use of atomic weapons, nor had American policy been declared toward those areas of the third world not immediately involved in the politics of superpower diplomacy.

The main architect of American foreign and military policy from 1953 to 1959 was Secretary of State John Foster Dulles. And, in his view, the many problems facing the United States in 1953 were epitomized by the threat from the world Communist movement and the aggressive intentions of the Soviet Union. Yet it appears that Dulles not only misunderstood Soviet policies during this period (they were conservative and counter-revolutionary), but he also failed to grasp the rapidity with which technological developments were making obsolete the balance of power concept and, therefore, the strategy of thermonuclear bluff that he implemented. Thus, the failure of the rather elaborate alliance systems created by Secretary Dulles was matched by the equally futile effort on his part to implement a policy based on an unrealistic and highly dangerous bluff—massive retaliation.

Although the doctrine of massive retaliation and the establishment of a number of complicated alliance systems are closely related, it is desirable temporarily to separate them for analytical purposes. However, the reader should keep in mind that the strategy of massive retaliation and the surrounding of the Soviet Union (and China) with alliance systems were both part of the over-all American policy of containment, and on occasion were used in an attempt to strengthen the unstated but implied policy of "liberation."

This policy called for an American attempt to "roll back" the Iron Curtain to "free" those countries with Communist governments. Although at times the rhetoric of such a policy was present in official government statements, the fact remains that during the Eisenhower Administration the United States had no military alternatives outside the use of atomic weapons; and nuclear weapons could not "roll back" the Iron Curtain without serious risks to the United States. The best example of this was the inability of the United States to react in any military manner to the Soviet suppression of the Hungarian revolution in 1956. Five American divisions, or twenty NATO divisions in Central Europe simply could not challenge the Red Army in Hungary with any prospect of success.

Following the Korean conflict, there was a great deal of revulsion and frustration in the United States concerning the limited application of American power in this "police action."

Many Americans were aware of this nation's great nuclear strength and believed in the invincibility of the armed forces of the United States once this country mobilized. These Americans could not comprehend the subtle reasoning (or did not agree with it) behind fighting a war other than one aimed at total victory, particularly if the United States could win the war without the use of nuclear weapons.[1] One of the major forms in which this frustration manifested itself was the increasing demand on the new Eisenhower Administration for a clearly stated, applicable means of using the nuclear power of the United States to implement American policies.

The problem of defining American strategy was further complicated by the existing rivalry between the military services. The Army and the Navy emerged from Korea with their belief intact in the need for strong conventional forces and the ability to transport them to any point necessary. For them, Korea confirmed the lessons of World War II. On the other hand, the Air Force contended that no nation would risk aggression in the face of an overwhelming American Air Force that could deliver large numbers of nuclear weapons anywhere in the world. They maintained that American air power should be able to destroy the atomic capability of any nation and that if this capability existed, there would be no need for the specialized forces required to fight limited wars. The power of the Air Force would be sufficient to deter any type of Soviet aggression. As will be seen, with the introduction of the doctrine of massive retaliation, the Air Force emerged as the most powerful of the military services with by far the largest percentage of the defense budget allocated to it.

Although the doctrine of massive retaliation was not officially stated until January 1954, its foundation and underlying philosophy became apparent during the first year of the Eisenhower Administration. In President Eisenhower's State of the Union message in February 1953, he stated that the free world could not leave to the aggressor "the choice of the time and place and means to cause the greatest hurt to us at the least cost to himself."[2] He then set forth his Administration's policy for obtaining national security without excessive defense spending:

To amass military power without regard to our own economic capacity would be to defend ourselves against one kind of disaster by inviting another. . . . The biggest force is not necessarily the best.[3]

The President's goal of balancing military requirements and economic capacity of the United States proved to be difficult to achieve. The Eisenhower Administration became ensnarled in the same dilemma that frustrated the Truman Administration. In more precise terms, the dilemma was how to maintain United States security and the military posture believed necessary to conduct foreign affairs while at the same time following a domestic policy of solvency and expansion of essential domestic programs.[4]

The traditional American approach of preparing for war by planned mobilization of manpower and industrial resources over an extended period of time appeared to be outmoded in the nuclear age, and the new strategy of deterrence through readiness accentuated military versus nonmilitary claims on scarce resources.[5]

President Eisenhower continued to state many of the more significant aspects of the doctrine of massive retaliation before its formal announcement. In his second State of the Union message, he announced: "We shall not be the aggressor, but we and our allies have and will maintain a massive capacity to strike back."[6]

The formal announcement of the doctrine of massive retaliation was made by Secretary of State Dulles on January 12, 1954. The original doctrine had two basic precepts—one dealing with the cost of deterrence and the other with the response of the United States to aggression. The Secretary of State declared: "We want for ourselves and for others a maximum deterrent at bearable costs."[7] In order to secure the two goals of security and solvency, the Eisenhower Administration initially adopted a dual posture to prevent Soviet aggression. Strategically, the policy of threatened massive retaliation emerged to deter Soviet aggression. On the tactical level, especially in Western Europe, it was felt that should deterrence fail, the United States would have the option of conducting tactical nuclear war rather than being forced to choose between capitulation or all-out war in the event of Soviet aggression. This dual strategic and tactical task was to be accomplished by getting "more bang for the buck" than would have been possible under more conventional forms of defense planning.

By publicly articulating the official doctrine of massive retaliation, Secretary Dulles exposed it to open scrutiny and debate. The debate was not long in coming, and it revealed that a degree of ambiguity and confusion arose from the original statements. The combination of continued debate and the subsequent Administration attempts to clarify the new doctrine continued until the concept changed and was eventually discarded.

The first express criticism raised the question of the President's constitutional authority to initiate massive retaliation,[8] and other critics questioned its credibility in the mind of a potential aggressor.[9] The problem of constitutionality was never seriously discussed, but the question of credibility was a constant factor throughout the debate.[10]

Due to the criticism and confusion arising from the original statement in January, Secretary Dulles attempted to clarify the doctrine and to answer his critics in the April 1954 issue of *Foreign Affairs.* He began by restating what he believed to be the basic question concerning the maintenance of free world security, that is: "How should collective defense be organized by the free world for maximum protection at minimum cost?"[11] Mr. Dulles believed that to allow the aggressor to dictate the battle conditions and thereby to engage the "free world" in a struggle involving manpower was to encourage aggression. He thought that the aggressor would be tempted to attack in places and by means where, at a minimum cost to himself, he could impose the greatest burden on the United States. If the "free world" responded to this strategy, it could bankrupt itself and not achieve the security required.[12] Secretary Dulles attempted to forestall any act of aggression when he stated:

> The potential of massive attack will always be kept in a state of readiness, but our program will retain a wide variety of means and scope for responding to aggression.[13]

Despite the reference to a "wide variety of means," this policy was based on the belief that it was impossible for the "free world" to build up adequate conventional defense forces around the Communist perimeter. By claiming that the United States could choose the time, place, and means of warfare, there was a strong implication that local conflicts might be escalated as to the place and methods of retaliation. The doctrine of massive retaliation implied the threat of and preparation for total war in an effort to prevent not only all-out war but also limited warfare.

Despite this clarification, the exact response of the United States to any given act of perceived Soviet aggression remained vague, probably on purpose. By not stating exactly what aggressive act would initiate instant retaliation, or the exact nature of the retaliatory act, Secretary of State Dulles hoped to prevent all types of aggression.

However, the doctrine and its clarification had hardly been announced, when just the type of "aggression" that it was allegedly intended to prevent was succeeding. In Indochina, a supposedly Russian-directed war was rapidly approaching its decisive stage, and it was becoming apparent that the French would be forced to abandon the area unless substantial American military forces were forthcoming. Although some consideration was given to the use of American forces, both conventional and atomic, the decision was made in Washington not to do so. Thus, the first test of massive retaliation as a doctrine resulted in American inaction.

For complete credibility, such a doctrine should have been based on a United States counterforce posture—United States ability to strike first at the enemy's nuclear capability, destroying enough of its delivery system to prevent an unacceptable second strike by the enemy. Unless the United States possessed this capability, it made no sense to retaliate massively against limited aggression if the United States would suffer unacceptable damages in return. Ironically, Secretary Dulles announced the new doctrine almost at the time that the United States was losing its ability to attack the Soviet Union without the certainty of an unacceptable Soviet counterattack. Prior to 1954–1955, the United States could have launched an atomic attack on

Soviet territory and not received a single atomic bomb on its soil in retaliation. But by the time of Dulles' announcement, the Soviet Union had 300–400 nuclear and thermonuclear weapons and was beginning to produce operational long-range bombers to deliver them.[14] After 1955 there could be no certainty that the United States would not receive a devastating nuclear attack on its major cities in the event of war with the Soviet Union.

Massive retaliation could deter local aggression only so long as there existed a reasonable prospect of an immediate victory in all-out war and so long as the potential aggressor understood this. However, the possibility did exist that the doctrine of massive retaliation, even though not supported by a guaranteed American counterforce posture, would still be an effective deterrent to limited war if a potential aggressor was convinced that American prestige and honor were so involved in a dispute that the United States would respond massively to limited aggression. Nonetheless, as Soviet nuclear strength increased, the credibility of massive retaliation weakened.

Except for an atomic attack on the United States, the doctrine of massive retaliation was—in its simplest terms—a bluff. From 1956 on there was no way that the leaders of the United States could be *certain* that this country would not be seriously damaged in the event of a thermonuclear exchange with the Soviet Union. It made no sense to base American military policy on a threatened reaction that could lead to the destruction of American society. Yet, many contend that even if the policy was a bluff, it worked in that there were no examples of overt Soviet aggression during the period 1954–1960. This assumption, of course, was based on the belief that the Soviet Union was an aggressive nation during the 1950s just waiting for the chance to attack. Outside Eastern Europe there is really no evidence to support this contention. The best example of Soviet aggression during the Eisenhower Administration was the suppression of the Hungarian revolution; American inaction during this conflict is well known. On a more hypothetical level, let us assume the worst and speculate for a moment on the American reaction to a Soviet invasion of Turkey. Here would be a classic case of clear aggression and the application of Dulles' doctrine of massive retaliation. For the United States to respond to this aggression by entering into a race of mutual annihilation with the Soviet Union hardly seems to be a rational reaction. It can certainly be argued that the destruction of fifty of America's largest cities is an incredibly high price to pay, especially when existing Soviet ground forces would have probably overrun Turkey anyhow. The doctrine of massive retaliation and its accompanying weapons systems meant that the United States was left with only a nuclear response to any military action it perceived as hostile or aggressive.

TACTICAL NUCLEAR WEAPONS AND NATO

As it became increasingly evident that American military power could deter an all-out attack on the United States, but not necessarily stop more limited aggression, the question arose as to the means by which limited aggression could be prevented. In keeping with the desire of the Administration to provide security and solvency, the decision was made in 1954 to equip ground, air, and naval forces with tactical nuclear weapons.*

As early as 1951 the United States had successfully tested tactical nuclear weapons, and American leaders began to discuss the possibility of using them in the initial stages of limited hostilities rather than resorting to the use of strategic weapons.[15] The Navy rapidly developed the capability to launch carrier aircraft with atomic bombs, and the Army began development of the "atomic cannon." By 1953, the United States had over $10 billion invested in its atomic program, with over 90 percent of it for military purposes. By this same year, the United States was approaching a stockpile of 10,000 atomic weapons, and production costs for each additional weapon were down to about $1 million each. Finally, the appropriation of $3 billion in

---

* The distinction between tactical and strategic nuclear weapons is difficult to make. But, for the purposes of this study, it would mean that the United States and the Soviet Union might use "low yield" tactical atomic weapons (2–100 kilotons) against hostile forces engaged in Europe, but would not resort to "high yield" strategic weapons against each other's homelands.

1953 for atomic facilities guaranteed the existence of an extremely large American nuclear stockpile.[16]

In 1951, in recognition of the impact of tactical nuclear weapons, Senator Brian McMahon had called for a sixfold increase in American atomic production,[17] and by 1953 he summed up the results of this program:

> Five years ago neither the professional soldiers nor the atomic scientists foresaw what will turn out to be the great military revolution —the use of atomic energy as firepower in the hands of troops, sailors, and airmen. It was this revolution that brought about the requirements for great numbers of atomic bombs.[18]

But Senator McMahon had only stated the most obvious result of the decision to arm American conventional forces with nuclear weapons. What he did not state was the fact that the American decision to deploy nuclear weapons in Europe was a direct result of the fact that the North Atlantic Treaty Organization (NATO) nations had failed to meet troop quotas established at an earlier date.

By the end of 1949 or early 1950, the United States had made the dual decision of *attempting* to confront Soviet military power in Europe with a conventional response and of completely reassessing its policy toward rebuilding and eventually rearming Germany. Obviously these two decisions were closely interdependent. It did not make much sense to rearm Western Europe without rearming Germany. As later events demonstrated, even with Germany completely rebuilt and rearmed, the NATO allies have never had the conventional capability of defending Western Europe against a Soviet attack.

Officially, NATO was formed in 1949, and its initial military goals were the establishment of 20–22 divisions. But no amount of *feasible* rearmament could have protected Western Europe against a conventional attack if the Soviet Union had launched one. The decision to rearm this area placed a heavy burden on the already strained economies of these nations. The reality of the conventional rearmament program in conjunction with the growing American atomic capacity is certain to have appeared as a threat to the Soviet Union, if for no other reason than as an apparent attempt on the part of the West to remove Western Europe as a hostage in the event of an American atomic attack of Russia.

By 1949, the Soviet Union had 50–60 well-equipped and combat-ready divisions in Eastern Europe and the western part of the Soviet Union. Against this force, the five European nations could boast a maximum of six divisions—three French, one British, one Belgian, and one Dutch.* The United States could have possibly added one or two divisions to this force, while the Soviets could have brought their total strength up to 150 divisions within a month.[19] This discrepancy among conventional forces was recognized by Western leaders. In 1952 at the Lisbon Conference the NATO allies approved a plan that called for 50 NATO divisions (half active, half reserve) by the end of 1952, 70 by the end of 1953, and 97 by the end of 1954.[20] These goals were never met. The fact is that at no time since World War II has the NATO Alliance had more than 25 combat-ready divisions in northern Europe (and most of the time less than this).

When it is also recognized that many of these Western divisions were stationed in areas other than the crucial North German Plain invasion route, including at a later date the entire United States Seventh Army, the inadequacy of the NATO conventional forces in Europe becomes even more apparent. As will be shown in Chapter III, contrary to the Pentagon's public relations effort, at no time since World War II have the NATO forces had a credible nonnuclear response to a Soviet attack on the North German Plain (roughly a line running from the German cities of Kiel, Hamburg, Hannover, and Giessen). Without adequate conventional defensive forces in this area, and in the absence of the use of atomic weapons, it would probably have taken the Soviet Union about eight days to take the critical ports of Antwerp and Amsterdam.

---

* The number of men in a division varies greatly, but roughly Soviet divisions were approximately 10,000–12,000 men, with Western divisions running approximately 15,000 men (sometimes reinforced from 18,000 to 20,000 men).

By 1953, the NATO powers were nowhere near the 70 divisions envisioned at Lisbon; as a matter of fact, NATO combat-ready strength in Central Europe at this time was under twenty divisions and showed no signs of significantly increasing. It was in this context that the decision was made to deploy tactical nuclear weapons instead of the manpower that the European nations were either unwilling or unable to contribute. This represented a major shift in NATO strategy. And, although it was not realized at the time, the decision to attempt the defense of Europe with atomic weapons in 1954 was the final admission that the NATO powers could not or did not feel it necessary to defend Europe with conventional forces, and never again were the high goals of the Lisbon Conference set by the NATO nations.

The controversy over the efficacy of the substitution of firepower for manpower began almost immediately and still has not been resolved. The United States initially placed a great deal of faith in the concept of the use of tactical nuclear weapons to *defend* against an attack on Western Europe. But as the weapons systems evolved and the age of nuclear plenty became a reality, the validity of this belief became open to doubt, and some serious observers began to regard the existence of thousands of tactical nuclear weapons in Europe as more of a deterrent force than as a viable defense against Soviet attack.

As the number of tactical nuclear weapons in Europe continued to grow during the 1950s, two fundamental questions arose concerning the value and possible use of these weapons should the need arise to fight with them. The first question concerned tactical military function; the second question was fundamentally a humanitarian and moral one.

The debate over whether tactical nuclear weapons would militarily favor the offense or the defense in the event of hostilities has not been resolved. Since they have never been used in a tactical situation, the exact effect is not known.[21] However, it does appear that their use would place a large premium on well-trained manpower reserves, mobility and dispersion of forces, and maneuvering territory available to the opposing forces. If this is the case, and tactical nuclear weapons are considered as a defense force in Western Europe, the advantage would appear to rest decisively with the Soviet Union. For, throughout the arms race in Europe, Soviet superiority in these critical areas seems to be fairly clear.

But the humanitarian question overshadows this military problem and reduces it to meaninglessness.* As the number of tactical nuclear weapons increased in Western Europe, the real possibility began to emerge that the use of these weapons would result not in the defense of this area, but in its destruction. During the 1950s American leaders and some scholars† advocated and planned for the use of these weapons to defend Western Europe; but it would seem that the morality and efficacy of this plan could be seriously challenged by concerned Europeans and, of course, that is exactly what happened. First DeGaulle and then progressively more European leaders began to wonder about the wisdom of defending Western Europe by destroying it. It is one thing for the leaders of the United States and the Soviet Union to speak of a land war in Europe which would almost inevitably result in the use of tactical nuclear weapons; but it is quite another matter for Europeans, both east and west, to contemplate this approach with equanimity.

In spite of the growing awareness of the destructiveness of tactical nuclear war and the fact that the use of these weapons would probably favor the Soviet Union if they favored either side, NATO did not develop an adequate conventional defense against any major attack on the main front of Central Europe. The early acceptance of the idea that tactical nuclear weapons diminished the need for troops naturally tended to counteract efforts to build up a conventional shield force in Europe. As a consequence, in Europe there was almost no capacity for defense by conventional means. If deterrence failed, there would be no choice but to surrender Europe or run the risk of destroying it.

* The reader should be reminded that the average tactical nuclear weapon has an explosive power of about 20 kilotons—the same size weapon as that used on Nagasaki.

† See Henry Kissinger, *Nuclear Weapons and Foreign Policy.* Kissinger later changed his mind about the use of tactical nuclear weapons in the defense of Western Europe.

The American decision to emphasize manpower over firepower and the attempt to implement the doctrine of massive retaliation and its lesser corollary—deploying tactical nuclear weapons—meant that during the Eisenhower years the Air Force had won the interservice rivalry for budgetary funds. From 1955 to 1959 military appropriations were divided among the services in the following manner: Air Force, 45 percent; Navy-Marines, 28 percent; and the Army, 23 percent.[22] During this period, the number of men in the Army and Navy declined, as did the number of combat-ready Army divisions and active naval ships. At the same time, the number of men in the Air Force and the number of Air Force wings increased substantially.[23] However, almost inadvertently, an important long-range consolation prize was given to the Army in the form of its new atomic missions—atomic artillery and eventually air defense. In the long run this meant additional appropriations for the Army which placed it in the technological position to challenge, temporarily, the Air Force missile programs (see next chapter). More important, the Army combined this early technological progress and its assigned air defense mission to the early Nike antiaircraft systems and eventually to the much more lucrative ABM (antiballistic missiles) systems that were developed (Nike-Zeus, Nike-X, Sentinel, and, in 1970, Safeguard).

Samuel Huntington has contended that the original Dulles announcement of massive retaliation represented the "New Look" of the Eisenhower Administration and that this doctrine aimed at superiority in strategic weapons while accepting inferiority in conventional forces. Mr. Huntington further contends that this policy was changed about 1956 by the introduction of the "New, New Look" which assumed superiority in neither, but adequacy in both.[24] Yet throughout the Eisenhower Administration the United States remained vastly superior in strategic weapons and maintained a very limited conventional capability. This situation was probably best reflected by the fact that at no time during this period did the NATO allies have a conventional option in Europe in the event of a strictly conventional attack. The reality of this policy was demonstrated at a later date when the United States was strapped for a conventional force of approximately six divisions for an invasion of Cuba after the Bay of Pigs operation had failed.[25]

COLLECTIVE SECURITY

In an effort to make the doctrine of massive retaliation more credible, Secretary of State Dulles not only continued the alliance-building of his predecessors, he expanded the American attempt to guarantee the protection of its national interests and contain communism through collective security arrangements. The promise to respond "at places and with means of our own choosing," so the thinking went, would certainly be more believable if the United States had a tighter set of alliance systems surrounding the periphery of the Soviet Union and China.

Thus, by 1955 the United States had literally allied itself with every nation near the Soviet Union or China that would enter into a collective security pact or associate itself with the United States or its allies. These alliances, both multilateral and bilateral, were set up without regard to the political system of the nation involved, so long as the governments did not call themselves Communist. The keystone of this system of collective security was NATO.

The American decision to establish a European alliance system effectively reduced the future options of American foreign policy and proved to be one of the critical decisions in solidifying and guaranteeing the continued development of the Cold War. At this point, a few examples will illustrate some of the costs of establishing this alliance. In terms of Soviet-American relations, the most costly of these sacrifices can be traced to the decision to rebuild and then rearm Germany. This decision produced predictable Soviet hostility and eventually the Warsaw Pact. Likewise, part of the price for French support of German rearmament was increased American support for French attempts to maintain its colonial empire in Indochina and then Algeria.

The efforts of John Foster Dulles finalized American policy toward Europe for many years. Although his threats of an "agonizing reappraisal" initially failed to gain French support for the European Defense Command, the French finally approved of West German rearmament and the acceptance of West Germany into NATO. In addition, Dulles' efforts to apply the doctrine of massive retaliation to Europe meant that it was then possible for a world-wide thermonuclear war to be fought without European consultation, much less approval.* The introduction of American-controlled tactical nuclear weapons meant that an atomic war might take place on European soil before the governments of Europe had a chance to prevent it. Neither of these latter possibilities proved to be particularly appealing to the thinking European.

However, there appears to have been a deeper, more fundamental difference between the American and European approach to European Security—a difference that has constantly weakened the NATO Alliance and will probably destroy it in the long run. As early as 1953, this difference was noted by Hanson Baldwin when he stated: "Europe simply does not take the threat of imminent war as seriously as the United States does. . . ."26 While American strategists and politicians planned for the invasion of Western Europe by the Soviet Union, Western Europe gave some lip service to this threat, offered token defense forces, and then proceeded to allocate their resources, first toward the rebuilding of Europe and then toward the extension of European prosperity. (Germany is the possible exception to this statement.) European support was greatest during the early years of the Alliance when these nations were dependent upon the good will of United States capital and foreign aid; but once currency convertibility and relative prosperity had been achieved, European ardor for rearmament and NATO cooled noticeably. This tendency was apparent by 1953, when it became obvious that the NATO nations were not going

* In March 1954, Secretary Dulles announced that he interpreted the doctrine of massive retaliation and the NATO commitment to mean that the United States President could retaliate "instantly" without consulting Congress in the event of an attack on American allies in Europe. *The New York Times,* March 17, 1954.

to fulfill even the minimum force levels agreed upon at the Lisbon Conference.

The argument that the introduction of tactical nuclear weapons obviated the need for conventional forces is a classic evasion of the issue. The American decision to introduce these weapons into Europe was based on the clear recognition that the European nations were not going to rearm sufficiently and therefore the introduction of tactical nuclear weapons was the only alternative open to the United States unless this country wanted to undertake the conventional defense of Europe by itself.

By 1955, American diplomacy had succeeded in placing tactical nuclear weapons in Europe. It had also succeeded in gaining approval for the rearmament of Germany and the admission of West Germany into the NATO Alliance. But two months following the admission of West Germany, the Soviet Union responded by forming its own alliance system in Eastern Europe—the Warsaw Pact.

Yet even the formation of the Warsaw Pact did not seem to disturb unduly the defense plans of Western Europe. If the nations of Western Europe had truly feared a Soviet invasion, they would have spared no effort to arm themselves with adequate forces for the conventional defense of Europe. Western Europe had the manpower and the industrial capacity by the mid 1950s; the failure to use it was based on their assessment that a Soviet attack was not imminent.

However, the finalization of NATO was not Dulles' major contribution to the American policy of collective security. Dulles formulated and implemented two other major alliance systems to contain what he viewed as the aggressiveness of communism. At the primary initiative of the United States the Baghdad Pact (later, Central Treaty Organization—CENTO) and the Southeast Asia Treaty Organization (SEATO) were formed. Even at the time, the efficacy of both of these systems as meaningful collective security arrangements was open to serious doubt. By the end of the Eisenhower Administration, Iraq had pulled out of CENTO, and this alliance was in a state of steady decline and irrelevance.[27] On the other hand, by 1960 the SEATO agreement was just beginning to be used as one of the major justifications for American involvement in Southeast Asia. And, as of 1970, the damage done to American and world interests because of the manner in which this alliance has been interpreted is not yet over, and is staggering.

Although Dulles constructed the underlying diplomatic-military system that was to continue throughout the Eisenhower Administration, the President seemed to demonstrate an awareness of the meaning of the thermonuclear age that his Secretary of State lacked. This tendency on the part of the President to be doing or saying one thing while members of his Administration were reacting in a different or opposite fashion reappeared throughout this Administration. (See below on the missile gap period.)

President Eisenhower stated as early as 1954:

> We have arrived at that point, my friends, where war does not present the possibility of victory or defeat. War would present to us only the alternative of degrees of destruction. There can be no truly successful outcome.[28]

This solid analysis by the President was confirmed several months later by a report of the Atomic Energy Commission on the hydrogen bomb tests of March 1954 which had polluted an area of 7,000 square miles with deadly radioactive fall-out. Several years later, Secretary of Defense Charles Wilson warned Congress that the atomic stockpiles of both the United States and the USSR were approaching the point where they could "practically wipe out the world."[29]

This growing awareness of the power of thermonuclear weapons did not serve as a brake on the arms race; rather, it seems to have escalated it. As seen above, as early as 1951 United States Air Force spokesmen had begun to cast doubts on the ability of United States strategic forces to deter an attack by the Soviet Union.[30] With the arrival of the thermonuclear era in 1953, this fear evidently persisted as Pentagon strategists began to calculate that the strategic balance was turning against the United States.

THE BOMBER GAP

In view of the fact that the Soviet Union did not possess a bomber that could reach the United States, it seems reasonable to speculate that the threat perceived by the Air Force was not the Soviet Union, but a budget-conscious Republican administration. An administration committed to stabilizing, if not reducing, the military budget was a threat to all the military services, but particularly to the Air Force with its large share of the existing budget. The bulk of the Eisenhower Administration's reductions in the Truman budget had occurred in the Air Force allocations. President Eisenhower had also abandoned the Truman target of 143 Air Force wings by 1956, with the new goal being 114 in Fiscal Year 1954 and 120 for 1955.[31]

Thus, by 1955, the foundation for the "bomber gap" had been laid. In the next chapter we will go into considerable detail as to where the later "missile gap" came from, the forces that produced it, the weaknesses in American decision-making it illustrated, and the degree of interservice rivalry involved. Therefore, in dealing with the bomber gap the discussion will be limited to the basic facts surrounding this example of myth creation in American defense policy, rather than examining the bomber gap in great detail.

The bomber gap, in its most basic form, was the belief by many American leaders that the Soviet Union had the capability and desire to mass produce a large number of Bison bombers in preparation for an attack on the United States that would destroy the American ability to retaliate. Although a number of civilian and military leaders had believed all along that the Soviet Union was preparing to attack the United States, the Soviet Air Show in July 1955 seemed to offer them proof of this contention. At this air show, for the first time the Soviet Union displayed their *first* intercontinental bomber, the Bison (officially the M-4, a rough equivalent of the already operational

American B-52). The Soviets not only displayed this bomber flying in squadron formation (ten planes), but also appeared to have large numbers of Bisons in the air that day. It was from this allegedly impressive display of air power that many Americans, especially the Air Force, contended that the United States was in danger of losing its strategic advantage and would be imperiled by a Soviet Bison attack in about two years. (It should be noted that the period of "maximum danger" had shifted from 1954 to 1957.) American estimates indicated that the Soviets *could* quickly build over 600 of these aircraft.[32] The belief that the Soviet Union would maximize this capability led U.S. Air Force General Curtis LeMay, to comment that this huge Soviet bomber build-up could lead to a 2–1 Soviet advantage over the United States.[33]

Later evidence indicated that the Soviet Union had attempted to create the illusion of strength to conceal their weakness in long-range delivery systems. To create this impression, they had their one existing squadron of ten Bisons flown repeatedly around the review stand in a wide circle.[34] Evidently the Soviet Union had the *capability* to produce large numbers of Bisons, but they simply chose not to allocate their resources in this manner. As a matter of fact, the Soviet Union has *never* possessed at any one time more than 300 bombers capable of reaching the United States, while under the impetus of the "bomber gap" the American strategic bomber force soon reached about 500 long-range B-52 bombers and over 1,500 medium-range bombers capable of reaching the Soviet Union from either foreign bases or with the aid of in-flight refueling.[35]

The Soviet attempt to create an illusion of strength succeeded only too well. Many Americans believed that the Soviet Union had achieved strategic superiority over the United States, and this country began a massive build-up of its strategic forces. Thus, when the "bomber gap" did appear, it appeared in favor of the United States by about a 5–1 ratio. Common sense would indicate that the Soviets might have learned a lesson about the American reaction to a possible strategic inferiority, but they repeated exactly the same error at a later date during the "missile gap" period and with exactly the same results—an overwhelming increase in American missile superiority. In the long run, this Soviet error cost the Soviet Union a great deal of money and led to an escalation of the arms race that they neither wanted nor could afford. In trying to create an illusion of strength in the face of American superiority, Soviet leaders played right into the hands of the American military and their numerous allies.

Thus, the Soviet Union seems to have learned the wrong lessons from the "bomber gap." Instead of realizing the extreme dangers of arms escalation because of American sensitivity to possible threats to its strategic superiority, they learned only that some forces in the United States could be falsely led to believe (or claim to believe) that America's strategic power was inferior. Obviously, the American willingness to propagate its own strategic weakness in the face of projected Soviet forces is at least partially traceable to the military-industrial drive for more funds for future weapons systems. The forces supporting higher military budgets had learned early in the arms race that there is no better method of increasing the military budget than that of convincing Congress of some *future* threat to American security by the Soviet *capability* to produce a weapons system. The fact that the Soviets have never developed these systems in the form predicted has not in the least reduced the effectiveness of this tactic.

At a later date, some observers claimed that the Soviet Union had tricked the United States into believing that they were mass producing bombers when actually they were engaged in a "crash" missile-production program.[36] There does not appear to be much doubt that the United States was tricked by the Soviet Union, but this was not because the Soviets were engaged in a "crash" missile-building program. It seems more likely that the Soviet Union was diverting some resources to missile development (but not necessarily to programmed missile production), and that they were using the remainder of their available military resources for the modernization of the Red Army.

It would appear that during the postwar period the Soviet Union explicitly rejected the idea of surprise attack both in theory and in the weapons systems built. The fact that the Soviet

Union had the *capability* to build large numbers of Bisons but chose not to do so, even in the face of overwhelming American superiority, is another indication of the soundness of this analysis.

Theoretically, the Soviet Union explicitly rejected the decisiveness of a surprise thermonuclear attack in 1955. Raymond Garthoff, quoting Soviet Marshal Rotmistrov, in an article in *Military Thought* (February 1955): "Surprise attack by itself still does not and cannot provide complete victory in war or in an operation."[37] Under both Stalin and his successors, the leaders of the Soviet Union had spoken of "peaceful coexistence" and had repeatedly denied any intent to attack the United States.[38] And, in 1956 at the 20th Party Congress, Premier Khrushchev denied the inevitability of war for those that might have missed the message earlier. It appears that at first the Soviet Union rejected the ability of nuclear weapons to be decisive in a new war; then they gradually began to realize that no one would "win" the next war.[39] This debate in the Soviet Union, as in the United States, continues to this day, but no civilian Soviet leader since World War II believed in the efficacy of an atomic surprise attack to meet Soviet national goals. Suffice it to say that behind the bomber gap was the underlying American assumption that the Soviet Union was preparing a first strike against the United States, and this was not true. Likewise, the Soviets had really given no indication that this was the case.

The belief in the bomber gap was not destroyed by comparative data on American and Soviet bomber forces. The bomber gap was simply submerged and replaced by the panic that accompanied the first Soviet testing of an ICBM in August 1957 and then by the successful orbiting of an earth satellite by the Soviet Union in October of the same year. The myth of the bomber gap and the danger of a bomber attack on the United States was replaced in 1957 by the myth of the missile gap and the imminence of a Soviet missile attack sometime around 1961.

III

THE MISSILE GAP: A Study in Myth Creation

(1957–1961)

The period of the "missile gap" (1957–1961) is a classic illustration of myth creation by forces within and outside of the United States government, and serves as an excellent example of the assumptions and forces at work in the development of American defense policy. The components in the American system which produced the missile gap were not new and certainly have not disappeared as of the 1970s. Therefore, if this complex and difficult process can be explained and understood it should aid in an understanding of the problems facing American defense policy makers, not only at present, but also in the future. Many of the lessons to be learned from a detailed study of the missile gap can be of value in an assessment of the AMB, MIRV, and SS-9 debate presently taking place and of the ULMS (undersea long-range missile system) debate which is assured for the future. Therefore, substantial detail will be devoted to the missile gap in the hope that by using this as a basic case study some light can be shed on previous and future arguments that inevitably surround a given weapons system.[1]

The basic assumptions of those who accepted the myth of the missile gap are fairly simple. In August 1957 the Soviet Union successfully tested the first ICBM, and in the following October they placed the first earth satellite in orbit. From this point on, it was the commonly accepted belief by many in the United

States that the Soviet Union would mass produce ICBMs, so that by about 1961–1962 they would have roughly 1,000–1,500 missiles (to less than 100 American ICBMs), which could then be used in a surprise attack to destroy the strategic power of the United States.

Whether intended or not, the creation of the missile gap accomplished the following:

(1) It led to a drastic increase in the budgetary allocations for the military, particularly for the Air Force.

(2) The Democratic Party gained substantial advantages, particularly in the 1960 elections, from the illusion that the Republicans had allowed the missile gap to occur.

(3) The belief that the Soviet Union was the avowed enemy of the United States, prepared to attack at any time, was perpetuated and strengthened.

(4) The NATO Alliance was shaken by the weakening of American nuclear credibility and the other forces released by the belief in the missile gap.

(5) American intelligence system was reorganized (DIA).

(6) Relations between the Soviet Union and China were considerably weakened by Mao Tse-tung's belief in the missile gap myth.

(7) The United States military was given an excuse to place IRBMs and MRBMs on the periphery of the Soviet Union (particularly in Turkey, Germany, Italy, and Great Britain).

Once the missile gap myth had been destroyed (1961), it became possible to attempt to answer some of the perplexing questions raised by this controversial period in the history of American defense policy and the arms race. The creation, perpetuation, and eventual destruction of this myth raised serious questions concerning the fundamental assumptions of American military planners and the means by which these individuals attempted to gain a given weapons system or budget allocation.

Due to the complexity of these questions, this analysis is divided into three major parts:

(1) Soviet strategy, American intelligence, and the missile gap

(2) Budgetary, partisan, and military effects of the missile gap

(3) The impact of the missile gap abroad

SOVIET STRATEGY, AMERICAN INTELLIGENCE, AND THE MISSILE GAP

Well before the intercontinental ballistic missile became a reality, the psychological foundation for believing in Soviet strategic superiority had been laid. The surprise attack on Pearl Harbor had left an indelible imprint on American strategic thinking and led to what can be called a Pearl Harbor psychosis. Coupled with this fear was the definition by American leaders of the Soviet Union as an enemy so cunning, so inherently evil, so antithetical to the "American way of life" as to be desirous of launching a surprise thermonuclear attack on the United States the instant it thought this could be accomplished at a level of "acceptable" damage.

It was believed that this situation would exist when the Soviet Union possessed a first-strike nuclear force strong enough to destroy the United States nuclear retaliatory forces. It was also believed that this was the ultimate goal of the Soviet Union and that it was pursuing this goal with all the technological and natural resources at its disposal. This alleged Russian doctrine was based on the belief that the Soviet Union was pursuing a "counterforce" strategy. Those who accepted this interpretation as the basic military philosophy of the Soviet Union tended to overestimate Soviet missile programs and to accept (or create) those missile projection figures which appeared to substantiate their position.

The fear that the Soviet Union is preparing for a surprise attack on the United States still exists, but at no time during the missile gap period did the Soviet Union fully mobilize its production capacity for bombers or missiles. The Soviet Union apparently produced only those weapons it felt were needed to deter an attack on Russia by the United States. In fact, it would appear that between 1957 and 1962 the Soviet Union built less than 4 percent of the ICBMs and only 20 percent of the heavy bombers that American intelligence estimated its economy could have sustained. In its relations with the United States the Soviet Union apparently pursued the policy of minimum deterrence, threatening an all-out blow only in retaliation for use of nuclear weapons against Russian territory.[2]

An analysis of the estimated weapons production of the Soviet Union, including some "official" Pentagon figures (see Appendix A) supports the minimum deterrence theory.[3] The Soviet Union possessed a limited number of long-range bombers (and, later, ICBMs) and a large conventional military force to meet less than all-out nuclear aggression. With these conventional and nuclear forces, Russia could protect its land mass from a conventional attack and deter a United States nuclear attack by possessing a large enough striking force to threaten the *possible* destruction of American population centers. The Soviet Union did not have to possess enough deliverable nuclear weapons to create the *absolute certainty* that it could destroy major American metropolitan areas; Russia only had to create an element of *uncertainty* among high American officials to prevent an attack.[4]

Apparently Soviet leaders believed that this strategy not only guaranteed their military security, but also offered an additional advantage: by not building a large operational nuclear delivery system, Russia could wait for the development of the next, more sophisticated, weapons generation before beginning large-scale production, and therefore scarce Soviet resources could be channeled into other facets of the economy.[5]

However, in the long run this advantage was reduced, if not destroyed, by the Russian leaders (especially Khrushchev) who attempted to take maximum diplomatic advantage of the American belief in the missile gap. The Russian boasts of missile superiority and "rocket rattling" reinforced this belief. It is probable that the United States would have engaged in large-scale missile building anyhow, but the Soviet statements certainly did nothing to weaken those forces in the United States intent upon another escalation of the arms race—an escalation that the Russian leaders were either unwilling or unable to compete with on equal terms.

The apparent fact that the Soviet Union had adopted a mini-

mum deterrent strategy was not believed by those responsible
for formulating American military policy. The basic assumption
throughout the period of the missile gap was grounded on the
belief that the Russians were utilizing the maximum capability
credited to them by U.S. intelligence. This assumption was
changed only when "hard" information become available which
indicated that the Soviet Union was not using its maximum
capability, and even then it was not accepted by all agencies
of the intelligence community.

The threatened bomber gap, the successful Soviet ICBM
test, and the Sputnik earth satellite caused many American
officials to raise their estimates of Soviet capabilities and added
a strong element of uncertainty within government circles in the
calculation of Soviet strategic nuclear power. This American
lack of certainty caused serious alarm, and efforts were made by
the United States government to obtain accurate information on
Soviet missile and bomber programs, but the exact extent of
these intelligence efforts were not known to the public. However, numerous public reports have reflected an awareness of at
least two of the major sources of information on Soviet missiles
available to American intelligence.

The first source appeared in various public reports indicating
that in July 1955 the United States had installed missile tracking stations in Turkey which could monitor Russian long-
range missile tests. These radar stations reportedly could track
Russian missiles up to a range of 4,000 miles.[6]

The second major source of intelligence information was not
known to the public until May 1960. The U-2 photo reconnaissance aircraft began flying its high altitude photographic
missions as early as June 1956, and was reported to have found
the Soviet ICBM testing center at Tyura Tam (near the Aral
Sea) before the first Soviet ICBM test in August 1957.[7]

At the time, the most authoritative statement on the value
of the U-2 photographs was made by Secretary of Defense
Thomas Gates:

From these flights we got information on airfields, aircraft,
missiles, missile testings and training, special weapons storage, sub-

marine production, atomic production and aircraft deployment. . . .
These results were considered in formulating our military programs.[8]

Later, Allen Dulles stated that the U-2 photos had given "hard"
intelligence to American analysts and claimed: "The intelligence collected on Soviet missiles has been excellent as to the
nature and quality of the potential threat."[9]

Various other claims have been made with respect to the
accuracy and value of the U-2 photographs, but perhaps the
strongest and, if true, the most significant was the claim that
the U-2 could photograph all of the operational first-generation
Soviet ICBMs, which were installed along the Trans-Siberian
railroad route since their large and cumbersome size prevented
their emplacement far from a major railroad.[10] If this was the
case, then the U-2 had only to fly along the railroad route periodically and photograph new missile sites or those under construction.

However, the classified nature of the American radar stations
in Turkey and the U-2 photographs did not make it possible for
the American public to determine the comprehensiveness and
accuracy of the intelligence sources available to the U.S. government. The possibility also existed that the Eisenhower Administration had other sources of intelligence that still have not
been made public.[11]

But from the published information during the missile gap
period, the Eisenhower Administration apparently had valuable
intelligence sources upon which to base estimates of Soviet
strategic delivery means.

The debate over the missile gap constantly reverted to the
confusing question of the numerous intelligence figures that
appeared, indicating that a number of different assessments existed on projected Soviet missile strength. The reasons for the
confusion within the government were numerous and could not
be traced to one source. However, upon analysis, certain basic
interrelated reasons for the emergence of the missile gap appear.
The first of these is that there were numerous sets of intelligence
estimates available within the United States government at any
given time during the period 1959–1961. The exact number of

estimates available at any given time is impossible to determine, but the following possible situation existed at times: (1) The CIA annual estimates that contained figures based on an "orderly" (low estimate) Soviet missile building program and an estimate based on a "crash" program (high estimate); (2) An Air Force estimate based on its own intelligence sources and its own interpretations of the U-2 photographs; (3) An Army-Navy estimate based on their own sources; and (4) The existence of the previous year's estimates that were still accepted by some even though they had been replaced with more up-to-date estimates. Added to this inherently confusing situation was the secrecy that surrounded the whole debate and the willingness of the military services to selectively "leak" their own estimates to the press in order to strengthen their case for a given weapons system or force level.* It is to an analysis of this complex situation that we will now turn.

Initially, the CIA resisted the pressure from the Department of Defense to provide intelligence projections on Soviet missile strength. In the past, when estimates had proved faulty, the CIA had borne the brunt of public criticism and was not eager to assume responsibility again. But the Department of Defense persisted, saying that it had to have this information to compensate for the long "lead times" needed to produce a given missile system (at least 18–30 months). Finally, the CIA admitted that they were the agency that should do this job and began work on this project.[12]

The CIA believed that the Soviet ICBM test in 1957 had shown a high degree of competence in this field. But the basic question that faced the experts was to determine as closely as possible how the Soviet Union would allocate its total military effort. Obviously, Russian emphasis on heavy bombers, fighter

---

* The reader who is dubious about the power or influence of the individual military intelligence service efforts should keep in mind that in 1970 it was revealed that the three services would spend $2.9 billion on intelligence. This money did not include any CIA operations, nor the tactical intelligence operations of the services in Vietnam. *The New York Times*, May 19, 1970, quoting Assistant Secretary of Defense Robert F. Froehlke in testimony before the House Appropriations Committee.

planes, or conventional weapons would cut down on the funds available for missile programs. Therefore, the early CIA estimates on projected Russian missile strength were based on a combination of proven Russian capabilities, "our view of their intentions," and an over-all assessment of Russian strategy.[13]

With these essential guidelines established, the CIA began to collect information on the Soviet missile effort (presumably from the U-2 flights and the radar stations in Turkey). As "hard" facts became available, the intelligence experts attempted to estimate the actual programming of the Russian missile system. As more evidence was gathered, CIA estimates were revised downward since "hard" intelligence indicated that the Soviet Union had not engaged in a crash missile production program. However, the continued existence of the earlier, more pessimistic, estimates for a given year meant that there were several different projections in existence, produced at different times, but for the same year in the future. As will be seen below, these downward revisions by the CIA were not necessarily accepted by the Air Force or by spokesmen friendly to this military service. The resulting confusion deserves some attention.

The first evidence during the missile gap period of confusion within the United States intelligence community apparently occurred in 1957 concerning the so-called Gaither Report. In 1965, President Eisenhower admitted that this report indicated that United States retaliatory forces would become vulnerable to Soviet missile attack by about 1959, but that he had "other information" on American strategic posture and therefore did not accept the conclusions of the Gaither committee.[14] The former President never explained the source of his "other information" or what it was. In view of the fact that the Gaither committee supposedly had access to all essential classified information needed to conduct their study, it appears that some intelligence information was not turned over to this committee (possibly the U-2 interpreted photographs or an even more sensitive source).

In the summer of 1958, Senator Symington offered the first concrete evidence that there was more than one set of intelligence figures on Soviet missile programs in circulation within the United States government. He sent a secret letter to President Eisenhower and charged that the United States was lagging unjustifiably behind the Soviet Union in missile development and gave "as his authority his own intelligence sources." He further claimed that the full extent of the danger had not been accurately estimated by the CIA.[15] Senator Symington's "own intelligence sources" were never disclosed, but before the missile gap debate was over evidence indicated that his source was the Air Force. (Senator Symington was a former Secretary of the Air Force.)

This secret Symington letter to President Eisenhower was not made public until 1959 when it became apparent that the CIA had made its first downward revision of projected Russian missile strength. No definitive evidence was found as to exactly when the CIA made its revision; however, when the public statement was made early in 1959, it appeared to be based on the assumption that the United States and the Soviet Union had both reached the same negative conclusion concerning the value and efficacy of mass-producing large numbers of first-generation intercontinental ballistic missiles.[16]

By 1959, at the latest, the United States government had decided that first-generation liquid fuel ICBMs were not worth the investment required to produce in large numbers. The Atlas ICBM was heavy, cumbersome, and expensive. In addition, it took thirty minutes to prepare, fuel, and launch, making it highly vulnerable to surprise attack and therefore primarily a first-strike weapon. It was decided to produce a limited number of them and move on to the development and production of the more sophisticated and cheaper second-generation Minutemen. The same reasoning applied to the substitution of the Polaris for the Regulus.[17]

The government had decided to rely, temporarily, on its superiority in manned bombers, plus a limited number of first-generation ICBMs as the major strategic military instrument to implement its foreign policy until the second generation of American missiles became operational.[18]

Secretary of Defense McElroy appeared to confirm this policy when he testified early in 1959:

It is not our intention or policy to try and match missile for missile in the ICBM category of Russian capability *in the next couple of years*. Our position . . . is that our diversified capability to deliver the big weapon [nuclear warheads and bombs] is what we are going to count on as our ability to deter general war.[19]

The Secretary of Defense also admitted that in a year or two Russia could have more ICBMs than the United States.[20]

Evidently, early in 1959 the Soviet Union also had decided not to produce first-generation ICBMs in large numbers. Like the American decision, it was not possible to determine exactly when this became official policy. However, according to the United States Defense Department, by 1961 the Soviet Union had produced only a "handful" of ICBMs and even by 1964 was credited officially with less than 200.[21] If the Soviet Union had embarked on a "crash" missile production program in 1959, they certainly would have had more than a "handful" in 1961 and far more than 200 by 1964 (in 1964 the United States had 750 operational ICBMs and 192 Polaris missiles). In spite of the claim by Khrushchev that Russia was producing missiles in "serial production" and that one factory produced 250 missiles per year, the Soviet Union decided upon a very limited production program for first-generation ICBMs.[22]

Early in 1959, the CIA accepted the possibility that the Soviet Union was not engaged in a large build-up of first-generation ICBMs. Therefore, the first downward revision of intelligence estimates of projected Soviet missile strength was made. This fact came out during the *Joint Hearings*, 1959, when Senator Symington stated that during 1958 he had been briefed by the CIA four times, and that although he disagreed with their estimates based on "other information I had," the CIA figures had been the same all four times. Then he claimed that even lower estimates allegedly from the CIA had been given by Secretary of Defense McElroy in an earlier secret hearing before a different congressional committee.[23]

Simultaneously, the United States government purposely produced two sets of figures in the National Intelligence Estimate based upon different assessments of the number of ICBMs the

Soviet Union *could* produce. Due to a lack of certainty on the part of the intelligence community as to exactly what programs were being pursued by Russia, the National Intelligence Estimate for 1959 attempted to cover two possible contingencies. The smaller projected number represented an "orderly" Soviet missile program based on the missile production capacity credited to the Soviet Union. The larger, second figure attempted to cover the possibility that the Soviet Union might use this capability to engage in a "crash" missile program.[24]

Later in 1959, Secretary of Defense McElroy publicly implied for the first time the possibility of two sets of figures. He stated that the missile gap arose only when the number of missiles the United States actually planned to produce were compared to the number the Soviet Union "could" produce. The Secretary further stated that it was impossible to overemphasize the importance of the word "could" in this "type of estimate," and that United States estimates were not intended to mean that the Soviet Union actually would produce this large number of missiles. To support his argument, he referred to the bomber gap and the fact that at the time of this supposed gap, the American estimates said the Soviet Union could produce 600 to 700 Bisons, but it chose not to do so.[25]

The existence of two official sets of intelligence figures produced in 1959 did not become public until 1960. When they were openly discussed they caused a great deal of confusion, even after it had been explained that official American estimates had rejected a "crash" Russian production program and believed that the Soviet Union had adopted an "orderly" program.[26]

By the end of January 1959, there was a real possibility that there were three sets of secret intelligence figures being discussed within government circles—the two sets in the National Intelligence Estimate ("orderly" versus "crash" production programs) and Senator Symington's "other information."[27]

But the confusion did not stop there. At the same time that the "revised" intelligence estimates were being given to congressional leaders, Secretary of Defense McElroy apparently admitted that by the early 1960s the Soviet Union would have a 3–1 advantage over the United States in operational long-range ballistic missiles. The transcript of the congressional hearing where he allegedly made this statement was never released. But a vast number of reports of this statement were made and it was never denied by Secretary McElroy.[28] The public was never told which set of intelligence figures was used by Secretary McElroy in arriving at his prediction of a 3–1 Soviet missile advantage in the early 1960s.

Politically, whichever set of figures was used by the Secretary was not relevant. This alleged statement gave Democratic critics of the Eisenhower Administration an "official confirmation" of the existence of a future missile gap.

The accuracy of the press coverage of the missile gap controversy is certainly open to question. Claims of "leaks" and of the possession of "official estimates" could not be certified, and even if these claims were true, they could not be admitted by the government officials concerned. The press also displayed many of the political biases and subjective opinions so often found in its treatment of any controversial issue. In spite of these real handicaps to objectivity—and the lack of objectivity—an interesting pattern of reporting on the comparative strategic American-Soviet power appeared in newspaper and periodical analysis.

The earliest public estimates of the missile gap for the year 1962 gave the Soviet Union a projected ICBM lead over the United States of from 8 to 14 ICBMs to one ICBM for the United States. According to these earlier figures, by 1962 the Soviet Union was supposed to have between 1,000 and 1,500 ICBMs while the United States allegedly was programmed to have only 130. Following the first American downward revision of projected Soviet missile strength in 1959, the publicly predicted Russian strength was reduced accordingly to 500 ICBMs. Also, several of these new projections appeared to follow Secretary McElroy's predicted 3–1 Soviet advantage, rather than the earlier predictions of a Soviet advantage of roughly 10–1. It is impossible to determine if the figures in the media were "leaks" from government officials, however throughout the missile gap period many newspapers and periodicals closely paralleled the later figures claimed by the government to be the "official intelligence estimates."[29]

The confusion on estimates that occurred in 1959 took place for the most part in secret; it was not until early 1960 that the almost chaotic situation within the intelligence community became apparent in public sources. This confusion, which continued through 1960 and for most of 1961, was never cleared up in public sources and only disappeared when the missile gap illusion itself disappeared in late 1961.[30]

Throughout this time President Eisenhower attempted to assure the American people of the basic nuclear strength of the United States, while he called for increases in bomber forces and development of missile forces.[31]

Yet while the President proceeded in this manner, his military personnel seemed to be purposely undercutting his effort. The commanding officer of SAC, General Thomas S. Power, gave a speech in January 1960 claiming that the 100 American nuclear launching installations virtually could be destroyed by a limited number of Soviet missiles. General Power stated:

> . . . it would take an average of three missiles in the current state of development to give an aggressor a mathematical probability of 95 percent that he can destroy one given soft target some 5,000 miles away. This means that, with only some 300 ballistic missiles, the Soviet could virtually wipe out our entire nuclear strike capability within a span of thirty minutes.[32]

Needless to say, General Power followed up this warning with a call for a large-scale SAC airborne alert, the production of more long-range bombers, and the development funds for the new B-70 bomber.[33]

In spite of this foreboding prediction of the ability of 300 Soviet ICBMs and IRBMs to destroy the American retaliatory forces, *the fact remains that in 1960 the Soviet Union did not have anywhere near 300 missiles (at the most 10 ICBMs)*, and had only 150 long-range bombers. Arrayed against this force was a large, diversified American deterrent force that even General Power called "the most powerful retaliatory force in the world."[34] This deterrent force consisted of almost 600 B-52's, 1,200 B-47's (with in-flight refueling), and over 200 carrier-based aircraft dispersed on 14 American attack carriers (plus an unknown number of American fighter bombers with a nuclear capability stationed at various American bases throughout the world).[35] No one, not even General Power, questioned existing American security, but the debate continued to revolve around the estimates of future comparative missile strength.

The alarm caused by General Power's speech was demonstrated during the *Joint Hearings, 1960*. According to General Power, the predicted missile gap would arrive when the Soviet Union had the 150 ICBMs and 150 IRBMs. At this time, SAC could be destroyed as an effective retaliatory force. Therefore, the *Joint Hearings, 1960*, concentrated on the question of the predicted Soviet missile strength. This question had to be answered by the American intelligence community, but this community offered "several" conflicting and contradictory answers.

During 1959, a series of unconfirmed reports indicated that the Soviet Union had run into difficulty in its ICBM testing and development programs. There were also indications that the Russian missile program had placed a serious strain on its economy. These reports presaged the second major downward revision of American intelligence estimates in 1960 on projected Soviet missile strength.[36]

This revision occurred early in 1960 when Thomas Gates, the new Secretary of Defense, stated that the Russians had engaged in an "orderly" missile production program and therefore earlier estimates based on a "crash" Soviet missile program were too high.[37] Simultaneously, CIA director Allen Dulles produced a less optimistic, different set of intelligence figures, and the Air Force came up with a third set that was higher than either of the first two. The exact figures used in these estimates were never made public, nor were the reasons for the confusion stated.

It appears now that there were three reasons for the chaotic situation within the United States intelligence community in 1960 and in early 1961. (1) In spite of the continued downward revision of projected Soviet missile strength, several individuals within the government apparently continued to accept the earlier, more pessimistic, projections. (2) The existence of at least two official sets of figures in the National Intelligence

Estimate ("orderly" versus "crash" Soviet programs) until 1960 gave some spokesmen the supposed option of accepting either a "high" or a "low" set. (3) The fact that the military services continued to produce their own estimates of future Soviet missile strength gave rise to at least two additional possible sets of figures—one set from the Air Force and one from the Army-Navy coalition.[38]

In considering these three factors within the intelligence community, logic would indicate the possibility of at least six different sets of figures in 1960 purporting to be the projected number of Soviet missiles for a given year. However, this does not appear to be the case. The real possibility exists that there was a great deal of overlap and duplication within intelligence circles. For example, the "crash" estimates rejected by the Department of Defense could have been the same as the "high" Air Force estimates, while the "low" Army-Navy estimates could have been the same as the "orderly" Department of Defense figures. By 1970, the reasons for this confusion still had not been clarified for the American public.

The almost unbelievable confusion in American intelligence apparently continued until the fall of 1961. At that time, President Kennedy managed to combine the various estimates of the military services under the control of the Secretary of Defense and the newly created Defense Intelligence Agency (DIA). Once this was done, the Air Force apparently accepted the lower figures of the Army-Navy estimates, and the military services finally agreed upon one set of projected Soviet ICBM figures.[39] Even though the creation of the DIA seemed to resolve the differences concerning missile projection estimates, it did not solve the problem of competition between the intelligence agencies.

Once again the mass media appears to have reflected the downward revisions of the United States government. The 1960 downward revision by Secretary of Defense Gates was represented in many periodicals, and showed the Soviet Union with a maximum advantage over the United States of 3–1 by 1961–1962.[40] Early in 1961, the published projections still showed a Soviet ICBM lead, but a reduced lead compared to earlier projections, and by the end of 1961 most published reports claimed either missile parity between the two superpowers or a slight United States lead.[41]

Surprisingly, there have not been many published reports that attempt to explain "where the missile gap went," or to assess the blame for its creation. Spokesmen for the Kennedy Administration attempted to blame statements made by President Eisenhower and his Administration for creating the missile gap illusion.[42] Others claimed that Kennedy's statements were made in "good faith."[43] Still other sources blamed American "politicians," "sensation-seeking journalists," "the Military-Industrial complex," and in some cases the blame was placed entirely on the "bravado" of the Soviet Union.[44]

One of the major personalities involved in the creation of the missile gap, Senator Stuart Symington, came up with his own interesting version of how the missile gap was created and where it went, although he did not deal with why it was created.[45] Senator Symington blamed the CIA and its constant downward revision of national intelligence figures based on Soviet "intent" rather than "capability" as the major cause of the missile gap myth. To prove his point, Senator Symington quoted alleged official figures for projected Soviet missile production for the years 1961–1962. In order to avoid going into the classified number of missiles involved in these secret projections, he used the percentage of predicted Russian missile production as of 1959 compared with the new percentage used in 1961. (See Tables I and II.) According to the figures used by Symington, the official United States government estimates of Russian missile production had been reduced by 96.5 percent from December 1959 to September 1961. So that as of September 1961 the Soviet Union was given credit for the production of only 3.5 percent of the missiles that the United States had said in 1959 the Russians would produce.[46]

When Senator Symington confronted Secretary of Defense McNamara with these figures, McNamara answered rather lamely that those who had discussed the missile gap had based their comments on national intelligence estimates and "were speaking of the missile gap in good faith."[47]

TABLE I

TOTAL HIGH ESTIMATED SOVIET MISSILE PRODUCTION FOR 1961–1962*

	December 1959	February 1960	August 1960	June 1961	September 1961
100%	100% (1,500 ICBMs)				
80%					
60%					
40%		34% (512 ICBMs)			
20%			30% (450 ICBMs)		
				15% (225 ICBMs)	
0%					3.5% (52 ICBMs)

* The figures in parentheses represent the number of Soviet ICBMs projected by public sources for late 1961 to early 1962. The 1959 prediction is used as the base year. The December 1959 figure of a projected 1,500 ICBMs was used here to present the most pessimistic public estimate used at the time.

Due to the fact that Senator Symington had been a major protagonist in the missile gap debate, it was logical that he would attempt to find an explanation for its creation that did not damage his own reputation or political image. Nonetheless, his rationalization of the missile gap appears to be one of the few *public* statements made by anyone who had access to classified information and was connected closely with the development of the missile gap.†

† In view of the recent skeptical attitudes of Senator Symington toward the ABM debate, it is possible that he learned a valuable lesson from his earlier experience.

TABLE II

LOWER ESTIMATED SOVIET MISSILE PRODUCTION
FOR 1961–1962*

100% 100% (1,000 ICBMs)				
80%				
60%				
40%	34% (340 ICBMs)			
20%		30% (300 ICBMs)		
			15% (150 ICBMs)	
0%				3.5% (35 ICBMs)
December 1959	February 1960	August 1960	June 1961	September 1961

* The figures in parentheses represent the number of Soviet ICBMs projected in public sources using a lower base number of ICBMs (1,000). The projected number of Soviet ICBMs can be found in Appendix A. Both sets of percentage figures were given by Senator Symington in place of classified missile figures. See U.S. Congress, Senate, *Hearings*, January–February 1962, p. 49; Stuart Symington, "Where the Missile Gap Went," *The Reporter* (February 15, 1962), 26:22.

If Senator Symington's percentages are analyzed in an attempt to gain a picture of how the missile gap appeared to those who accepted its existence, the following picture emerges.[48] By using the highest 1959 Soviet ICBM projection for 1962 (1,500 ICBMs) as a base figure and then reducing the number of projected missiles as the estimates were revised downward (according to Senator Symington's percentages), the most pessimistic view of the missile gap seen by those who accepted the downward revision is apparent.[49] (See Table I.) If the lower 1959 prediction of 1,000 Soviet ICBMs for 1962 is used (Table II), then the potential gap is reduced but remains substantial.

From this analysis an interesting observation can be made. A check on the figures presented in Appendix A reveals that the figures in Table II (in parentheses) resemble many of the public estimates presented from 1958 to 1961 in the popular journalistic treatments of the missile controversy.

A comparison of Senator Symington's figures and those presented to the public gives rise to two tentative conclusions. First, the possibility existed that Senator Symington's percentage projections offer enough evidence to create a relatively accurate reconstruction of at least one set of intelligence figures found in the United States government during the missile gap controversy. And, second, the apparent accuracy of published accounts of at least this set of missile projections offers strong evidence that classified information was being revealed to some reporters. These conclusions are tenuous, but there is enough evidence to warrant their serious consideration as a valid reconstruction of how the missile gap appeared to those who accepted a substantial United States missile inferiority. If, in fact, the Soviet Union had possessed between 1,000 and 1,500 ICBMs by late 1961, the missile gap (but not necessarily a deterrent gap) would have been a reality, but the fact remains that at this time the Soviet Union was credited with the possession of less than 100 ICBMs.

At the same time that Senator Symington attempted to explain the missile gap, an Air Force spokesman admitted that the Russians had the "capability" to create the gap, but "they [the Russians] did not do what our intelligence people thought they would do."[50]

The evidence available indicated that the United States government was fairly accurate in determining the Soviet "capability" to produce long-range ballistic missiles, but misinterpreted and exaggerated the "intent" of Russian policy makers in assuming that they would use this capability to its fullest possible extent. And, as far as the intelligence community is concerned, this misinterpretation was the basis of their faulty assessments leading to the belief in the missile gap in the first place. The Soviet Union had the capability to mass produce large numbers of ICBMs, but they had no reason to do this. They simply were not attempting to assume a first-strike posture toward the United States, and to build the missiles would have been a waste of resources. On the other hand, the American willingness to believe that the Soviet Union would maximize this capability once again demonstrated a degree of American paranoia that was not warranted, based on an assessment of either postwar Soviet policies or strategy.

The acceptance of the missile gap by many individuals in the United States had a definite domestic impact on American policies, and this question deserves considerable analysis.

BUDGETARY, PARTISAN, AND MILITARY EFFECTS OF THE MISSILE GAP

The domestic impact of the missile controversy on the United States can be divided into three general, interrelated categories:

(1) Defense expenditures and interservice rivalry
(2) Partisan politics and the missile gap
(3) American military strategy and missiles.[51]

The budgetary procedures of the United States government are difficult to analyze, even for those with access to the classified details on the process of defense appropriations and expenditures.[52] The budget categories conceal the nature of American preparedness for various military contingencies, and the figures available are "written in a jargon that defies comprehension."[53] In addition to these handicaps, the increasing complexity of technological developments in the defense field make the whole process of defense appropriations confusing. As a result, Congress usually allows the major budgetary decisions to be made in the executive branch, and contents itself with minor revisions or, at most, dramatic proposals that still are left to the White House for final action.[54]

These serious difficulties, inherent in American budgetary

procedures, greatly complicate the task of analyzing defense expenditures during the period of the missile gap.

The prime ingredient of the struggle among the military services was the constant fight for a higher budgetary appropriation so that each one could carry out the mission it visualized for itself. In order to justify the requests for these appropriations and to maximize its future role, military doctrines on limited and all-out war were articulated and defined by each of the military services and their business, political, and journalistic allies.

The post–World War II debate over American strategic doctrine cannot be totally attributed to the selfish demands of the military for larger appropriations, but neither can it be denied that this was a significant aspect of interservice rivalry, and it played an important part in the missile gap controversy. It was not a blind search for truth that led the Air Force to believe in a counterforce doctrine (or a variation on this doctrine) and led the Army and Navy to accept a form of minimum deterrent strategy. No doubt it was felt these expenditures would best serve the military interests of the United States. Nevertheless, they added appreciably to the appropriations for the military services.

Along with the constant statements on national security, the military services also mobilized their "independent" organizations and publications to support their position. The Air Force, politically by far the strongest of the three services, presented its case through the Air Force Association and the Air Force unofficial publication, *Air Force* (later renamed *Air Force and Space Digest*).[55] The politically weaker, but still potent, Army and Navy positions were presented by the Association of the United States Army (*Army Magazine*) and by the Navy League (*Navy: The Magazine of Sea Power*), respectively.[56]

The military services also found valuable allies in the weapons industry and among congressmen who represented districts (or states) where weapons industries were located. The industries advertised in the service periodicals as well as in national periodicals with a broader circulation. With huge defense contracts at stake, it was to their advantage to do everything to obtain funds for the development and production of a weapons system in which they were involved. Therefore, for example, in the Thor-Jupiter (IRBMs) struggle, the Chrysler Corporation, under contract to develop the Army Jupiter, and with major plants in Alabama, heralded the ability of the Jupiter and was joined by the Alabama congressional delegation. Simultaneously, Douglas Aircraft supported the Thor missile, and was joined by the California delegation. The same picture emerged from the conflict between the Army Nike-Hercules (antiaircraft missile) versus the Air Force Bomarc systems: Western Electric supported the Nike system and Boeing Aircraft backed the Bomarc antiaircraft systems.[57]

This coalition of military and industrial interests led President Eisenhower to warn of the potential threat of the "military-industrial complex." The same theme has been dramatized and expanded by several authors who came to the conclusion that the pressures for increased defense spending can be traced almost exclusively to this "military-industrial complex."[58]

The mass media is one aspect of the military-industrial complex that has yet to receive adequate examination, and is probably the least understood of the components of American military programs and policies. (Another would be the role of labor unions.) The influence of the press is obviously of prime importance, since many Americans tend to believe everything they read, hear, or see. In fact, the creation of the missile gap and its wide public acceptance was a direct function of the means of mass communication in the United States. Every mass periodical but one accepted and propagated the missile gap myth at one time or another during the period 1957 to 1961. The exception was *The Nation*, but such liberal periodicals as *The New Republic* and *Commentary* joined the more conservative *Time*, *U.S. News & World Report*, and *Newsweek* in propagating the myth. *The New York Times* also found itself supporting the belief in the missile gap most of the time.

The influence of the mass media is extremely wide, and varies from the journalist who constantly presents a particular military point of view, to the newscaster who will read anything put before him by the Department of Defense; from the special-interest periodicals, to the wire services that present as fact any news release from the public relations establishment in Saigon and elsewhere.

There was a substantial amount of support for the missile gap belief among the nationally syndicated journalists in this country, and a prime example of this was the repetitive sounding of the alarm by Joseph Alsop.[59] These journalists were joined by politicians and scholars,[60] as well as scientists, such as Werner von Braun and Edward Teller, who allegedly provided more scholarly and "scientific" explanations for the existence of the missile gap. It is interesting to note that it would seem that not one journalist, politician, scientist, nor scholar had his reputation even slightly damaged for his part in the creation of the missile gap myth.

During the missile gap period, military appropriations increased but the services continued to obtain roughly the same percentage of the defense budget they had received before the crisis arose. Throughout the missile gap period, the Air Force received approximately 46 percent of the defense budget, while the Navy maintained 28 percent and the Army 23 percent.[61] The one major exception to this unwritten budgetary rule occurred in 1957, when the Air Force received a rather substantial budgetary increase over the Army and the Navy.[62] (See Table III.) However, the crisis atmosphere created by the missile controversy, along with the above-mentioned factors, led to an annual over-all increase in the United States defense budget from 1956 to 1959. When American defense expenditures were reduced in 1960, this reduction apparently was the result of three factors. First, 1960 was an election year and the Republican Administration attempted to create what it believed would be viewed as a favorable economic climate. Second, this decrease in defense spending reflected the earlier decision by American leaders not to mass produce first-generation missiles, but to wait for the more sophisticated, cheaper, second generation. And, finally, the Eisenhower Administration's willingness to

TABLE III

NATIONAL SECURITY EXPENDITURES FOR THE ARMY, NAVY, AND AIR FORCE
1956–1962
(in millions of dollars) *

	1956	1957	1958	1959	1960	1961	1962
Army	8,702	9,063	9,051	9,468	9,392	10,332	11,559
Navy	9,744	10,398	10,906	11,728	11,642	12,313	13,193
Air Force	16,749	18,363	18,435	19,084	19,066	19,816	20,883
Total Defense Budget	40,641	43,270	44,142	46,426	45,627	47,494	51,107

* Not included in total expenditures: Direction and co-ordination of defense, other central defense activities, civil defense, military assistance, development and control of nuclear energy, stockpiling and other defense-related activities. "United States Defense Policies in 1964," The Library of Congress, Legislative Reference Service (Washington, D.C.: U.S. Government Printing Office, June 4, 1965), 89th Congress, 1st sess., House Document No. 285, p. 179.

cut the defense budget may have reflected President Eisenhower's personal belief that United States security would not be seriously affected by this move.

In 1961, American defense expenditures again began to increase. But before these additional funds could have any impact on American deterrent posture, President Kennedy had convinced the American people that there was no missile gap.

The fact that the defense expenditures of the United States did increase during the period of the missile gap is indisputable, and there does not appear to be much doubt that the pressures of the alleged missile gap added to defense costs. However, numerous other factors were working simultaneously to increase the appropriations Congress and the executive branch allocated for security.

One of the factors which created pressure for additional funds was the substantial role played by partisan politics in the missile gap controversy. In theory, a two-party democracy should have a party of the "opposition" and in this case the party of the opposition was the Democratic party. At the national party level, the conflict between the Democratic and Republican national committees continued throughout the missile debate, and the Democratic Advisory Council was the constant critic of the defense policies of the Eisenhower Administration.

At the outset of this discussion, it should be emphasized that although the Democratic party must take the major blame for the creation of the missile gap because it was the party out of power, during other periods of the arms race the exact reverse was true when the Republicans were out of power (e.g., Nixon in 1968—"security gap"). During the first twenty-five years of the arms race, American partisan politics has been completely onesided in the sense that the opposition always called for more defense spending rather than for less.

The politicians who propagated the missile gap thesis appeared to be reacting to at least three interrelated stimuli: prospects for partisan advantage; loyalty to a military service, to a strategic concept, or an industrial friend; and a sincere concern for the defense posture of the United States.

The missile debate was not sufficiently developed in 1958 to play a major role in the congressional elections of that year. When the debate did become an issue in the 1960 presidential elections, it was transformed from the question of a missile gap to one of American prestige, based on United States military and space achievements. Senator John F. Kennedy attempted to exploit this "prestige" issue in October 1960, and during this period public opinion polls showed definite gains in his vote-getting ability. However, with the multitude of issues involved and the impact of the "great debate," it cannot be claimed that the transformed missile gap question proved decisive—only that it was a factor.

The most interesting observation on the long-run partisan effects of the missile gap debate is that none of the major participants was damaged politically by their mistaken advocacy. Senators Symington and Jackson have since been re-elected and Johnson became President of the United States in a "land-

slide" election in 1964, with hardly a murmur of his past activities in connection with this critical issue of national defense.[63]

Right after President Kennedy's inauguration in January
1961, the House Republican Policy Committee attempted to
answer the Democratic charges on the missile gap and submitted
a set of figures on comparative United States-Soviet Union
military strengths that later appeared to be the official Pentagon
figures for January 1961. This estimate of comparative strategic
strength showed the following:[64]

UNITED STATES	SOVIET UNION
16 Atlas ICBMs	35 T-3 ICBMs (8,000 miles)
32 Polaris missiles	None comparable
600 long-range bombers	200 long-range bombers

President Kennedy did not believe that the United States had
a consistent, coherent, military strategy. He instructed the new
Secretary of Defense, Robert S. McNamara, to conduct a special
study of defense strategy and weapons systems and to make
recommendations to the White House by the end of February.

Almost immediately after President Kennedy announced the
establishment of a committee to study United States defenses,
an event occurred that presaged the end of the belief in the
existence of the missile gap. This event in itself did not end the
debate, but it laid the foundation upon which the missile gap
myth was eventually destroyed. Early in February 1961 strong
evidence indicated that Secretary of Defense McNamara had
stated in a "background briefing" to the press that there was "no
missile gap." The briefing reportedly was given February 6, and
the following day the front page of *The New York Times* carried
a lead article entitled: "Kennedy Defense Study Finds No Evidence of 'Missile Gap.' "[65]

The White House reacted immediately; it denied the alleged
report by Secretary McNamara that there was "no missile gap,"
and stated that this report was "absolutely wrong."[66] The next
day, in a press conference, President Kennedy was asked to
clear up the record on the reported "background briefing" by
McNamara. President Kennedy avoided answering the question

by simply stating that he had not received the defense report from his study commission on United States defense policy and that "it would be premature to reach a judgment as to whether there is a gap or not a gap."[67]

In spite of the fact that Secretary McNamara later denied he had made a statement negating the existence of a "missile gap,"[68] three major periodicals commented on his February "background briefing" in articles highly critical of President Kennedy and the role he had played in the development of the missile gap thesis.[69] One of these periodicals went so far as to declare that if there was a missile gap, the gap favored the United States and not the Soviet Union, and then listed supposed official intelligence figures to support its case.[70] Even the periodical that allegedly served as the unofficial spokesman of the United States Air Force reported the statement Secretary McNamara was said to have made on the missile gap.[71]

Throughout February and March 1961 the press corps in Washington continued to pressure President Kennedy for a definitive answer on the missile gap question, and each time the President replied that he was waiting for the completion of the defense study he had ordered undertaken by the Department of Defense. On March 1, 1961, President Kennedy said that the study would be completed in several weeks, and at that time he would make his recommendations to Congress. On March 8, the President stated that the study would be completed in several days and then he would indicate "what I believe to be the relative defense position of the United States."[72] But, for some reason, from March 8 until early October 1961 the Washington press corps discontinued its questions on the missile gap and the issue was ignored in presidential news conferences during this period.[73] Why the press let President Kennedy ignore the question during this period is not known. However, any lingering doubts about the possibility of a significant missile gap was finally laid to rest by Undersecretary of Defense Roswell Gilpatric in October 1961. *The New York Times* quoted Mr. Gilpatric as saying that the United States had a *second strike* capability which was at least as extensive as what the Soviet Union could deliver by *striking first* [emphasis added]. In other words, the United States would have a larger nuclear delivery system left *after* a surprise attack by the Soviet Union than the nuclear force employed by the Russians in a first strike.[74] In November, President Kennedy claimed that his statements of American military inferiority had been based on the best information available to him, but that at the present time the military power of the United States was "second to none."[75] Finally, by late 1962, Secretary of Defense McNamara claimed that he was "absolutely confident" that the missile gap was a "myth."[76]

Once the missile gap controversy ceased in early 1962, politically this issue did not appear again until 1964. Then, when it was discussed by the Republican presidential nominee, Barry Goldwater, he did not attack the earlier creation of this myth. Instead he attempted to create a new "deterrent gap" based on his belief that American missiles were not reliable and that the United States should rely on manned bombers rather than on untested missiles.

Any assessment of the total impact of the missile gap debate on partisan politics in the United States is by definition a subjective matter. Although the missile debate raged for over four years and at times assumed an almost completely partisan nature, most of the evidence indicated that it played an important but not a lasting role in the American political process. Evidently the American people and their leaders did not learn much from this experience in myth creation. As a political issue, it helped Senator Kennedy get elected, and in view of the closeness of the 1960 election, a case could be made that it was one of the important factors in his election.

The partisan and budgetary effects of the acceptance of the missile gap were closely related to the impact it made on the development of American military strategy.

An attempt to isolate the missile gap and attribute any basic shifts of American military strategy exclusively to this question would misrepresent the development of American strategy during this period. Such factors as the growing number of nuclear weapons available to both sides, the changing nature of the Cold War, the growth of American economic capacity, shifts in military strategy as it related to the third world, are examples of factors that played an important part in the calculation of American strategy. Nonetheless, an analysis of the missile gap debate in conjunction with these factors does offer some significant insight into the formulation of American military policy during this period.

Once the missile gap illusion was destroyed, the following question was asked by many observers, Was the United States, at any time during the missile controversy (1957–1961), in danger of having the American retaliatory forces destroyed by a surprise Russian attack? The answer to this question was an unqualified no. At no time during this period did any major military or political leader claim that at that moment the Soviet Union could destroy American nuclear power. The "period of maximum danger" of the missile gap always was placed some time in the future, and when this date arrived, a new period was defined. It became apparent that during the ICBM controversy the United States consistently possessed a nuclear delivery system that was far superior to that of the Soviet Union.

Until early 1961, United States nuclear superiority was based primarily on the fact that it had many more long-range and medium-range bombers (with in-flight refueling or foreign bases) than Russia had. As ICBMs became operational, the United States relied on the mixed-forces concept of using missiles and bombers to provide superior retaliatory force. By late 1961, it became apparent that the United States possessed a superiority over the Soviet Union in long-range bombers *and* in intercontinental ballistic missiles.

From 1957 to 1961, officials of the Eisenhower Administration claimed that there was no "deterrent gap," and all the available evidence indicates the truth of this contention. Even if at some time during the 1957–1961 period the Soviet Union had possessed more ICBMs than the United States, a successful surprise attack by the Soviet Union on American retaliatory forces would have been impossible to coordinate. One group of experts estimated that it would take from four to six Soviet ICBMs to destroy one American SAC base.[77] The dispersal of about 100 SAC bases with between 400 and 600 aircraft on ground alert further complicated the Russian task. The Soviet Union also would have had to find and destroy 12 to 14 American attack aircraft carriers with a nuclear capability.

The United States had entered the period of the threatened missile gap with a strategic military approach to deterrence that had evolved from the earlier concept of massive retaliation. As nuclear weapons became more plentiful and their delivery means more sophisticated, this doctrine had been so modified that many observers believed it was obsolete as a strategic concept to meet less than an all-out nuclear attack. By the time the new Kennedy Administration revised American strategic doctrine, it was admitted that the United States had a substantial superiority over the Soviet Union in both missiles and bombers, but even this superiority did not make the doctrine of massive retaliation an effective instrument for preventing limited aggression. A detailed analysis of Secretary McNamara's "second strike counterforce doctrine" will be dealt with in the next chapter. At this point it is sufficient to say that this new doctrine would have been impossible without a recognized American strategic superiority.[78]

The American nuclear superiority over the Soviet Union was the result of numerous interrelated factors. Certainly, the pressures exerted on behalf of the expected missile gap led to an acceleration of the missile program. President Eisenhower decided to produce only a limited number of first-generation ICBMs, but the military critics of his Administration caused the number of these missiles actually produced to be increased. Concurrently with the decision to limit first-generation missile production, President Eisenhower assigned the highest priority to the development and production of the more sophisticated second-generation Minuteman ICBMs and Polaris IRBMs. Therefore, when President Kennedy was inaugurated, the second-generation Polaris was operational and the Minuteman ICBM was less than a year from being operational. The new President's decision to accelerate these two missile programs assured continued American superiority over the Soviet Union.

Militarily, probably the greatest irony of the missile gap debate is the fact that while many American government officials questioned the nonexistent strategic military inferiority of the United States, the real American weakness was a very limited capability to fight a conventional war. This limited capacity was a weakness only when viewed in the light of the almost unlimited American political-military commitments throughout the world to either defend other nations against aggression, or, more important in this case, the American commitment to uphold status quo governments in the face of challenges from their own people. Army and Navy spokesmen had emphasized this fundamental American weakness for several years, but no decisive action was taken by the Eisenhower Administration to correct this deficiency. Thus, when Kennedy assumed office he found that the United States had a scant eleven combat-ready Army and Marine divisions.[79]

The total impact of the missile gap controversy on the budgetary, political, and military situation in the United States proved to be rather large in scope. The missile debate was a factor in the increased American defense spending, the election of President Kennedy, and the misallocation of resources among the military services. In this sense, it was almost an all-encompassing consideration in the development of American policies during this period.

THE IMPACT OF THE MISSILE GAP ABROAD

It would be easy to overestimate the impact of the alleged missile gap on American policy and the policies of the other major world powers. Just as different individuals within the United States accepted or rejected this gap, so various nations (or national leaders) adopted their own attitudes toward this critical question. Also, the distinction should be made between the public attitudes expressed by these leaders and their personal knowledge of existing and future American power and the United States willingness to use this power. Nonetheless, there were three general areas in which the missile gap illusion figures rather prominently: (1) Soviet policy toward Western Europe and the partial fragmentation of the NATO Alliance; (2) the Cuban missile crisis; and (3) the Sino-Soviet dispute.

The fundamental question posed by a possible missile gap to the Western European allies of the United States was, Does the United States deterrent remain credible in the face of Soviet strategic superiority? Or, as was later asked, Even if there was no missile gap, could the United States be relied upon to deter a Soviet attack on Western Europe in the "age of nuclear parity"? The doubts created by the missile gap among Western European leaders hastened the process of questioning American nuclear credibility, but it would appear that even if there had been no missile gap illusion, the increasingly plentiful supply of American and Soviet nuclear weapons and their delivery systems would have created similar attitudes.

Concurrent with the supposed weakened posture of the American strategic deterrent capability in Western Europe was the growing realization by many military experts that tactical nuclear weapons probably would aid a Russian military offense in Western Europe more than the NATO defense of this area. And that in any case, a tactical nuclear war in Europe probably would destroy the very area defended.[80]

If this was the case, then Western Europe would have to be defended with conventional armed forces and this was a capability that few Western leaders believed the NATO Alliance possessed. America's European allies had never met the conventional force requirements agreed upon by the NATO Alliance, and the United States possessed a very limited capability to fight a conventional war.

Thus, the credibility of the American nuclear deterrent to prevent an attack on Western Europe was weakened at the same time that many observers doubted the ability of the armed forces of the NATO Alliance to defend this area without destroying it in the process. The Eisenhower Administration had been too preoccupied with the strategic nuclear balance and increased national defense costs to provide the funds essential for a large number of combat-ready conventional divisions.

The situation during the alleged missile gap presented the Soviet Union with an opportunity that it did not pass up. On numerous occasions, the leaders of the Soviet Union attempted to exploit the unanswered questions that surrounded "deterrence and defense" for Western Europe. The American IRBM bases in Europe, the use of NATO (and other) airbases for U-2 reconnaissance flights, the United States presence in Berlin, and the very existence of the Alliance were all situations that Soviet diplomacy wanted to change. When the opportunity presented itself, the leaders of the Soviet Union had no compunction about threatening America's NATO Allies with "nuclear blackmail" based on the alleged Soviet strategic superiority.[81]

The period of the alleged missile gap had occurred simultaneously with other military, economic, and political changes that led inevitably to a crisis within the NATO Alliance. The role of the missile gap in this crisis appears to be twofold: (1) In Europe, the doubts created by the missile gap helped to reduce the credibility of the American deterrent posture, and (2) In the United States the possibility of a missile gap encouraged the allocation of military resources for development of strategic weapons at the expense of a conventional capability. The former gave rise to the demand for an independent nuclear force by at least one European ally, while the latter eventually led the Kennedy Administration to an increased American emphasis on the development of the capability to conduct limited war (both conventional and unconventional). By 1970 neither of these problems had been resolved, and the NATO Alliance was still in a state of flux.

A second area in which the events surrounding the missile gap and its resultant American strategic superiority appear to have been an important factor was the Soviet decision to place intermediate- and medium-range ballistic missiles and medium-range bombers in Cuba in October 1962. (A detailed analysis of the Cuban missile crisis will be undertaken in the next chapter in the general context of the military-political strategy of the Kennedy Administration.)

The final major area in which the alleged missile gap played an important, though very limited, role was in the field of Sino-Soviet relations. A detailed study of this dispute is far beyond the scope of this book. Nonetheless, the missile gap controversy evidently added an additional element of friction to the developing split between these two Communist nations.

The acceptance of the missile gap thesis by many Americans and the Russian claims of missile superiority caused the leadership of Communist China to accept the existence of a missile gap favoring the Soviet Union. Apparently, Mao Tse-tung incorrectly assumed that the Soviet development of the ICBM in 1957 had brought about a decisive change in the balance of strategic power in favor of the Soviet Union. Based on this belief, the Chinese leader hoped that the Soviet Union would embark on a more militant foreign policy in an attempt to achieve the elimination, or at least the reduction, of American power in Asia. When the Soviet Union did not appear to exploit sufficiently this supposed military advantage, the Communist Chinese resented the cautious foreign policy pursued by the Soviet Union and accused Russia of ceasing to be a revolutionary power.[82]

As has been seen above, the Soviet Union itself added credence to the belief in the existence of the missile gap whenever possible. The boasts and bravado of Premier Khrushchev had been one of the fundamental causes of the creation of the missile gap. However, viewed in retrospect, it appears as though the Soviet Union paid a high price for very little, if any, temporary gains in its attempt to militarily bluff the United States. Diplomatically, during the period of the missile gap (1957–1961), the leaders of the Soviet Union made no solid gains, although negatively it was possible that the Soviet Union had managed to keep the diplomatic initiative. Soviet leadership eventually had to face the consequences for their willingness to exploit the possible missile gap. The Russian statements on Soviet missile strength had added strong impetus to the belief in the missile gap in the United States and therefore helped to encourage an escalation in the arms race which the Soviet Union could ill afford. Soviet claims and diplomacy managed to disillusion Communist China and led to a major diplomatic defeat in Cuba in October 1962.

By 1962, the Soviet Union was faced with a possible "deterrent gap" because of the overwhelming superiority of American strategic forces. The United States had 30,000 megatons stored and ready to deliver—this represented roughly the equivalent of ten tons of TNT for every man, woman, and child on the earth. To deliver this megatonnage, the United States possessed over 50 ICBMs (Atlas and Titan), 80 Polaris missiles, about 90 Thor and Jupiter missiles on stations overseas, 1,700 bombers capable of reaching the Soviet Union, 300 carrier-borne fighter bombers with an atomic capability, and approximately 1,000 supersonic land-based fighters with an atomic capability. In contrast, the Soviet Union possessed between 50 and 100 ICBMs and less than 200 long-range bombers capable of reaching the United States.[83] Once this American superiority became known in 1961 it greatly complicated not only Soviet policy, but also laid the blame for Soviet inferiority at the feet of Premier Khrushchev. This American superiority could easily be interpreted as an American preparation for a first strike on Soviet territory and there were still Americans around who thought that this might be a good idea.[84]

Finally, it should be emphasized that even if the Soviet Union had built a large missile force, this would have in no way negated the deterrent force of the United States. With part of SAC on airborne or ground alert and much of the remainder of this force spread throughout the world on American bases, there was no way a surprise attack could have destroyed this force. It was physically impossible for the Soviet Union to find and simultaneously destroy such a diversified force. In addition, the Soviet Union had to find and destroy the fourteen American aircraft carriers with a thermonuclear capability. In short, the United States, even had it faced a large Soviet missile superiority, would not have been in danger of the feared Soviet attack.

IV

The Kennedy Administration: Flexible Response and Second-Strike Counterforce

(1961–1963)

By the start of the Kennedy Administration, American nuclear superiority was firmly established and was to become a permanent reality of the 1960s. The only agency seriously to challenge this was the Air Force and its allies; their challenge and predictions of doom were always for several years in the future, never for the present. As has been seen, the Kennedy Administration, after some initial bungling, managed to destroy the myth of the missile gap without serious political damage to itself or the Democratic party.

As a matter of fact, recent accounts of the Administration of John F. Kennedy have claimed that by February 1961 President Kennedy knew America's nuclear strength exceeded its needs for defense, but claimed that he did not dare to challenge Congress on both bomber and missile reduction. So, according to Arthur Schlesinger, Jr., President Kennedy decided to back McNamara in challenging the "vociferous B-70 boys in Congress," while at the same time going along with the supporters of increases in the Polaris and Minuteman programs. And, although the new manned bomber (B-70) was delayed, the United States escalated its missile production.[1] Thus, even in the face of a recognized American superiority in missiles, the Kennedy Administration felt constrained by military and political pressures to escalate the arms race regardless of the comparative strategic power of the United States and the Soviet Union.

President Kennedy's awareness of American nuclear superiority evidently led him to understand properly the very limited diplomatic-military purposes to which this superiority could be applied. It was this awareness of the limited efficacy of nuclear weapons that led Kennedy and his new Secretary of Defense, Robert S. McNamara, to attempt once again a clear definition of American military strategy—the first such effort since the early attempts of the Eisenhower Administration.

It should be emphasized that the amount of military strength needed by the United States during any given period of this study depends upon how American policy makers viewed the role of the United States in the world and the extent of American commitments to its allies and to the maintenance of the status quo throughout the non-Communist world. It was the growing exaggeration and distortion of the perceptions of this role that led the United States increasingly to escalate the arms race in the face of what it believed was a sustained, planned form of aggression from Moscow (and then China). During the Eisenhower years, the common belief was that the United States could fulfill its role in the world with a superiority in thermonuclear weapons and a stated intent to use them. It was only with the advent of the Kennedy Administration that American leaders came to believe that this massive amount of strategic power was of no avail in such complex situations as had developed in such diverse areas as Hungary, Iraq, Cuba, and Indochina. Thermonuclear weapons were of absolutely no value in the Hungarian crisis of 1956, and they had failed to stop either Ho Chi Minh in Vietnam, Kassem in Iraq, or Castro in Cuba.

In order to correct this deficiency in existing United States military forces and to expand the military alternatives available to the United States government, the "two and half war" doctrine was developed by Kennedy and McNamara. McNamara contended that the United States should be prepared for major military actions in Europe and Asia, while at the same time keeping forces available for action in the Western hemisphere. Although this was not clearly articulated at the time, McNamara later put it this way:

> Therefore, we had to provide, in addition to our NATO requirements, the forces required to meet such an attack in Asia [by China] as well as fulfill our commitments in the Western Hemisphere.[2]

As is well known, by the time Kennedy was assassinated the United States still had a large number of troops committed to NATO and had begun to develop the force levels necessary to place over 500,000 men in Vietnam, with American reserve strength still available for the Dominican invasion.

Therefore, it should have come as no surprise that immediately upon assuming office, Kennedy moved to increase American military spending. If the liberals, who had been mainly responsible for putting Kennedy into the White House, had any illusions about his willingness to tackle the influence of the military-industrial alliance, they were sadly disillusioned, for less than three months after assuming office, Kennedy sent a special message to Congress requesting an additional $650 million for the Defense Department for the Fiscal Year 1962.[3] (It should be noted that this spending was requested over five months before the crisis surrounding the building of the Berlin Wall in August 1961.)

By the time the new Administration had completed its requests for additional funds for Eisenhower's original 1962 fiscal budget, President Kennedy had added $5 billion to the earlier requests.[4] After fourteen months in office, the Administration was proudly proclaiming the addition of over $9 billion in defense funds. Only one third of this additional funding went to nuclear striking power, and the remainder had gone for increases in the flexibility of the United States to respond to perceived limited military aggression.[5]

The rationale for the additional spending was not hard to find. Kennedy stated that the object of the additional budget funds was to insure that:

Any potential aggressor contemplating an attack on any part of the Free World must know that our response will be suitable, selective, swift, and effective.[6]

But the articulation of the new strategy of the Administration was left to McNamara. This strategy consisted of two parts— on the tactical level the doctrine endorsed a "flexible response"; on the strategic level it invoked a "second-strike counterforce" doctrine (see Glossary). It was hoped that with the development of a "flexible response" capability the United States would have a nonnuclear alternative to what it defined as aggression. The second-strike counterforce was supposed to give the United States a "rational" use of atomic weapons in the event of an attack on the United States or some close ally (e.g., Western Europe). The doctrine of massive retaliation was officially discarded[7] and replaced by one which was intended to give the United States a larger number of alternative responses to various types of "aggression."

The importance of these two American doctrines is hard to overestimate; the fact that "second-strike counterforce" and the "flexible response" are still the basis of American military-diplomatic thinking demonstrates their critical nature of these policies. Therefore, it is imperative that a clear understanding of these doctrines be gained in order to analyze critically their efficacy and relevance in today's world. For the purpose of analysis, we will temporarily separate the two doctrines, studying the concept of flexible response first and then the second-strike counterforce strategy. The two halves can then be reunited and an effort can be made to see how the Kennedy (and later the Johnson and Nixon) Administration applied this definition of American power and its uses to the various situations that faced the United States.

FLEXIBLE RESPONSE

In its simplest terms, the military problem perceived by Kennedy was one of finding a doctrine which would bring American military power to bear on the rest of the world without the use of atomic weapons; the doctrine of a "flexible response" was the answer. Like all shifts of American military doctrine, indications of this change had appeared in the years preceding its formal announcement in 1963.

Throughout the Eisenhower Administration the Army had felt that it was being shortchanged in the fight for military appropriations. This frustration had peaked in 1959 with the retirement of General Maxwell Taylor and the publication of his book *The Uncertain Trumpet*. In this work, General Taylor strongly criticized American defense policies, especially the United States failure to develop a conventional capability and to establish a large Army force capable of carrying out this type of mission. The following year, Lyndon Johnson's Senate Preparedness Investigating Subcommittee conducted an investigation into Army modernization and found, not surprisingly, that the Army had fallen far behind its Soviet counterpart in modernization and re-equipment in the post-World War II period.[8] In a strict military sense, these charges appear to have been well founded. The United States Army in 1960 did have a limited combat capability—both in Europe and in the rest of the world. In the 1956 Hungarian crisis, the United States had no conventional options in the face of the Russian suppression of the Hungarian revolution. Likewise, the Lebanon crisis in 1958 had placed great strains on the Army and Navy capacity to land and maintain a relatively small number of troops in that country; this was done only at the expense of the reserve forces of both the Sixth Fleet in the Mediterranean and the Seventh Army in Europe. Although the estimates vary, it would appear that when Eisenhower left office, the Army had somewhere between eleven and fourteen divisions and the Marines had approximately three.[9] Of these divisions, the United States had five committed to the Seventh Army in Europe and two committed to the Republic of (South) Korea. Therefore, at this time, the combat reserves available to the Army were somewhere between four and seven divisions, some of doubtful combat effectiveness. One member of the Kennedy Administration contended that the United States had only three divisions in reserve.[10]

Kennedy came to the White House determined to change what he perceived to be this fundamental weakness in American power and the military alternatives available to the American President. He increased the budgetary allocations for these services and brought General Taylor out of retirement as special adviser to the President for military affairs. From the start of the Kennedy Administration the major change in military policy was the strengthening of the American ability to engage in limited conflict.[11] Thus, by 1965, on the eve of the Vietnamese escalation, Johnson had sixteen active Army divisions and six National Guard and reserve divisions to work with in his contingency planning for Vietnam.[12]

The rationale for the doctrine of "flexible response" was set forth by Secretary McNamara in the clearest possible terms:

> Suppose you were to start from the premise that nuclear war is unthinkable and that you are not capable of fighting a nonnuclear war. If that is true, then you have no military foundation at all for your policy.[13]

But the doctrine of "flexible response" went beyond the abstraction of offering a nonnuclear alternative and served notice on Communist or Communist-defined forces that in the future they would be confronted with American military power. Secretary McNamara made this clear in testimony before Congress when he stated:

> Our Communist opponents have greatly extended the range of conflict to cover virtually every aspect of human activity. And we, together with our allies, must carefully allocate our defense effort to insure that we can meet the challenge on every front and at every level.[14]

McNamara continued in his testimony: "We must be in a position to confront him [the enemy] at any level of provocation with an appropriate military response.[15]

In order to be in a position to "confront him at any level" Secretary McNamara established the United States Strike

Command by placing the Strategic Army Command (regular reserves of United States Army) and the Tactical Air Command of the Air Force under joint command. This force was to provide an:

> . . . integrated mobile, high combat ready force, available to augment the unified commands overseas or to be employed as the primary force in remote areas.[16]

This was no vague threat of massive retaliation; it was a specific statement of American intent to engage in conflict "on every front and at every level." After the events in Cuba, Laos, Cambodia, Vietnam, and the Dominican Republic, nobody can say that the United States public was not warned of the intentions of the Kennedy and then the Johnson administrations.

The American decision to develop a conventional alternative in the conduct of its foreign and military policy should be understood for exactly what it was—an American decision to engage in this type of conflict whenever the leaders of this country perceived a "Communist" or "Communist-inspired" form of aggression. It seems safe to assume that the Kennedy-McNamara willingness to develop the capacity to fight a conventional war meant a willingness on their part to fight just such a war if they felt American interests demanded it. Obviously, the very existence of the capacity to fight a nonnuclear war increased the chances of one.

SECOND-STRIKE COUNTERFORCE

At this point in the arms race, the American decision to develop a conventional capability could have had at least one positive effect if the United States had decided simultaneously to reduce its massive nuclear striking force to a minimum deterrent posture. Or, put another way, if the United States had reduced its strategic striking force to approximately the same low number of delivery vehicles possessed by the Soviet Union, no longer would the possibility have existed of a surprise attack on the Soviet Union. If this had taken place, the United States would have then been following roughly the same strategic doctrine that the Soviet Union had followed since 1955, that is, the possession of enough nuclear delivery power to deter an attack on its homeland and a large conventional army capable of defending and patrolling the periphery of its empire. In Pentagonese, this translated into a doctrine of minimum deterrence.

However, the Kennedy Administration did exactly the opposite. Instead of reducing the number of American delivery vehicles, it increased them. It not only promised to be able to withstand a Soviet first strike, it promised to be able to absorb such a first strike and still be able to destroy not only Soviet cities, but also the remaining Soviet nuclear force. This "second-strike counterforce" doctrine accepted the existing American superiority in delivery systems and promised an escalation of the arms race for the maintenance of this superiority. There was no system of logic or reason known to man to prevent the Soviet Union from perceiving this force as being a potential first-strike force against the Soviet Union; the only way for them to end this potential threat was for the Russians to increase their own nuclear delivery system.

Secretary of Defense McNamara demonstrated his awareness of American nuclear superiority when he announced the new doctrine in the most precise and rational-sounding terms:

> Our nuclear strength . . . makes possible a strategy designed to preserve the fabric of our societies should war occur. The United States has come to the conclusion that to the extent feasible . . . principal military objectives, in the event of nuclear war . . . should be the destruction of the enemy's military forces, not of his civilian population.[17]

Later, he continued his explanation of the forces necessary for such a policy:

> Such a force should have sufficient flexibility to permit a choice of strategies, particularly the ability to 1) strike back decisively at the entire Soviet target system simultaneously, or 2) strike back

first at the Soviet bomber bases, missile sites, and other military installations associated with their long-range nuclear forces to reduce the power of any follow-up attack—and then if necessary, strike back at the Soviet urban and industrial complex in a controlled and deliberate way.[18]

But "such a force" as could be left over *after* a Soviet attack would by definition be large enough to be viewed as a potential American first-strike force by any objective observer.

An essential corollary to the new doctrine was the absolute necessity of a substantial American civil defense program. Official reasoning was that to accept a first strike, you must have shelters for the population. Or, in the vernacular of the time: "The United States could have more confidence in its Sunday Punch if it were associated with some capacity to absorb punishment."[19] Therefore, one of the first moves of the Kennedy Administration was to start the process of alerting the American public to the need for shelters and the allocation of $207 million in the first six months of his administration for a shelter program.[20] After an initial period of success in galvanizing the public (and industry) to build shelters, the program failed and led mainly to a shelter program for high government officials, and for the very rich. The not-so-powerful or affluent gained a number of signs marking "shelter" on public basements and a growing awareness that the shelter program was completely impractical in the thermonuclear age.

Secretary McNamara's new doctrine was intended to deter an attack on the United States. But the fact remains that less American power would have accomplished the same purpose even if the Soviet Union had been planning a surprise attack on the United States. In the process, the McNamara strategy of continued American superiority was perceived as a threat to the security of the Soviet Union and inevitably led to a *needless* escalation of the arms race. McNamara had not learned that in the thermonuclear age an increase in arms may mean a decrease in national security. The leaders of the United States have yet to learn this lesson.

At a later date, I. F. Stone succinctly pointed out the folly of McNamara's "second-strike counterforce" when he stated: "The finely spun concepts of deterrence and second strike give a rational appearance to an essentially irrational process, the mindless multiplication of weaponry."[21] And, of course, that is exactly what happened under the Kennedy and then the Johnson administrations. The missile gap debate in the United States had already led to a major American escalation of the arms race, and McNamara's new doctrine demanded even greater increases in military spending by the government of the United States.

Therefore, on the strategic level, the Kennedy Administration began to insure the continued United States superiority over the Soviet Union in delivery systems. The new Kennedy budget submitted in January 1962 called for 13 Atlas squadrons to be operational in 1963 (130 ICBMs); 12 Titan squadrons totaling 108 ICBMs; and funds for additional Minutemen, bringing the total to 850. In January 1963 another 150 Minutemen were added to the existing goals, to bring the total projected Minuteman force to 1,000.[22] In addition to these planned increases, "the increase in the strategic bomber force to fourteen wings of B-52s and two wings of B-58s was completed in 1963." The number of SAC bombers placed on 15 minute alert was increased by 50 percent.[23]

Although all of these goals were not met because of changes in the need for certain systems and the introduction of large numbers of Polaris missiles, the fact remains that this build-up began at a time when the Soviet Union had less than 100 ICBMs and fewer than 300 long-range bombers capable of reaching the United States.[24] By November 1963 the United States plans called for 1,000 Minutemen, over 650 Polaris, and over 1,000 long- and medium-range bombers capable of reaching the Soviet Union. But throughout this period, Soviet strength grew very little in proportion to the American increases, with the Soviet Union holding its strategic forces at approximately 300 ICBMs and under 300 long-range bombers until some time after 1966. And, when the Soviet Union finally did begin its own large-scale missile-building program, it appears to have been in part a reaction against the proposed American ABM, the possible development of the B-70 bomber, and possible MRV (Multiple Re-entry Vehicle) on the Polaris A-3 missile.

At this point, the alert observer will ask, But what about all of the savings by McNamara due to his "cost effectiveness program" and his willingness to tell the generals no? And the answer is that there obviously were substantial savings involved in the refusal of the Kennedy Administration to give the military everything they asked for. Probably the two most important areas of at least temporary savings were Kennedy's decisions to halt development of the atomic airplane and his decision not to spend the funds for the Nike-Zeus ABM system.[25] The atomic airplane had cost the American taxpayers over one billion dollars over a fifteen-year period before Kennedy stopped it. And, as is known, the initial decision to deploy an ABM system has already been approved by President Nixon and the Congress; the total costs of this program are unknown (see below).

The major fight between the White House and the Pentagon during the Kennedy Administration (and the Johnson Administration) was, to no one's surprise, the effort on the part of the Air Force to gain additional funds for more bombers and the development of the B-70 long-range supersonic bomber. This drive for funds followed the now-classic pattern of obtaining funds from a reluctant President or Congress. "How Far Is the Red Air Force Ahead?" ran the title to an article in *Air Force and Space Digest* in September 1961. In this article it was contended that the Soviet Union was ahead of the United States in the field of bomber development, and called for more money for the Air Force so that this deficiency could be corrected.[26]

The early stages of this new "bomber gap" centered around the Air Force claim that the Soviet Union had developed a long-range Mach 2 (supersonic) bomber—the Bounder. Therefore, so the reasoning went, the United States should have such a bomber immediately. This claim was also supported in 1963 by the prestigious *Jane's All the World's Aircraft,* at least to the extent that *Jane's* mentioned its existence. But at a later date it became evident that the so-called Bounder was a Soviet test aircraft, references to it in future issues of *Jane's* were dropped, and the Air Force finally quit speaking of the threat from this nonexistent bomber force.[27]

The reader should keep in mind that the threat of the Bounder appeared simultaneously with reductions in the Air Force budget. Secretary McNamara had cut the development funds for the B-70 bomber from $358 to $220 million and had refused to spend the $525 million for the building of a new wing of 45 B-52 bombers.[28] McNamara's reasons for cutting back on the bomber force were not to slow down the arms race but to conduct it more efficiently. He claimed that to develop and procure a "modest force" of these planes would have cost $10 billion. But the planes were not even bombers in the traditional sense: they would carry no "bombs," but a very complex air-launched missile. "The question was not bombs versus missiles. The debate was about alternative launching platforms and alternative missile systems."[29]

Throughout his term, McNamara continued this running battle with the "bomber generals" and succeeded at least to the extent that he prevented a substantial building program for the B-52 or B-58; he also stopped the Air Force from starting construction of the various names under which the B-70 was disguised. Yet in the long run, like the ABM system vetoed by Kennedy, it would appear that McNamara lost this fight also. By 1970, the Air Force seemed to have gained a commitment from the Congress for $10 billion for the B-70 (later renamed the B-1).

McNamara's temporary success in frustrating the grandiose schemes of the Air Force generals led not only to increasing acrimony between the Secretary and the Air Force, but also laid the foundation for the attempted development of a "bomber gap" theme in the 1964 presidential campaign. In spite of the best efforts of General Curtis LeMay and Republican nominee Barry Goldwater, this issue never really caught on, in part because McNamara released to the press the official intelligence estimates of Soviet bomber strength as of 1964 as less than

300,[30] and hopefully in part because the American people had learned something from the earlier bomber and missile "gaps" and were not quite ready to believe another defense myth.

Paradoxically, the total effort of both Kennedy and McNamara was to save the American taxpayer money while simultaneously increasing the military budget of the United States. Money was saved by McNamara's "cost effectiveness" in the sense that the atomic-powered bomber and the ABM system were not built; nonetheless American military spending increased substantially during the Kennedy Administration. Perhaps Noam Chomsky best summed up the achievements of Secretary McNamara in this field when he said: "No doubt McNamara succeeded in doing with the utmost efficiency that which should not be done at all."[31]

The Kennedy Administration had barely begun before it was confronted with three of the continuing "crisis" areas facing the United States—Vietnam, Berlin, and Cuba. It is these three areas that will now be briefly examined.

VIETNAM, BERLIN, AND CUBA

Like all of the other early problems of the Kennedy Administration, the Vietnam crisis was a continuation of the difficulties of the previous Administration. During the 1950s, American aid to the Diem regime in South Vietnam had averaged over $300 million a year and by 1960 the United States had 685 military men in South Vietnam. After some initial hesitation, President Kennedy acceded to pressure from advisers (primarily General Maxwell Taylor and Walt W. Rostow) to commit American military forces in Vietnam to maintain the status quo. It was hoped that the number could be kept at a low level, but General Taylor estimated that it would take approximately 10,000 Americans to "show them how to get the job done."[32]

Thus, at a very early stage in the Kennedy Administration, the doctrine of flexible response was implemented. By the end of his first year, the President had sent 3,200 men to Vietnam; and at the time of his assassination, there were 16,300. During his first year in office, 11 Americans were killed; during 1963, 78, and 218 were wounded as the American commitment continued to expand.[33]

But Kennedy's major historical role in relation to Vietnam was found not so much in the early escalation of the war as it was in the fact that he decided to build up the Army's conventional and unconventional warfare capability. It was this 1961 decision to dramatically increase the size and capability of the Army that enabled Johnson to increase the number of troops in Vietnam from 23,300 in 1964 to 385,000 in 1966. Had the earlier build-up under Kennedy not taken place, Johnson would not have had this option, because the troops would not have been available. Therefore, although historians may argue as to whether Kennedy intended to pull out of Vietnam after the 1964 elections, the fact remains that it was his policy that made a massive land war in Vietnam possible in the first place.

The 1961 crisis over Berlin was a continuation of the Soviet pressure tactics since the end of World War II. In 1958, in the face of the alleged missile gap in favor of the Soviets, Premier Khrushchev had announced his intention to turn Berlin over to the East Germans. An authority who should have known better, D. F. Fleming, attributed this Soviet move to the reality of the missile gap favoring the Soviet Union and the belief that the Soviets were acting on the basis of their lead in the nuclear arms race.[34] Arthur Schlesinger attributes the 1958 Soviet pressure on Berlin to "the changing balance of nuclear forces."[35] Obviously, this was not the case, although Khrushchev evidently thought that he could obtain some diplomatic goals by bluffing in the face of the American belief in the missile gap, and this appears to be exactly what Khrushchev was doing in the case of Berlin, both in 1958 and in 1961. By early 1961, the Soviet leaders are certain to have known that it was a question of months before the obvious American superiority became common knowledge.*

The last chance for the Soviet Union to use the "missile gap" apparently was at the June 1961 meeting in Vienna between

* It is well to keep in mind that the U-2 had been flying over the Soviet Union from 1956 to 1961. Once the U-2 was grounded, the intelligence mission of this aircraft was taken over by equally competent earth satellites.

Premier Khrushchev and President Kennedy. At this meeting Khrushchev made his last bluff based on the alleged Soviet superiority and threatened a separate peace with East Germany unless the Berlin question was resolved. By this time, President Kennedy knew that there was no missile gap and that the United States was superior to the Soviet Union in nuclear forces and would remain so for the foreseeable future. Premier Khrushchev's demands were not met, for they were recognized for exactly what they were—a bluff.[36] Once it became obvious that the United States could not be tricked out of Berlin, the Soviet Union decided that its only other means of closing this exit route to Western Europe was to seal off the city. The Soviet Union proceeded to do just that when it began building the Berlin Wall on August 13, 1961.

The United States feared that another Berlin blockade was being attempted and almost immediately sent a battle group (approximately 1,200 men) down the Helmstead Autobahn to Berlin to establish access rights to the city. The battle group was not challenged, and the fear of blockade lessened. However, President Kennedy used this occasion to augment American military spending, increase the size of the armed forces by 225,000 men, and received authority to call up an additional 250,000 reservists at any time.[37] Access to the allied sector of Berlin continued for the Western powers, and the Berlin crisis subsided.

On the other hand, the continuing crisis surrounding Cuba presented a more dangerous threat to world peace.

The Cuban crisis can be broken down into two related crises, one in 1961—the Bay of Pigs—and the other in 1962—the Cuban missile crisis. The blame for the Bay of Pigs fiasco must be jointly shared by Eisenhower and Kennedy. The successful American-sponsored invasion of Guatemala in 1954 had overthrown the Arbenz regime and led to the establishment of a more pro–United States, pro–United Fruit regime in this unfortunate Latin American nation. Based on this earlier success, certain people in the Eisenhower Administration became convinced that the same tactics would work to overthrow Castro in Cuba and thereby destroy the Cuban Revolution. One of the first Eisenhower spokesmen to advocate some type of invasion of Cuba was Vice-President Nixon in April 1959.[38] Eventually, the idea of a Guatemala-type invasion gained the acceptance of the CIA and some in the higher echelons in the Pentagon. President Eisenhower approved of the invasion plan in March 1960; Cuban exiles were then trained and equipped by the United States in Guatemala and Nicaragua. The invasion was set for Spring 1961. When Kennedy came to office he approved of the invasion plan for April 1961 with the understanding that no United States forces would be directly involved.[39]

The invasion was an abysmal failure. Apparently the Cubans had no desire for a return of an American-supported Batista type of government, and they failed to "rise-up" and challenge the forces of Fidel Castro. The failure of the invasion was a distinct blow to the prestige of John Kennedy, and the new President emerged from this crisis determined not to allow such faulty intelligence and planning to reoccur in the future. President Kennedy attempted to place a buffer between the presidency and the CIA in the form of McGeorge Bundy as a special adviser to the President for national security affairs. And, significantly, a short time later the President ordered the Joint Chiefs of Staff to draw up the contingency plans necessary for the future invasion of Cuba.[40]

After the Bay of Pigs failure, many in the United States were critical of President Kennedy for not salvaging American prestige and launching an American invasion of Cuba. However, at the time of the invasion, it is doubtful if the United States could have mustered the forces necessary for an invasion of Cuba without stripping American military forces of all reserves. As Arthur Schlesinger has pointed out:

> . . . the United States could not even have invaded Cuba after the Bay of Pigs without drawing troops from other parts of the world and thereby inviting communist moves on other fronts.[41]

The Bay of Pigs had demonstrated to Kennedy how limited his conventional military options were in view of his determination to control foreign revolutions and internal conflicts. As has been seen, the President and his Secretary of Defense had already begun to expand the conventional forces of the United States and to extend American alternatives to include the use of large-scale conventional/unconventional operations by the armed forces.

But before this expansion of conventional power could take place, the United States was confronted with another Cuban crisis, this time not directly of its own making. By October 1962 it had become apparent that the Soviet Union was installing intermediate-range ballistic missiles (IRBM—approximate range 1,500–2,000 miles) and medium-range ballistic missiles (MRBM—range 1,000 miles), along with a small medium-range bomber force (Ilyushin 28—1,500 mile range). The exact number is open to question, but the following figures are probably accurate—IRBM, 12–16 missiles; MRBMs, 24 missiles; and 48 IL 28 bombers.[42] This Soviet action was taken in the face of an overwhelming American strategic superiority. The United States had over 1,600 bombers capable of reaching the Soviet Union, compared with less than 300 Soviet bombers that could reach the United States. In addition, the United States had almost 300 missiles that could reach the Soviet Union, while Russia had less than 100.[43]

The attempt to place missiles so close to the United States was obviously a dangerous move and one that Soviet leaders must have thoroughly examined in a detailed manner. The Soviet Union was aware of the American U-2 reconnaissance capability and is certain to have known that the risks of discovery were high, if not certain. Therefore, the question must be asked (and answered) as to why Khrushchev was willing to take such risks in the face of an American nuclear force that could survive a Soviet surprise attack, with or without missiles in Cuba, and then proceed to obliterate the Soviet Union.*

A number of explanations for the Soviet action were put forward in the United States, but there was no simple answer.

---

* It should be pointed out that only the 12–16 IRBMs were capable of reaching American SAC and missile bases in the north and north central United States. The MRBMs and Ilyushin 28 did not have the range to reach most of these targets.

However, it does appear as though there was *one predominant* reason for attempting to place Russian missiles in Cuba, with other motives playing only a supporting role.

The most simplistic reason given for the Soviet move was the belief that it once again demonstrated the highly aggressive nature of the Soviet Union and its desire to upset the balance of power and threaten a first strike against the United States.[44] In view of American strength at this time this argument hardly deserves comment.

A more logical explanation is that by 1962 the United States had upset what Khrushchev believed to be the balance of terror. As has been seen, at this time the Soviet Union was not only inferior to the United States in ICBMs, but also had decided *not* to build large numbers of first-generation ICBMs, and to wait until they had perfected their version of second-generation missiles. In the meantime, United States strategic forces appeared ominous and threatening to the security of the Soviet Union. Therefore, the logical way to close this perceived deterrent gap was for the Soviet Union to deploy some of their numerous medium-range missiles in Cuba as a temporary stop-gap until the second generation of Soviet ICBMs became operational.[45]

If American and Soviet leaders understood the deadly game of thermonuclear diplomacy and the reality of the accompanying weapons systems, then they knew that the deployment of approximately 42 missiles in Cuba did not upset the balance of terror. The Soviet missiles were not of sufficient range to reach most of the strategic delivery systems of the United States. (At most, 16 had the needed range.) In view of the American superiority in delivery systems, the Soviet move in Cuba might serve to re-establish the *certainty* of mutual annihilation that had been temporarily upset; but it could in no way lead to a first strike on the United States, with its advantage in delivery systems that ran over 4–1.

The decision to place IRBMs and MRBMs in Cuba was greatly facilitated by the fact that the Soviet Union had developed a large number of these medium-range missiles in keeping with their doctrine of being able to defend the entire periphery of the

Soviet Union against attack. This could explain the fact that while the Soviet Union was only building several hundred long-range bombers in the late 1950s and early 1960s, they had produced literally thousands of Mig-15 and Mig-17 interceptor aircraft, and were to later produce large numbers of Mig-21s.[46]

Even a few Soviet missiles in Cuba would vastly complicate any American effort to launch a surprise attack designed to *simultaneously* destroy Soviet delivery systems in Russia and in Cuba. The complexity of timing and coordination of such an attack would in itself be enough to prevent the United States from attempting such a difficult task. Thus, Soviet security would be assured until second-generation missiles (or more first-generation missiles) were available.

On the other hand, some experts have contended that the Soviet missiles were placed in Cuba in an attempt to prevent an American invasion. In view of past American actions, the fear of an invasion appears to have been a real one. And it is possible that one of the main reasons that Castro allowed the emplacement of missiles was to prevent such an invasion. However, it is hard to believe that the Soviet Union would risk its existence *only* to prevent an invasion of Cuba. There would appear to be a reason more closely related to Soviet security.

The precise motives for the Soviet action may never be known. But, Soviet leadership could have rationalized such a risky act along the following lines. At the invitation of a friendly Turkish government, the United States had deployed Jupiter missiles near the Soviet border on Turkish territory. If such an act was legal and justified, then why could not the Soviet government accept the invitation from a friendly Cuban government and deploy missiles in Cuba? Throughout the arms race the United States had deployed medium-range bombers and then missiles on allied territory close enough to the Soviet Union to effect a strike on Soviet territory. This had been done in the name of national security. Thus, in the face of the overwhelming American strategic force, why could not the Soviet Union deploy missiles in Cuba to maintain a balance of terror that it felt had been upset to the detriment of their national security?

Of course, America did not see the logic of the Soviet position.

Either the Kennedy Administration misunderstood the reality of the balance of terror, or, more likely, the President's reaction was based more on domestic political considerations than on the military reality of the existing status of the arms race. Possibly President Kennedy felt that the intricacies of the balance of terror were too complicated to explain to the American people. Whatever the case, Kennedy characterized the Soviet act as a ". . . deliberately provocative and unjustified change in the status quo . . ." that could not be accepted by the United States. Kennedy further contended that the Soviet act was a "definite threat to peace" and that the United States had never transferred missiles to any other nation "under the cloak of secrecy."[47] One wonders if the Jupiter missiles in Turkey and Thor in Britain were not a threat to peace since they had been sent there openly in the face of Soviet impotence.

The President then set up a naval "quarantine" (a peacetime blockade, which under international law is an act of war) and threatened further dire action should the Soviet Union refuse to remove its missiles from Cuba. Within 24 hours, the United States had committed an act of war, bypassed both the Charter of the United Nations and that of the Organization of American States, and taken the entire world to the brink of thermonuclear war.

Premier Khrushchev recognized that he had made a serious error in judgment in assessing the American reaction to his Cuban policy. He also recognized that no possible gain in or around Cuba could justify going any closer to war than the situation already indicated. Soviet missiles were withdrawn, and the United States promised not to invade Cuba. With very few exceptions, President Kennedy's handling of the whole crisis was praised as a diplomatic victory and the height of statesmanship. (Of course, there were some who thought that the United States, at last, had been adequately provoked to justify a war against Cuba.)

And yet, the major lessons of the Cuban missile crisis seemed to have been missed by most Americans, both in and out of the government. For the most part, the fact that the Soviet Union was primarily trying to redress a threatening American superiority in thermonuclear delivery systems was ignored at the time. If this had been understood, it might have generated some pressure for a reduction of current missile production programs; however, these programs continued unabated and the result was an increasingly dangerous American superiority, and, of course, eventually a Soviet missile build-up. The ability of the leaders of the United States to convince the American people that Jupiter missiles in Turkey and Thor missiles in England were defensive while similar Soviet missiles in Cuba were offensive epitomizes the double standard by which the United States has fought the Cold War.

In addition, the fact that the American people had so willingly and uncritically followed the President to the brink of thermonuclear war should have served as an indication of a distinct lack of awareness on the part of the American public of the perils of all-out war. Certainly, such ignorance is a dangerous situation in the thermonuclear age, and efforts should have been made to correct this misconception. Such was not the case.

There was at least one encouraging conclusion to be drawn from the Cuban crisis. If there had been any doubt before 1962 that the Soviet Union understood the informal workings of the balance of terror, this doubt *should* have been removed in 1962. The Soviet Union recognized that it had mistakenly backed the United States into a corner from which it felt it had no alternative but to react in a military manner. Once this was fully realized in the Kremlin, the Soviet Union backed down. Unfortunately, some American observers drew the wrong conclusions from this act of wisdom. Some believed that it was simply an example of foiled aggression, while others were convinced that it demonstrated that all the United States needed to do was to rattle its weaponry and at some future date the Soviets would back down again. There are still Americans who, failing to distinguish the uniqueness of the Cuban crisis, think that this is the solution to problems as diverse as Vietnam and the Middle East.

Many Americans were simply not willing to admit that the leadership of the Soviet Union had progressively rejected total war with the United States as a rational instrument of national policy. As has been seen, Stalin had rejected the inevitability of war between the two superpowers. Khrushchev repeated this in 1956, and by 1960 the Soviet Union specifically rejected the notion that a third world war would lead to the end of capitalism.[48] Khrushchev officially accepted the concept of "mutual deterrence" and claimed that only a "madman" would start a war under the existing circumstance.[49] Just prior to the Cuban missile crisis, the 21st Party Congress in 1961 had not only reaffirmed the Soviet belief in peaceful co-existence but had also endorsed the concept of "different roads to socialism."[50]

After the crisis in Cuba had subsided, Premier Khrushchev clearly announced in the Communist party newspaper *Pravda* the Soviet recognition of the horrors of thermonuclear war:

> According to the calculations of scientists the very first blow [in a thermonuclear war] would destroy between 700 and 800 million people. All large cities, not only in the United States and the Soviet Union, the two leading nuclear powers, but also in France, Britain, Germany, Italy, China, Japan and many other countries would be razed to the ground and destroyed. The consequences of atomic-hydrogen bomb war would persist during the lives of many generations and would result in disease, death and would cripple the human race.[51]

If this rhetoric had been accompanied by a massive building program in bombers and missiles that could have threatened a first strike on the United States, then American leaders could have relegated such statements to the category of propaganda and left it at that. But the statements were accompanied by a distinct lack of a massive Soviet effort to build up its strategic power to the point that it could even vaguely threaten a first strike on the United States. During the 1950s and 1960s, Soviet statements on the undesirability of thermonuclear war underlined their failure to produce weapons systems that could threaten the balance of terror. Unfortunately, American actions were not as consistent with American statements and the United States continued to maintain a threatening superiority over the Soviet Union in strategic delivery systems.

THE TEST BAN TREATY

It is possible that the Cuban missile crisis had one beneficial result—an agreement between the United States and the Soviet Union in 1963 to ban nuclear tests in the atmosphere. The fact that the world had gone to the brink of thermonuclear war over Cuba evidently had a sobering effect on both Kennedy and Khrushchev. The cessation of nuclear testing by the two superpowers was to the credit of both nations. However, the fact that this period of détente and limited good will was not expanded to include nuclear arms reduction represented another opportunity lost to end the insanity of the arms race.

There were numerous ramifications of the Test Ban Treaty, but perhaps the most encouraging was the fact that the two major powers acted in a manner that can be described as enlightened self-interest. Scientists had long known the lethal aftereffects of atomic explosions and as early as 1958 a report by the Federation of American Scientists stated:

> . . . with a stockpile . . . that now exists it is possible to cover the entire earth with a radiation level which for ten years would remain sufficiently intense to prove fatal to all living things.[52]

As evidence increasingly indicated that nuclear testing in the atmosphere was creating danger to human life and future generations, it was logical that the nations with highly developed nuclear technology would attempt to prevent further discharges of nuclear debris into the atmosphere, particularly Strontium 90 and Iodine 131. That the Soviet Union and the United States succeeded in this goal is one of the few encouraging aspects of the arms race.

On the other hand, there was a more insidious motive to be found among some Americans who eventually acquiesced to the Test Ban Treaty. As President Kennedy surveyed the forces working within American society against approval of the treaty, he found that there was substantial opposition from the military, the scientific community, and among some of the political leaders of both parties.[53] In order to reduce the opposition to the treaty and insure its passage by the Senate, President Kennedy had to offer certain "safeguards" to these powerful opponents. It was first pointed out that the treaty insured Soviet "acquiescence in American nuclear superiority."[54] Then President Kennedy promised the Joint Chiefs of Staff the following safeguards:

> . . . vigorous continuation of underground testing; readiness to resume atmospheric testing on short notice; strengthening of detection capabilities; and the maintenance of nuclear laboratories.[55]

In addition, Secretary McNamara guaranteed the Senate that he would move in the near future to raise "the megatonnage of our strategic alert forces."[56]

By promising the "vigorous continuation of underground testing," the arms race merely moved underground,[57] but with one very important exception. The fact that all Soviet and American future tests of atomic weapons would take place underground meant that the nation with the most sophisticated testing and the most generous allocation of resources would inevitably have a distinct advantage over the less technically advanced, poorer nation. In both instances, the advantage went to the United States. Although exact figures on the number of Soviet and American underground tests are difficult to find, it would appear that by 1969 the United States had conducted 186 "announced tests" compared to 28 for the Soviet Union. Likewise, the United States was apparently spending over $200 million a year on underground testing.[58] It was this effort that produced multiple warheads and the antiballistic missile system and led to a continuation of the roughly four-year military-technological advantage enjoyed by the United States.

NATO

Although the United States had received diplomatic support from most of its NATO allies during the Cuban missile crisis, the willingness of the United States to act in such a decisive manner without even consulting with its allies led to further estrangement within the NATO Alliance. American and European perception of the Soviet threat had begun to differ sharply by the mid-fifties, and this continued into the Kennedy Administration of the 1960s.

By 1962 the European tendency to play down the Soviet threat had matured considerably. President DeGaulle openly challenged the two basic assumptions of American NATO diplomacy: (1) that the Soviet Union was preparing or desired to attack Western Europe; and (2) that the United States would risk all-out war in the defense of this territory even if an attack took place. Numerous American efforts to discredit the challenge from DeGaulle or to represent "Gaullism" as an isolated phenomenon had failed in the face of growing restiveness within the Alliance. As shall be seen, this fragmentation of NATO was a gradual process dependent on numerous forces within the dynamics of world politics; but by 1962 the major thrust of the disintegration of NATO had been defined. The strength and unity of the alliance system has progressively deteriorated ever since. (The fragmentation of NATO has been accompanied by a similar process within the Warsaw Pact.)

Until the Kennedy Administration, American military strategy toward Western Europe had been based on a confusing combination of relying on the doctrine of massive retaliation, tactical nuclear weapons, and the claim that Europe could be defended by conventional means. From the outset, the new Administration recognized and admitted that there was no conventional option in Europe and stated its declared intention to correct this error. In McNamara's words: "In Europe, we lack the 'conventional option.' And we are not going to achieve that option in the near future."[59] A little later, McNamara unequivocally declared:

> With regard to Europe, the presently programmed United States forces, together with the present forces of other NATO countries, would not be able to contain an all-out conventional Soviet attack without invoking the use of nuclear weapons.[60]

The Secretary then called for large increases in the budget for the Army to increase this conventional capacity.[61]

In keeping with the new doctrine of flexible response and the increased military budget, McNamara was able to increase the size of the Army from 11 to 16 combat-ready divisions. Ironically, none of these went to Europe.*

Since its inception, many NATO supporters have claimed that the NATO forces in Europe were capable of a conventional defense of Western Europe. Was this true at any time in the past and is it true today? Does NATO have a nonnuclear alternative in the face of Soviet-Warsaw Pact strength should war occur? The answer must be a firm no. That the United States and its allies did not have a conventional capability during the 1950s and early 1960s is admitted by most, but certainly not by all, observers.[62] So the question legitimately can be asked, What has changed by 1970 to give NATO this capability today? And the answer must be nothing.

The importance of the question obviously does not hinge on the belief that if the United States and NATO lack this capability it should be developed; the importance of the question is in the fact that it is one of a long list of myths created by the United States military establishment that should be examined and serve as a warning for the future.

In spite of McNamara's efforts at increasing the conventional capability of United States forces in Europe, the American conventional strength in Europe today is *less* than it was in 1961— because of very limited troop withdrawals, but mainly because of the progressive reductions in combat effectiveness due to equipment and skilled personnel shortages caused by the war in Vietnam.

However, a great deal has been said and written about the American airlift capacity and its growing ability to re-enforce American NATO forces (especially when the C5A becomes operational). The American taxpayer sees millions of dollars used to demonstrate that one Army division can be moved from Texas to Germany under ideal conditions in a short period of

* As a matter of fact, by the time McNamara left office, the United States had withdrawn 34,000 military personnel from Europe. (See U.S., Congress, Senate, Authorization for Military Procurement, Research & Development, Fiscal Year 1969, and Reserve Strength, 90th Cong., 2d sess. (February 2, 1968), testimony by Secretary of Defense McNamara, p. 103.

time; then the public is told that this demonstrates the fact that the United States can defend Europe with reserve forces stationed in this country. Even as astute and critical an observer as Marcus Raskin seems impressed with the American airlift capability. In his perceptive book (along with Richard Barnet) on NATO, Mr. Raskin speaks of the "spectacular air operation, transporting an armoured division from Texas to Germany in a matter of hours."[63] After leaving office, McNamara claimed: "The United States can more than double its combat ready divisions in Central Europe within several weeks of mobilization."[64] Yet the claim that the United States could adequately re-enforce its NATO strength in time of war is simply not true. Those who speak of an airlift distort the ability of American aircraft (including the C5A) to penetrate a European war zone and land troops under combat conditions. A conventional war in Europe would have to be fought with the forces in being, or turned into a tactical nuclear war that would devastate the Continent and maybe beyond.

If there was a conventional Soviet attack on Western Europe —and it should again be made clear that the writer does not believe the Soviet Union is planning or wants such an attack— the situation would be something like this: the Warsaw Pact nations would immediately assume at least temporary air superiority and destroy all major airfields designed to receive re-enforcements. The reasons for this are fairly simple—the Soviet Union has more interceptor aircraft, more fighter– ground-attack aircraft, more light bombers, and medium-range missiles than do the NATO forces.[65]

	NATO	WARSAW PACT
Light bombers	50	450 (400 of them Soviet)
Fight ground-attack	1,500	1,650 (1,120 of them Soviet)
Interceptors	720	3,000 (2,000 of them Soviet)
Medium-range missiles	0	750 (Soviet)

In view of this Warsaw Pact superiority, it is absurd to claim that lumbering American Boeing 707s, 727s, 747s, or even a fleet of C5As are going to land American troops in Europe unhindered. Most would be shot down with the loss of not only the aircraft but also the strategic reserve forces of the United States. Those aircraft not destroyed in flight would have great difficulty in finding a place to land, and it is certain that the Soviets would not leave Rhine-Main Airbase intact to accept these re-enforcements. (Rhine-Main Airbase in Frankfurt, Germany, is the major American airbase in Western Europe.)

Some commentators on comparative NATO-Warsaw Pact strengths have attempted to make a case for their belief that the forces in being could defend Western Europe in a conventional manner, and they cite total troop strengths to prove their point. Thus, for example, McNamara in the late '60s claimed that NATO has about 900,000 troops deployed in all regions of continental Europe, compared with 960,000 Warsaw Pact troops.[66] Yet these figures are extremely misleading. First, McNamara is dealing with total NATO forces (counting, for example, Greek or Portuguese troops). Second, the key area in assessing European defensive capabilities is not southern Europe, or even Central Europe, but the area of the North German Plain, the traditional invasion route into the Low Countries and France. It is this area which would be hit the hardest and hit first. The United States Seventh Army (roughly five divisions) is located south of this invasion route and it is highly improbable that it could be pulled out and then placed on the North German Plain before the Soviet forces had begun to occupy it (that is, in three or four days). If this maneuver was attempted, it would probably result in the destruction of the Seventh Army as it was attacked in force from its eastern flank as it moved north. Therefore, the essential defense of Central Europe rests with the British Army on the Rhine (less than 50,000 men) and less than six German divisions. While fighting a minimal hold-action on other fronts, the Soviets could easily muster a 4–1 division advantage on the North German Plain.* A conservative estimate of the time that it would take a determined Soviet effort

---

* In 1963, Secretary McNamara estimated the number of Soviet divisions at 85, with 40 immediately combat ready. See *The New York Times,* November 19, 1963. Normal Soviet mobilization plans would have meant that the remaining 45 divisions would have been combat ready in less than 30 days. The NATO forces could not match this Soviet mobilization figure in Western Europe.

to break through the northern front would be less than a week. This would place Soviet forces *at the rear* of the United States Seventh Army in about eight days or less and in Antwerp in about ten days. There could be no Bastogne this time; the American forces would be flanked and would be lucky to make it to the Pyrenees safely before they were destroyed by a Soviet "wheeling action" at the base of the Swiss and French Alps.

Obviously this hypothetical situation is not going to take place. The Soviet Union is not about to attack Western Europe, and even if they did, the United States would have to use tactical nuclear weapons, and the exact military effect of these is not yet known. But in this event, a solid argument could be made for the case that not only would the societies of Europe be destroyed, but possibly *both* opposing armies. As pointed out before, if the United States has 7,000 tactical weapons for Europe *alone*, it would be unwise to credit the Soviet Union with less.[67]*

The belief that the United States (and NATO) has a conventional option for the defense of Europe is another classic example of myth creation by those who govern the United States. If this myth can continue to be sold to the American, and to a limited extent European, people, a number of objectives will be accomplished:

(1) The American and European populations can continue to live under the illusion that Europe is defended by conven-

---

* Secretary McNamara claimed in 1966 that the United States had 7,000 tactical nuclear weapons in Europe (see *The New York Times*, September 24, 1966). If this was the case, it seems safe to assume that the Soviet Union had as many atomic weapons available as it believed necessary to defend this area. Thus, a conservative estimate would place the total number of tactical nuclear weapons in Europe at over 10,000. These weapons are in the kiloton range and vary from about 2 to 100 kilotons, with the average being about 20—or the same size as the weapon dropped on Nagasaki. Simple arithmetic will indicate that in Europe today, excluding strategic arsenals, there are approximately 200,000 kilotons stored and deliverable, or roughly 10,000 times the amount of explosive power that destroyed Nagasaki. The use of even a small percentage of these weapons would result in the deaths of millions of Europeans and the destruction of the Continent.

tional forces and therefore the continued presence of American troops all over Europe can be justified.

(2) The United States Army is assured of continued budgetary support for these forces, along with the financial contribution for the supporting naval and air units.

(3) The producers of the overpriced and mismanaged C5A cargo plane stand a better chance of the continuation of the flow of funds into the Lockheed coffers. (Most recent estimates place the overrun cost of the C5A for 200 planes at over $2 billion.) Other NATO-related industries will also continue to benefit.

(4) The continued presence of American troops in Europe means that American policy makers have forces near at hand for operations such as the past ones in Lebanon or the Congo, or future ones to uphold the regimes in Spain or Greece. The very presence of these units serves not only to give the American government these options, but also the remote threat of their use for such a purpose is a powerful force for the maintenance of the status quo and a deterrent to revolutionary change.

(5) Finally, the continued presence of American forces in NATO nations leaves American policy makers at the least the vague hope that the policies, and particularly the nuclear policies, of these allies can be controlled.

Thus far, only American policies and perspectives toward NATO have been discussed with European attitudes and policies postponed until the reality of American policy had been defined. As has been seen, since its very inception NATO has been confronted with substantial problems within the Alliance itself. Although these problems existed in all 15 of the NATO nations at one time or another, the major crisis facing NATO centered primarily around two nations—Germany and France. Without the former, the manpower and industrial strength needed for even a semblance of a viable Western European defensive system could not exist. Without France, there was not enough territorial or logistical depth in Europe to conduct defensive operations without violating French territory. For the first six years of the NATO Alliance, the resistance to

German participation was sufficient to prevent effective German participation. At no time since the founding of the alliance system has France met the military requirements of NATO; since the early 1960s France has been either inactive in the Alliance or actively hostile toward it.

The politics and diplomacy of the Atlantic alliance go beyond the scope of this study. Those interested in this aspect of the problem of NATO should consult the excellent work by Richard Barnet and Marcus Raskin, *After 20 Years: The Decline of NATO and the Search for a New Policy in Europe.* For the purposes of this study concentration will remain on the relevant military developments that added impetus to the fragmentation of the NATO Alliance.

It is fairly common knowledge that the policies of France and of Charles DeGaulle were the major manifestation of the shift in European attitudes; but for a number of reasons an attempt has been made to make "Gaullism" appear as an isolated phenomenon, not related to the French people and certainly in no way related to the general feelings of Europeans.

Gaullism may have started out as a French reaction against complete dependency upon the policies and power of the United States; but as it has developed and spread throughout the NATO nations, it has become much more than a simple reassertion of nationalism based on a resentment of American preponderance. The efforts to decrease military dependence upon the United States have logically led to a substantive increase in the independent military policies followed by American NATO allies. Therefore, what started under the Fourth Republic (before DeGaulle) in France has now escalated to the effective removal of France from NATO, and the policy continues under a supposedly "non-Gaullist" successor government. But the foreign policy of Gaullism now extends well beyond the borders of France. The reductions in the British Army of the Rhine (in Germany), the threatened British "withdrawal east of Suez," and the reductions of the military budget of Great Britain are manifestations of the same phenomena. The recent announcement of Canadian reductions in Europe and the failure of

Prime Minister Trudeau to endorse the American antiballistic missile system are similar examples.

These developments in NATO have been a gradual and as yet incomplete evolution of European policies and attitudes. First, the move from dependence on the United States was simply a demand on the part of some Europeans for more independence in their own national policies. However, as time passed this demand was joined by a much more potent force— fear that the United States might involve Europe in a world war without its consent. The unilateral American actions during the two Cuban crises and the invasion of the Dominican Republic did nothing to forestall these fears. The coup de grâce as far as many Europeans were concerned took place in 1966. "Rusk Says Pacific Is Flank of NATO," ran the byline in *The New York Times*. Secretary of State Rusk contended that the "western flank" of NATO was in the Pacific and strongly implied that in the event of war between the United States and China, the NATO doctrine of "an attack on one is considered an attack on all" would come into effect.[68] Many Europeans could only view with horror the possibility that American misadventures in the Pacific would be the cause of World War III and the inevitable destruction of Europe.

Above are listed a number of the military problems facing the NATO Alliance during the 1960s, but one additional military problem deserves special attention; it was this problem and the failure of American policy makers to solve it that greatly accelerated the inevitable fragmentation of NATO. In its simplest terms, the origins of this problem are to be found in the demand by Secretary McNamara that in the event of war "NATO target systems must be indivisible."[69]

In layman's terms, indivisible targeting in nuclear war means that there must be one central planning unit that designates *all* targets in event that nuclear weapons are used. Needless to say, under the various plans put forward by the United States, this planning unit would be the American government.

The demand that the NATO target system must be indivisible was designed to accomplish two purposes. First, and most important, it would prevent the European nations from achieving the status of independent nuclear powers and thus assure a continued American monopoly in this area and likewise a continued European dependence on the United States. Second, an indivisible target system translated as the logical corollary to the American doctrine of second-strike counterforce; that is, the United States must have the sole, final say on when and where nuclear weapons will be used in the event of war. Without this guarantee, America's selective, "rational" nuclear response in the event of war was meaningless.

In order for this strategy to work, the United States had to deal with three basic problems—the three nations of Western Europe that could potentially develop an effective nuclear deterrent force of their own—Great Britain, France, and West Germany. The problems created by these three nations were different, and a formula was needed that would meet the demands of all three. The American answer, submitted with a straight face and in all sincerity, was the multilateral nuclear force (MLF). This plan went through numerous changes, but the sum and substance of the plan was to place all *European* nuclear capacity under either multilateral NATO control or under effective American control by designating the NATO commander (always an American) as the final decision maker. Under multilateral control, all fifteen NATO allies would have had to agree to use atomic weapons simultaneously, an almost impossible task, or the American NATO commander would make the decision. American strategic systems (SAC and American ICBMs) would not be subject to MLF control.

According to American reasoning, this would remove the British need for an independent bomber force equipped with American Skybolt missiles (air-to-surface missiles capable of penetrating Soviet defenses). The independent French force de frappe would no longer be needed and could be replaced with reliance on the NATO system. And, finally, the MLF would serve as a surrogate for those in Germany demanding possession of nuclear weapons. With these problems solved, the American monopoly on control of nuclear weapons and the powerful political-diplomatic instrument represented by this monopoly would be maintained. Somehow, the Europeans did not see it this way!

The American advocacy of the MLF and the European rejection of it is of prime importance in understanding the progressively deteriorating cohesion of the NATO Alliance; therefore, a more detailed discussion on a country-by-country basis is necessary.

By 1960, a respected and authoritative British military expert had joined those who doubted the credibility of American deterrent policy. Alastair Buchan wrote in *The Bulletin of the Atomic Scientists:*

> . . . confidence in the ability of the United States to guarantee the security of Western Europe is decreasing as Russia becomes a formidable nuclear missile power.[70]

In the same series, this opinion was shared by the American expert Klaus Knorr and the well-known French analyst Raymond Aron.

By this time, the British felt it necessary to develop their own small bomber force capable of reaching the Soviet Union with thermonuclear weapons. But with the advances being made in defensive surface-to-air missiles, serious doubts were being raised as to the ability of the British Vulcan/Victor bombers to penetrate Soviet defensive forces. The British, suffering under the economic strain of maintaining an appearance as a major world power, had decided to rely on the American Skybolt air-to-surface missiles rather than developing their own penetration system. But at the British-American Nassau meeting in early December 1962 the United States announced its decision not to build the Skybolt, and began to push MLF as an alternative to furnishing the British with Skybolt. Under this plan, the United States would *sell* Polaris missiles to Britain; then Britain would be responsible for producing the warheads and its financial share of the naval vessels needed for the system. At this point, the British had no choice but grudgingly to accept the American fait accompli on Skybolt production. On the other hand, if the United States could get the British to accept the

MLF rather than rely on their own deterrent force, then the "indivisibility" of targeting systems demanded by McNamara would have been achieved.

By 1964, the British had rejected the concept of MLF, and Lyndon Johnson let the system quietly disappear from consideration after Prime Minister Wilson's visit in December of that year. Later evidence indicates that the United States had applied substantial pressure on Great Britain to gain its adherence to the multilateral concept of deterrence for Europe, and that the United States had been willing to "pay a good price" in order to gain British acceptance of this concept.[71] The British still refused to accept the system.

If there ever was any doubt in Great Britain as to the efficacy of the MLF, this was certainly not the case in France. Well before DeGaulle became president of France in 1958, the leaders of the Fourth Republic had begun to carve out an independent foreign military policy including the removal of American nuclear weapons from French soil and the decision to proceed with the development of the force de frappe. This policy was continued and expanded under DeGaulle. However, it should be understood that DeGaulle's contention that the Americans would not meet their commitment to defend Western Europe was not so much an accusation of bad faith, but was based on DeGaulle's belief that "no nation will choose to fight to the death for another. . . ."[72] In conjunction with this conviction was DeGaulle's determination to establish the independence of French policy from that of the United States.

It was this realistic assessment of the limits of American power, along with the fear of an American-provoked world war, that fed the increasing restiveness of the major nations of the NATO Alliance. Perhaps the best summation of the French position came not from France but from a well-qualified British observer, Denis Healey:

> . . . France does not believe there is a substitute for purely national defense systems, and does not intend to be sidetracked from the pursuit of nuclear independence by meaningless formulas for collective deterrence. . . .[73]

The French had decided to follow their own concept of how best to obtain some semblance of security and national prestige in the thermonuclear age. This concept did not include the acceptance of a multinational nuclear force that would be unable to react in time of crisis or would be an American-controlled force.

Therefore, the French continued to develop nuclear weapons and the bomber force (the Mirage series) necessary to create the *possibility* of delivering a small number of thermonuclear bombs on Soviet targets. These French actions made McNamara's concept of indivisible targeting meaningless the moment it was proposed. The possibility that the independent French force *might* be able to drop several megaton-range bombs on Moscow and Leningrad ended the indivisibility of the Western target system and in a very real sense established a balance of terror between France and the Soviet Union.

The situation facing German-American relations was a very different one. The United States bore prime responsibility for not only the rearming of Germany and its participation in NATO, but also for the degree of permanency that has characterized the division of Germany into two states since the early 1950s.[74] Thus, when Germany demanded some say on the control of nuclear weapons, the United States was faced with the very difficult task of devising a formula that would make it look as if Germany had nominally become a nuclear power, but in reality, of course, had not. Of the three powers involved, Germany could have at least gained "symbolic" nuclear status and therefore was not as critical of the MLF as Britain and France. The MLF seemed to be the perfect formula to fulfill this purpose, but it never gained acceptance in Germany for the simple reason that the Germans also recognized that it was an unworkable and meaningless concept.

The attempt to force the multilateral nuclear force on to America's European allies was the last major effort on the part of the United States to change substantially its European military policy. Once the MLF had joined the other myths of American defense policy in oblivion, if not ridicule, the United States settled down under Johnson and then Nixon to an acceptance of the status quo in NATO. By 1970, the United States, in the face of a distinctly not expansive, conservative Soviet Union, had decided to place over 7,000 tactical nuclear weapons in Europe, go through the motions and rhetoric of the possibility of a conventional defense, and leave the situation substantially as it had been ever since the 1950s.

V

Johnson-Nixon: Logic Fulfilled

(1963–1970)

The policies of the Johnson Administration were a continuation of the past. President Johnson carried the assumptions and policies of the Kennedy Administration to their logical conclusion. The results have been an unmitigated disaster for the conduct of the foreign and military affairs of the United States. The Dominican invasion, massive land war in Asia, major escalations of the arms race, increased fragmentation of the NATO Alliance, and a general weakening of the world-wide moral position of the United States have been the major results of the administration of Lyndon Johnson. What John Kennedy had continued, Lyndon Johnson escalated.

The difference was one of the degree of power committed to a given policy, not to a different policy. Where Kennedy had supported a Cuban emigré invasion during Bay of Pigs and failed, Johnson landed Marines in the Dominican Republic in sufficient strength so as to preclude the possibility of military failure. Where Kennedy had committed up to 15,000 Americans to help a pro-American Saigon government maintain itself in power, Johnson committed 500,000 Americans to fight a war that the Saigon government had already lost. Where Kennedy went through the motions of supporting self-determination, following the Dominican invasion in 1965 Lyndon Johnson approved of the Seldon resolution in the House of Representatives justifying the unilateral use of American troops in Latin

American nations that considered themselves threatened by "international communism, directly or indirectly."[1] This resolution, although it was not legally binding, seemed to finalize the establishment of the Johnson doctrine—a virtually unlimited claim of American legitimacy for armed intervention by the United States in internal or external conflicts throughout the noncommunist world.

It appears that Johnson was overwhelmed by the increasing intensity of revolutionary forces throughout the third world and could not operate with the comparative restraint that had characterized the Kennedy Administration. American installed and supported status quo governments were increasingly challenged by the only instrument available to the forces for change in the third world—revolutionary resistance and warfare. And, at home, Johnson did not seem to possess the will, even temporarily, to resist the demands of the military and its allies in the constant drive for more funds and weapons systems. On the whole, Johnson was not as subtle or as restrained as Kennedy; this was the major difference between their administrations in the conduct of American foreign policy.

In spite of all its liberal rhetoric, the Johnson Administration was in its own way as much a hard-line, fearful, anticommunist administration as that of Eisenhower-Dulles. This fear and uncertainty was best represented by Johnson's statement:

> There are 3 billion people in the world and we have only 200 million of them. We are outnumbered 15 to 1. If might did make right, they would sweep over the United States and take what we have. We have what they want.[2]

In case there was any doubt as to the identity of these billions, Secretary of State Dean Rusk defined the challenge in a press conference in the following manner:

> Question: Why do you think our security is at stake in Vietnam?
> Answer: [Rusk] Within the next decade or two, there will be a billion Chinese on the mainland, armed with nuclear weapons,

with no certainty about what their attitude toward the rest of Asia will be.[3]

But the Chinese threat to American security was not limited to a billion Chinese: the threat was extended to all those forces demanding change in the socioeconomic structure governing their nations. Therefore, by implication, either Moscow or Peking must be involved in revolutionary efforts in the Third World. In Secretary Rusk's words:

> But what the Communists, in their upside down language, call "wars of liberation" are advocated and supported by Moscow as well as Peiping [sic]. The assault on the Republic of Vietnam is a critical test of that technique of aggression.[4]

With this perception of the world facing the United States, it is no wonder that American leadership was willing to take great risks to prevent being overrun by the masses of the world. These "risks" were defined as being unlimited. W. W. Rostow, Johnson's Henry Kissinger, probably said it best in an article entitled "The Test: Are We the Tougher?" Mr. Rostow claimed that "credible deterrence in the nuclear age lies in being prepared to face the consequence if deterrence fails—up to and including all out nuclear war."[5]

But a very important distinction in theories of deterrence is missing in this question. Simple deterrence of a Soviet attack could be accomplished with several hundred Polaris missiles. But more limited military actions for which the Soviet Union or China might be conveniently blamed, although not responsible, could not be deterred or stopped by threatening them. For example, it is highly doubtful that no matter how willing the United States was to go to all-out war against the Soviet Union to prevent Castro from coming to power, no matter how vehement the threats, he would have still assumed power in Cuba. The Soviet Union simply did not control Fidel Castro. The same point can be made for Ho Chi Minh's revolution in Vietnam. Rostow recognized the differences of the tactics of the challenge, but he, like the Administration he served, insisted on holding

Russia or China responsible for all challenges to the status quo throughout the world.

Two points should be emphasized: first, American policy makers viewed the world as billions of people hammering away at the edges of the American empire, rather than as peoples trying to develop their own nations without American intervention. Second, these policy makers saw these challenges as directed from either Moscow or Peking (or both) and therefore national suicide could be contemplated as a last-ditch policy to counter these challenges. It is within this context that American policy was made and must be analyzed if it is to be understood. It is then easier to comprehend United States behavior in the Dominican Republic and Vietnam; and why the United States has insisted on escalating the arms race despite massive strategic superiority.

By the mid-1960s, United States military policy had distinguished between the perceived threat from the thermonuclear power of the Soviet Union, and the different threat to American interests posed by alleged Russian (or Chinese) supported and controlled revolutions aimed at destroying the status quo that the United States wanted to preserve. McNamara calculated the changing nature of the challenges to American interests in the following manner:

> In the eight years through late 1966 alone there were no less than 164 internationally significant outbreaks of violence, each of them specifically designed as a serious challenge to the authority or very existence of the government in question.[6]

He went on to claim that only 15 of these 164 challenges were military conflicts between states, with the remainder (by implication) being indigenous in nature. McNamara also recognized the escalating nature of the insurgency forces demanding some kind of domestic change. In 1958 there ". . . were 23 prolonged insurgencies going on around the world. As of February, 1966, there were 40."[7]

This changed perception of threats to American interests produced a dichotomy in American military planning and weapons systems. To a limited extent, each challenge demanded its own military doctrine and its own weapons system or military force-levels. A large part of the history of the Johnson Administration centered around these questions.

At the strategic level (Soviet or Chinese direct threat), arguments flourished over the Sentinel ABM, the Soviet Tallinn Line, the B-1 bomber, and the Multiple Independent Re-entry Vehicle (MIRV). While on the tactical level (revolutionary challenges), the controversies surrounded more limited systems such as the C5A super transport aircraft, fast deployment logistic ships (FDLS), the TFX (FB-111) mixed-mission aircraft, and the nuclear aircraft carrier. One set of systems was designed for strategic reasons against the Soviet Union and to a limited extent China, while the other represented further preparation for the future Vietnams inevitable in a revolutionary world should United States policy remain unchanged.

For example, the pressures to build the C5A cargo plane and to deploy the fast deployment logistic ships (FDLS) were closely related and reflected future American strategy toward conflicts such as had taken place in the Dominican Republic or Vietnam. The C5A was designed to carry over 500 soldiers long distances (as well as military equipment if needed). The FDLS were designed as floating "barges" with equipment and supplies sufficient to equip two American divisions. The Pentagon scenario might read as follows. There is an attempted rebellion in Liberia against the pro-American government of President Tubman. A small, mobile American military force secures a beach head and an air field on the Liberian coast. At this time, the men from the air fleet of C5As are matched up with the equipment from the FDLS located in the Gulf of Guinea. By that time, a fleet of 80 C5As has placed 40,000 American military men in Liberia to suppress the rebellion and maintain President Tubman in power. With complete American air superiority in local regions of the third world, this operation could be done swiftly, and there are few revolutionary armies outside of Vietnam that could successfully withstand this preponderance of American power so rapidly brought to bear on a local revolution. The very existence of this force and its threatened use

would be a major bulwark for pro-American status quo government throughout the world.

Although we will distinguish between strategic and tactical
weapons systems, the reader should not be misled into believing
that functions of these systems were completely separate. American strategic power was certainly used in the narrow sense as
a deterrent against attack on the United States; but this same
system and American superiority were also designed in an
attempt to neutralize any Soviet and Chinese military responses
to American conventional and unconventional military actions
throughout the third world. For example, the willingness of
the United States actively to expand the Indochina War in 1970
to Laos and Cambodia was based on the belief that American
thermonuclear power would forestall any Soviet or Chinese
military response.

Before discussing these two types of systems, the reader
should be reminded of the fact that the B-1, the C5A, the TFX,
and the Minuteman MIRV are Air Force systems. The Sentinel
and Safeguard systems, along with the Cheyenne helicopter and
the new super tank were Army systems, while the Navy was
pushing during this same period for nuclear carriers, fast-deploy-
ment logistic ships, Poseidon, and their own carrier-borne version of a new aircraft. The importance of these facts will become
apparent below.

AMERICAN STRATEGIC SUPERIORITY

As has been seen, on a strategic level, the United States entered
the period of the Johnson Administration with at least a 4–1
advantage over the Soviet Union in the number of deliverable
warheads, and by the end of the Johnson Administration, this
same ratio remained, although both sides had engaged in substantial building programs during the interim.[8]

McNamara has claimed that this American superiority was
"greater than we had planned" but this is hard to believe in view
of the fact that McNamara learned almost immediately upon
assuming office that the Soviet Union was not engaged in a
large-scale missile-building program and that the missile gap

was a fiction. Yet he not only continued but escalated the American missile-building program even after he had learned of the Soviet refusal to build large numbers of first-generation missiles. As seen above, Arthur Schlesinger has argued that the early Kennedy Administration felt that it would not fight the forces of the Pentagon on both missiles and bombers, and therefore chose to resist building a replacement for the B-52 (renamed the B-1 in 1970), but felt compelled to proceed with its escalation of the Minuteman and Polaris building programs in spite of the known limited Soviet activity in missile-building programs. If these are the facts behind America's missile build-up of the 1960s, then it serves not only as an excellent illustration of the power of the military and its industrial allies, but it should also serve as a dire warning of the almost unlimited power exercised by the political/economic/military coalition that governs the United States.

However, it must be admitted that to the very end, Secretary McNamara resisted the forces pushing for the various versions of the B-1 supersonic bomber. General Thomas S. Power had supported this aircraft as early as 1960, and by 1962 the B-1 had the support of the Joint Chiefs of Staff. It is to McNamara's credit that he fought the production of this airplane until he left office.[9] Yet even after such effective resistance, by 1969 Congress had appropriated the initial funds for the production of the B-1. Before this system is completed (a total of 200 aircraft) the cost will run between $8 to $10 billion, if not more.[10]

The B-1 is scheduled to be operational by 1977, with a speed of 1,300 to 2,000 miles per hour and a range of 10,000 miles. This aircraft went through various designations by the Air Force and at times it was variously called the RB-70, RS-70, the B-70, the Advanced Manned Strategic Aircraft, and finally the B-1. For the purposes of this study, it will be referred to as the B-1.

Significantly, by the time the B-1 received congressional and executive backing, even its most ardent supporters no longer contended that it could function effectively as a bomber—its only function in the 1970s would be as an additional platform from which to launch air-to-surface missiles. This would mean that the United States was going to spend $10 billion for an additional set of platforms to supplement the over 1,500 existing Minuteman and Polaris-Poseidon platforms.[11]

It should be noted that the major effort by the Air Force for a new platform was accompanied by an Air Force demand for a brand new missile to be launched from this platform. The so-called SRAM, short-range attack missile, which was to replace the now obsolete Hound Dog air-to-surface missile, became a priority item for the Air Force. (The SRAM was to follow a long list of now obsolete Air Force air-to-surface missiles, including Crossbow, Rascal, Skybolt—with costs totaling $962.6 million.

The Air Force drive for the B-1 and SRAM was simply another case of a military service bringing all its substantial influence to pressure the executive and Congress for a given weapons system —a weapons system that was not too significant either in the strategic balance of terror or, except temporarily, as an escalating factor in the arms race. However, if the importance of the new manned bomber was primarily monetary, this *definitely was not* the case in the debate over the ABM-multiple warhead question. These two closely related systems and the apparent decision to build them led to an immense escalation of the arms race; maybe even more important, it is possible that with the deployment of these two systems even the slimmest hope for arms limitation agreements may disappear. This debate broke into the open in 1967 and really reached its first crescendo with the decision to provide the funds for the Sentinel and eventually the Safeguard ABM system.

As with all major weapons systems, discussion and argument about them had been taking place at higher government levels years before the public became substantially aware of the major problems involved (if the public became involved at all: it normally does not).*

The significance of the ABM-MIRV debate and the eventual decisions concerning them cannot be overestimated in any assessment of the arms race and the continued development of the strategic doctrine of the United States. These two systems

---

* This analysis of ABM-MIRV will cover both the Johnson Sentinel system and the Nixon Safeguard system due to the complete overlap in the nature of these systems and the debate that concerned them.

represented an eventual potential expenditure of well over $100 billion and thus were the richest set of potential contracts ever dangled by the Pentagon before the corporations of the United States. In addition to the commitment of resources in such gargantuan amounts, there were also those who believed that the military efficacy of the ABM was of the utmost significance if the United States was to control the world. In the words of Senator Richard Russell (Dem.-Ga.):

I have often said that I feel that the first country to deploy an effective ABM system and an effective ASW (anti-submarine warfare) system is going to control the world militarily.[12]

The debate over MIRV-ABM systems dominated the late 1960s, and American actions during this period led to another massive escalation in the arms race. Therefore, it is important to understand the exact steps in this escalation. The best place to start is to first look at the comparative strategic weapons systems of the United States and the Soviet Union from 1960 to 1969. Once this is done, an attempt can be made to clarify where the major escalations of building programs came from on both sides. In looking at these comparative figures, the reader should keep in mind that throughout the 1960s, both the United States and the Soviet Union possessed enough stored megatonnage to destroy the entire world several times over and could have built more if they desired to do so. The United States had roughly 30,000 megatons available, while the Soviet Union had 20,000 megatons.

Even a cursory look at these comparative figures leads to several basic conclusions concerning the nature of the arms race during the 1960s.

One, at no time did the Soviet Union maximize its ability to build long-range bombers; they never had even half the number possessed by the United States. Two, at no time did the Soviet Union attempt to maximize the in-flight refueling capacity of its large force of medium bombers so that they could reach the United States. Three, at no time did the Soviet Union build any type of aircraft carrier that would pose a threat to the

COMPARATIVE STRATEGIC STRENGTH—THE
UNITED STATES AND THE SOVIET UNION 1960–1969*

1960 At this time neither the United States nor the Soviet Union had more than a handful of ICBMs.

	UNITED STATES	SOVIET UNION
Long-range Bombers	585 B-52s	150
Medium-range Bombers (in-flight refuel or at foreign bases)	1,100	None capable of reaching the United States
Carrier-based Bombers	400	none
	2,085	150[13]

1962 Vehicles capable of reaching opponent's territory.

	UNITED STATES	SOVIET UNION
Long-range	650 B-52s 55 B-58s	70 Bears Less than 200 Bisons
Medium-range	1,000 B-47s Could reach Soviet territory	1,000 Badgers— Could not reach United States
ICBMs	100 Atlas	Less than 100 ICBMs
	54 Titans 20 Minutemen	

* The figures cited are taken from official United States government statements, *The New York Times,* and the Institute for Strategic Studies (London). After a number of years of surveying comparative weapons systems and comparing estimates with official United States government releases, the author has found the latter two sources to be the most consistently reliable. For more details of the 1960–1969 period, the reader should consult Appendix A. The figures listed below are not complete in the sense that they do not always reflect *all* American delivery systems, and therefore the total number of delivery vehicles at any given time tends to vary according to which delivery systems are included in the calculation. The totals listed below include only those vehicles capable of reaching an opponent's homeland.

1962   (continued)

	UNITED STATES	SOVIET UNION
Polaris	80	none
Vehicles capable of reaching opponent's homeland	1,959	300[14]

1964	UNITED STATES	SOVIET UNION
Long-range Bombers	540	270
ICBMs	750	200
Polaris	192	60
Thor (being phased out)	45	None near United States
Jupiter (being phased out)	60	None near United States
Vehicles capable of reaching opponent	1,587	530[15]

1966   These figures do not include the real possibility that the Polaris A-3 missile was equipped with Multiple Re-entry Vehicles.

	UNITED STATES	SOVIET UNION
Long-range Bombers	540	270
ICBMs	800 Minutemen 80 Minutemen II 54 Titan	300
Polaris	400 (possible MRV missiles)	125
Vehicles capable of reaching opponent	1,874	695[16]

1967   Official figures given by Secretary of Defense McNamara.

	UNITED STATES	SOVIET UNION
ICBM Launchers	1,054	720
SLBM Launchers (submarine-launched ballistic missiles)	656	30
Intercontinental Bombers	697	155

1969   (continued)

	UNITED STATES	SOVIET UNION
Total force loadings, approximate number of warheads	4,500	1,100[17]

1969	UNITED STATES	SOVIET UNION
ICBMs	1,054	1,000
Polaris	656 (possible MRV)	125
Long-range Bombers	500	150
Aircraft Carriers	23	none
	2,610	1,276[18]

1969   Projections of American missiles with Multiple Independent Re-entry Vehicles or MIRV. (In addition to much of the above firepower.)

UNITED STATES	
170 Minuteman III @ 3 each	510
Minuteman I & II	700
31 subs, 16 missiles @ 10 each	4,960
Single-warhead Minutemen	830
B-52s	500
Total	7,500[19]

security of the United States. Four, at no time during the period under consideration did the Soviet Union deploy more than one third of the Polaris-type missiles deployed by the United States. And, five, until 1966 the Soviet Union appears to have settled for a distinctly inferior position vis-à-vis the United States in the number of ICBMs. But by 1966 they had begun a major building program in ICBMs that would allow them to approach parity with the United States in ICBMs by 1969.

But, obviously, these figures and the above conclusions do not tell the whole complex story behind the arms race of the 1960s. Three fundamental questions remain unanswered. Why did the Soviet Union engage in a large-scale missile-building program in 1966 after accepting missile and bomber inferiority since the inception of the Cold War? What exactly did the Soviet anti-bomber and antimissile programs consist of during this period? And what is the state of development and mission assigned to the Soviet SS-9 and the fledgling Soviet MIRV program for the 1970s? Although these three questions are interrelated, they will be treated separately here in order to clarify an extremely complex set of problems.

Before going into a detailed analysis, it should be emphasized that as the arms race progressed through the 1960s and into this decade, the technological advances in weaponry and the complexity of the so-called strategies became even more difficult to understand, and the jargon surrounding these questions almost defies comprehension.

SOVIET ATTITUDES

Early in the decade of the 1960s, the leaders of the Soviet Union began to repeat the mistake they had made earlier during the missile gap period—they started to brag about weapons systems that they did not have and did not plan to build in the immediate future. In 1961, Marshal Malinovsky of the Soviet Union boasted of a Soviet solution to a defense against a missile attack.[20] This claim was followed less than a year later by Premier Khrushchev's famous statement that the Soviet Union had an antimissile missile that "can hit a fly in outer space."[21] These claims were later followed by various Soviet boasts on the capability of their antimissile missiles.[22]

The critical observer can legitimately ask why the Soviet Union would make such claims in view of the predictable American reaction to Soviet claims of superiority in *any* weapons system. And, although no definitive answer can be given, a logical conclusion would be that during this period the Soviet leaders knew that they were far behind the United States in strategic bomber and missile forces and that their bravado was an attempt to create some uncertainty on the part of American leadership as to the ability of the United States to destroy the Soviet retaliatory forces by a surprise attack.

There does not appear to be any doubt that the Soviet Union knew that it was far behind the United States in the arms race in 1962. Published Soviet figures of that year indicated that the United States had 162 ICBMs, 96 Polaris missiles, and projected American strength in 1966 to 1,040 ICBMs and 656 Polaris missiles. Therefore, when Khrushchev admitted in Berlin on January 19, 1963, that the Soviet Union only had 120 missiles capable of reaching the United States, it became obvious that the Soviets realized their inferior position.[23] (At this time, American superiority in numbers of bombers was an accepted fact.) In spite of this recognized inferiority, the leaders of the Soviet Union reduced their military budgetary expenditures for 1963–1964. The military budget was again reduced from 1964 to 1965 from 13.3 billion rubles to 12.8 billion rubles.[24] It was becoming obvious that Soviet leaders were willing to engage in the tricky game of bluff and bluster, but were not willing at this time to allocate a large portion of their resources for ICBMs, much less ABM production—this would come later under even stronger impetus and pressure from the United States.

It would appear that by 1964 the Soviet Union clearly grasped the realities of the balance of terror in the face of a 4–1 American advantage in delivery vehicles. By this time the Soviet Union specifically had rejected thermonuclear war as self-destructive; Mikhail Suslov, party theoretician, had stated that the "task of averting war has become especially urgent." Mr. Suslov, allegedly a "hard-liner" in the Soviet hierarchy, freely admitted that "if a thermonuclear conflict arose, it would be a most terrible tragedy for mankind and would, of course, be a heavy loss to the cause of Communism."[25]

The removal of Premier Khrushchev in 1964 did not substantially alter the belief among Soviet political leaders that there was no chance of "victory" in the event of thermonuclear war. In addition, by 1965, at least temporarily, statements by Soviet spokesmen seemed to reflect a more realistic assessment of the difficulties in producing an effective ABM system. One Soviet spokesman, G. Gerasimov, in the official *International Affairs*, claimed that the development of an ABM system capable of making victory possible would be a discovery ". . . bordering on a miracle." This same author contended that there is "no absolute defense against a missile salvo."[26] A Soviet general, N. Talenskii, wrote in the same journal a year later that it was a "dangerous illusion" that "it is possible to find acceptable forms of nuclear war."[27] The above statements are not intended to demonstrate that the debate over nuclear strategy had ended in the Soviet Union; it did not end in the 1960s and continues to this day. There are still advocates of the "hard-line" and the "soft-line" in the Soviet Union ("hawks" and "doves" in United States terms).

ABM AND MIRV

On the American side, the debate over an antimissile missile had been going on inside the high confines of the government for several years in the late 1950s.* As early as 1957, the United States government had given a contract to Western Electric to develop the Nike-Zeus antimissile system.[28]

In 1959, President Eisenhower conducted the first successful resistance to mounting pressure to install a $14 billion Nike-Zeus system that would have been obsolete before it was operational. When John Kennedy came to office, the pressure continued for the deployment of the Army Nike-Zeus system. This early debate took place before the massive Army build-up for Vietnam, and the ABM seemed to offer the Army a means of obtaining a large chunk of the defense budget that it felt had been denied by the Eisenhower Administration. There does not appear to be any doubt that the Vietnam build-up had the effect of reducing and delaying Army pressure for the ABM.

With the impetus offered by the original Malinovsky and Khrushchev statements, the ABM debate became public for a short time during 1963. Senator Strom Thurmond of South Carolina (at that time a Democrat) contended that the Soviet

---

*Under the Eisenhower Administration the decision had been made to give the Army the mission of air defense in the United States. Until 1958, this mission had been performed by interceptor aircraft and the Nike-Ajax system. By 1959, the Nike Hercules was operational, with an atomic warhead and range of 50–75 miles at altitudes up to 100,000 feet.

Union was building an ABM system around Leningrad and had "a lead of at least several years in the development of an active defense against ballistic missiles."[29] This alleged ABM system around Leningrad was later named the Tallinn Line. At the same time, Edward Teller was using this alleged Soviet ABM system as a reason to oppose the nuclear Test Ban Treaty. Teller further contended:

> An effective defense against ballistic missiles is one of the developments which can upset the strategic balance between the U.S. and the Soviet Union. In this the Soviet Union is at present ahead of us.[30]

In 1963, Dr. Teller did not indicate the unbelievable technical problems involved in the construction of an effective ABM system, nor did he indicate just how distant in the future, if at all, such a development might lie. Reports of the Soviet ABM system around Leningrad continued, and pressure mounted for an American ABM system.[31]

The conviction that the Soviet Union was building an ABM system around Leningrad was one of the most significant and misunderstood aspects of the arms race of the 1960s, and the continued impetus given to the arms race by this belief is still being felt. It was this belief, in part, which gave the rationalization for the American decision to equip the Polaris submarines with Multiple Re-entry Vehicles (MRV) when they became available (see below), created stronger pressure for the development of a more sophisticated American bomber, and led to demands for an increase in American ICBM and ABM programs.

By 1966 the pressures on the President to build an ABM in response to the Soviet Tallinn Line were increasing. The Army claimed that their ABM system (now the Nike X) would definitely work and would cost *only* about $8.5 to $10 billion. For this investment, the Army claimed that 25 American cities would be protected.[32] The Army claims for the Nike X were incorrect, and President Johnson successfully resisted these initial pressures for the Nike X. Three years later under President Nixon it would be admitted that American cities could not be defended against a Soviet missile attack. Yet this did not prevent the Army and the new President from successfully renaming the ABM system and claiming that it would protect American Minutemen sites. But, once again, if these sites were really as *vulnerable* as Nixon and the Army claimed, then they were obsolete and would eventually be replaced by underwater launching sites, Poseidon, and mobile Minutemen on railroad flatcars.

By 1967, Nixon and the Republicans increased the demands for an ABM system; this pressure promised to play an important role in the 1968 Presidential campaign, reminiscent of the missile gap in the 1960 election. President Johnson could not stop his critics: the easiest way to silence them was to go ahead with the deployment of a limited ABM system—the Sentinel. In November 1967 this decision was made by the Johnson Administration, and a reluctant McNamara attempted to sell the Sentinel system to the American people. It is interesting to note that even this effort by President Johnson did not prevent Nixon from developing a "security gap" theme in the 1968 campaign.[33]

Nonetheless, by the mid-1960s the American belief that the Soviet Union had begun to deploy an ABM system around Leningrad had given an added rationale to the following developments:

(1) Increased demands for the B-70 bomber
(2) Increased demands for a larger American ICBM program
(3) Increased demands for an American ABM system
(4) And, finally, demands for the deployment of Multiple Re-entry Vehicles (MRV) on the Polaris A-3 missile.*

---

* At this point the distinction between a multiple re-entry vehicle (MRV) and a multiple independent re-entry vehicle (MIRV) must be made. In both cases a single missile carries multiple warheads; normally the multiple warhead has three or more nuclear weapons. Also, the number of weapons in a given warhead varies from three to fifteen.

Multiple Re-entry Vehicle (MRV)—The multiple warhead on this type of system is *not* independently targeted. For example, a MRV with three warheads aimed at New York City would hit the city in the same manner

There was a fundamental fallacy in the American decision to increase its offensive or defensive strength in the face of the alleged Soviet ABM system around Leningrad. *The Tallinn Line was not an ABM system, but a new antibomber system* being built by the Soviet Union in response to increased sophistication of American bomber penetration devices and the very real possibility that the United States was going to enter into large-scale production of a new intercontinental, supersonic bomber—the B-1. (The Soviet Union had no comparable bomber.)

By 1967, the American intelligence community was split over the exact mission of the Tallinn Line—with the CIA claiming that it was antibomber and the DIA (Defense Intelligence Agency) still claiming that the system was an ABM system. (The DIA was created by President Kennedy to avoid confusion in the American intelligence community.) By 1968, Secretary of Defense McNamara officially admitted that the Tallinn Line

---

as a shotgun blast sprayed over a target, with each warhead striking somewhere in the general New York metropolitan area, but not specifically aimed at any given section of the city. Needless to say this type of attack would destroy New York as a functioning metropolis. The MRV is a technologically primitive system in that it is much easier to develop than the more complex multiple independent re-entry vehicle. It should be emphasized that although the MRV is an extremely effective weapon to destroy cities, it is not accurate enough to destroy an underground, hardened missile silo; therefore it is a counter-city weapon and is of little use in a first-strike surprise attack.

Multiple Independent Re-entry Vehicle (MIRV)—In this system, each warhead can be targeted independently. For example, a Minuteman III missile has three warheads per missile with an explosive power of 200–400 kilotons for each warhead. If New York was attacked with this system, an attacker could program the three warheads to strike Manhattan, Queens, and Brooklyn and be certain that they would strike their target. However, as this system's accuracy is further refined, it will be possible to aim one of the three warheads at the Empire State building and be assured of hitting within 500 feet of the building, with equal accuracy for the other two warheads. A system this accurate could obviously be used to try and destroy an underground missile silo. Therefore, the real danger of MIRV is that it is a potential first-strike weapon that could destroy an enemy's capability to retaliate. As the United States deploys this weapon it is certain to appear to threaten Soviet retaliatory systems.

was not an ABM system but an antibomber system.[34] This very fundamental mistake on the part of American intelligence analysis has passed almost unnoticed during the major debates on the arms race of the 1960s. The only authority this author knows of to correctly assess the importance of this mistake has been I. F. Stone. (*See I. F. Stone's Weekly*, June 16, 1969.)

By 1966, the Soviet Union had almost stopped its deployment of strategic weapons at approximately 250 ICBMs, roughly 200 long-range bombers, and 150 submarine-launched missiles (see Appendix A). At the same time the United States had reached its goals of 1,000 Minuteman ICBMs and 650 Polaris missiles, along with 500 B-52 strategic bombers.[35] If both sides had stopped here, it is possible that the Soviets would have accepted American superiority in view of the guaranteed destructive power represented by the Soviet second-strike system. But this was not the case.

The belief in the Tallinn Line, the increased tensions brought about by the expansion of the American war in Vietnam, and the normal economic-military forces at work in the United States seemed to dictate another major escalation of the arms race, in spite of the guaranteed security of the United States from a surprise attack due to its overwhelming superiority. There was no way that the inferior Soviet system could threaten to destroy the dispersed and hardened American delivery systems with a 4–1 American advantage. It was technologically impossible.

Nonetheless, in the mid-1960s, the United States decided to build the F-111 (TFX) with its mixed tactical and strategic mission,[36] work continued on the B-1, the commitment to the development of ABM-MIRV was solidified; and most important, somewhere between 1966 and 1968, the decision was made to deploy MRVs on the Polaris submarine-launched A-3 missile.

The decision to deploy MRVs on submarines has been one of the best kept secrets of the United States government, and the exact date of deployment is difficult to determine. The reasons for the secrecy are fairly obvious. First, the American government could not be sure if Soviet intelligence was aware of this deployment or not. Since the United States was increasing a superiority that already verged on a first-strike capacity, there was no reason to further frighten the Soviet Union by informing them of this threatening increase in American power. Likewise, in the face of the American superiority, the deployment of such a system might have raised questions in the United States as to the wisdom of such needless escalation of the arms race. It is this writer's opinion that it would be unwise to underestimate the ability of the Soviet intelligence activities; the Soviet Union probably knew of the deployment of MRV. If so, then the major reason for keeping the deployment of MRV secret was to prevent Congress and the people from learning of this escalation of the arms race.

I. F. Stone claims that the United States deployed MRV as early as 1966.[37] By 1969, there was a substantial amount of evidence to indicate that at least ten Polaris submarines were equipped with MRVs.[38] To the best of the author's knowledge, the United States government still has not officially indicated if American submarines are equipped with MRV or not. However, the apparent fact that the United States has already put multiple re-entry vehicles on at least ten of its submarines is significant in itself. Even if each of these MRV missiles has only three warheads instead of the 10 warheads per missile scheduled for the Poseidon, this still represents an increase of from 160 to 480 warheads for ten submarines.

But the real significance of the U.S. development of an operational MRV goes far beyond the quantitative number of warheads the United States can deliver on Russia or China. The real significance is in the technology itself. It is known that the MRV is much easier to develop and produce than the more sophisticated MIRV. At the present time (1970), American MIRVs are becoming operational in June 1970 on the Minuteman III and by October 1970 on Poseidon submarines.[39] As the United States moves toward this deployment, it is becoming more and more apparent *that the Soviet Union is just beginning to test MIRV warheads and is at least 18 to 24 months from deploying its first operational MIRV missile.*[40]

If, in truth, the Soviet Union has just begun to test MIRV, then Russia is from two to five years from the deployment of an independently targeted multiple warhead. If so, and there is substantial evidence that it is so, then the American decision to deploy MIRV in 1970 is not only the most recent massive American escalation of the arms race, but the United States is also guilty of purposely sabotaging the Strategic Arms Limitations Talks (SALT).

THE SOVIET REACTION

The question of whether the United States was purposely escalating the arms race by the deployment of MIRV well before the Soviet Union had even tested this weapon cannot be answered in a definitive manner at this time. But what is known is that the combination of American military programs and actions in the mid-1960s could not fail to produce a reaction on the part of the Soviet Union. No major thermonuclear power, faced with what it perceived as an implacable and strategically superior enemy, could afford to ignore the development of the F-111 supersonic fighter-bomber, the introduction of MRV into the American arsenal, the planned introduction of MIRV, and the decision to deploy an ABM system.

In addition to the challenge to the Soviet Union represented by the development of these American weapons systems, the massive escalation of the war in Vietnam in 1965–1966 raised serious questions in the minds of Soviet leadership as to the rationality of American leaders in the conduct of their foreign policy. This point has been well substantiated by William Zimmerman in his book, *Soviet Perspectives on International Relations, 1956–1967*. As early as September 1965 this feeling began to appear in Soviet thinking, and by 1966 A. N. Shelepin stated: "The events and facts of recent years show that the American imperialists are conducting themselves increasingly irrationally. . . ."[41]

In the face of an American arms escalation and of perceived American irrationality, the leaders of the Soviet Union could repond in only one manner consistent with the security requirements of the Soviet Union—build up their strategic forces to the point where there was *no chance* of them being destroyed by an American first strike; this is exactly what they proceeded to do. Starting in 1966, the Soviet Union possessed only 250 ICBMs (opposed to over 1,000 for the United States), but by mid-1967 they had increased this force to 570, and by 1968 they were credited with having 900 of these missiles. By 1969, the Soviet Union was given credit for having achieved "parity" with the United States in ICBMs, but *not* in the area of long-range bombers (United States, 500; Soviet Union, 150), *not* in Polaris-type missiles (656 to 125), and *not* in carrier-launched fighter-bombers (United States approximately 400; Soviet Union, none). Soviet "parity" existed only in the field of ICBMs, and in all other areas the United States maintained a distinctive superiority.[42]

Earlier, the question had been asked, Why did the Soviet Union engage in a large-scale missile-building program in 1966 after accepting missile and bomber inferiority since the inception of the Cold War? It appears that the answer must be that by 1966–1967 the United States had not only maintained a substantial nuclear superiority but also that reasonable projections of planned or anticipated systems would lead an objective observer to the conclusion that the future strength of the United States would be so great that it *might* destroy the entire retaliatory force of the Soviet Union in a single, surprise attack.

It is also necessary to point out the nature of the Soviet ABM effort during the 1960s. By 1968, it had been firmly established that the initial Soviet system around Leningrad (the Tallinn Line) was an antibomber system and not an ABM system as claimed throughout most of the decade. By 1969, it appeared as though the *entire* Soviet ABM system which had caused such a strong reaction on the part of the United States consisted of the Soviet Galosh system around Moscow with nothing around Leningrad. This system consisted of 67 obsolete Nike-Zeus-type ABMs that apparently even the Soviet Union had realized were worthless (evidence indicated that they had ceased building this system). By this time the United States had abandoned the Nike-Zeus system and was working on Sentinel, and was clearly ahead of the Soviet Union in ABM technology.[43]

The final question asked earlier in this chapter concerned the highly complex nature of the American and Soviet developments in the evolving technology of multiple warheads. Apparently, the United States had begun to deploy the simpler MRV around 1966. As early as 1965, the contract for MIRV had been given to Boeing, and in August 1968 the United States had tested its first MIRV. This placed the United States at least two years ahead of the Soviet Union in MIRV technology. (The first Soviet MIRV test did not occur until 1970, at the earliest.) Quietly and unobtrusively, the Johnson Administration had deployed an operational MRV system and had placed the initial contracts for MIRV before the public was even aware of the existence of these weapons systems.[44]

NIXON AND LAIRD

Thus, by the time the Nixon Administration assumed office, the United States had a demonstrable superiority over the Soviet Union in missiles and bombers. Likewise, the United States had an undetermined but substantial technological "lead-time" advantage over the Soviet Union in the development of ABM and MIRV systems.

In the face of this known Soviet inferiority American escalation of the arms race continued without regard to political party, personal philosophy, or White House occupant.

The election of Nixon in 1968 did not upset or change the Pentagon's plans for the future of the arms race. Nixon had attempted to gain campaign mileage in 1968 from a non-existent security gap, and if there were any doubts as to where he stood on defense spending, these were immediately dispelled by his attempt to make super-hawk Senator Henry Jackson (Dem.-Wash., location of Boeing Aircraft) his Secretary of Defense. When Jackson refused, he appointed Melvin Laird. For any who might have had any doubts about the attitudes of this Wisconsin member of the House of Representatives, a brief look at his book—*A House Divided: America's Strategy Gap*—served to quiet any fears that a critic of the Pentagon had been made Secretary of Defense.[45]

There is a curious, tragic logic to the appointment of Laird to the position of Secretary of Defense in the Nixon Administration. Since World War II a number of very different men had held this post—sensitive men, ardent businessmen, and a plain systems manager. But with the appointment of Laird, the first military man in civilian clothes was made Secretary of Defense —a man whose career has epitomized what the Pentagon and the Department of Defense have come to represent. At a time when the balance of thermonuclear terror was becoming obvious to all but the most obtuse, this man stated:

> Step one of a military strategy of initiative should be the credible announcement of our determination to strike first if necessary to protect our vital interests.[46]

However, the appointment of Laird was not so strange. He joined a chief executive who during the campaign had promised to put together just such a mythical first-strike force when he stated: "I intend to restore our objective of clear-cut military superiority."[47]

Lest there be any doubts as to the definition of America's "vital interests," Assistant Secretary of Defense Robert Moot defined them in the now traditional immodest terms:

> Our national interests extend across the North Atlantic in Western Europe, and the Mediterranean, south into the Caribbean and Westward in the Pacific countries bordering thereon.[48]

With a promise to "restore" American military superiority and a rather broad definition of American national interests, the Nixon Administration began by picking up where Johnson had left off on the development of ABM and MIRV systems.

The first military appropriation fight faced by the Nixon Administration was the effort to get through Congress the initial appropriation for Phase I of the newly named Safeguard ABM system. It was contended that this system was needed to protect about 350 Minuteman sites from a surprise Soviet attack that might destroy the missiles in their silos. Initial cost was estimated at $12 billion. The fact that the United States had a 4–1 delivery advantage over the Soviet Union was discreetly ignored by the proponents of the Phase I Safeguard or rationalized by some vague future Soviet threat. Likewise, the fact that the ABM (even if it worked) would in all probability be defending empty holes in the ground was also not extensively discussed. Nonetheless, although the fight for the funding for Safeguard was the most intense debate in the history of the arms race, the Senate finally voted the initial appropriation for Phase I Safeguard in 1969.

In 1970, it was predictable that the Nixon Administration would want to expand the Safeguard system. The Administration made the decision to proceed with Phase II of Safeguard. Phase II called for a partial shift of the fundamental rationale for Safeguard from primary protection of American Minuteman sites to the eventual protection of American cities against a Chinese missile attack. Phase II called for a third ABM complex to protect another Minuteman complex near Whiteman Air Force Base in Missouri and planned for five additional ABM sites across the country.[49]

There are serious doubts that an ABM system will work at all, but even if it did function with a relatively high degree of efficiency, *an ABM system would not be needed to deter a Soviet attack on American Minuteman sites* and would be useless against a determined Soviet attack on American cities. The very existence of a large, dispersed, and hidden American Polaris fleet with over 650 missiles means that no matter what happened to American Minuteman sites, the Soviet Union would be destroyed (100 Polaris missiles would be a sufficient deterrent). This submarine missile force could not be simultaneously found and destroyed by Soviet antisubmarine warfare methods or systems known at the present time or predicted for the future. As the director of Navy Strategic Systems Projects, Rear Admiral Levin Smith, has stated: "The Russians have no specific new antisubmarine warfare methods the Navy knows of that would make the Polaris fleet vulnerable to attack. . . ."[50] Likewise, even if the Soviet Union did develop the SS-9 missile and MIRV in large quantities, as the American government claimed, Minuteman silos would then be obsolete because of their vulnerability—if the Minuteman missiles were intended to "ride out" a first strike. In the face of this obsolescence, the United States would simply escalate the arms race one more step. One example of this would be deployment of an Underwater Long-range Missile System (ULMS—$44 million was requested for this system by Secretary Laird for 1971) under the Great Lakes or within the twelve-mile limit. Thus, it would appear that the deployment of an ABM system to protect Minuteman sites simply did not make sense.

But in moving from Phase I to Phase II, Mr. Nixon's confused rhetoric also indicated that Phase II would be designed also to protect American cities from a Chinese attack. Mr. Nixon claimed that such a thin defense was "absolutely essential" if the United States was to have a "credible foreign policy" in the Pacific.[51] He further contended that such an American system would be "virtually infallible" against a Chinese missile attack. And it is here that is found the real significance of the decision to escalate the American ABM system. By claiming that the American Safeguard system would be designed and built (at least in part) for the protection of cities against a Chinese attack, not only are the past assumptions of the Cold War arms race revealed, but also the future nature of this conflict are made crystal clear. In effect, Mr. Nixon revealed:

(1) That in the future the United States would consider the Chinese as the major threat to American security;

(2) That in order to keep American policy in the Pacific "credible," the United States would attempt to practice nuclear blackmail on China for as long as possible;

(3) That in the future the arms race with the Soviet Union would be replaced by one with China and that the emphasis would shift from a balance of terror to an American attempt to guarantee United States domination of the Pacific by "absolute" protection of the United States from a Chinese attack (an impossible task by the late 1970s).

(4) And, finally, that the acceptance of the belief that the Chinese would commit national suicide by attacking the United

States with 25 or 100 missiles indicated that either the Administration believed that the government of China was completely irrational or that the Administration was willing to perpetuate this myth to achieve its desired goals* (in this case, obtaining the funds for Phase II of the Safeguard System).

This fundamental shift of American foreign policy had obviously begun to take place years ago and only became blatantly obvious with the Nixon Administration. But as the Chinese thermonuclear capability and ICBM forces continue to develop, the leaders of the United States will probably have no difficulty convincing the American people of the "credibility" of this threat. China will become the "enemy" and a threat to the United States in spite of the enormous American thermonuclear superiority. Every attempt will be made to have the Chinese government appear as an irrational force that would destroy China for their own ends; and an attempt will be made to convince the American people that "Orientals don't really value human life the way we do" and that the Chinese therefore will run all risks even in the face of American superiority.

Unless something is done to change American policy and attitudes, the new "enemy" has been found and the new Cold War/arms race is under way.

In 1970, the Chinese thermonuclear threat to the United States could not be made credible; at the same time, the Soviet Union still possessed a formidable thermonuclear capacity. A potential lull in the arms race loomed, and it appeared essential to keep the Soviet threat alive for at least several more years. Thus, Mr. Nixon's protection of the Minuteman sites, and even more important, the American decision to deploy MIRV on the Minuteman III and the Poseidon. Since there was no way that MIRV could be explained as an answer to the nonexistent Chinese intercontinental delivery system in early 1970, the only

---

* In 1968, Secretary McNamara stated: "We estimated, that a relatively small number of warheads detonated over 50 Chinese cities would destroy half of the urban population (more than 50 million people) and more than one-half of the industrial capacity." See U.S. Congress, Senate, *Authorization for Military Procurement, 1969,* 90th Cong., 2d sess., February 2, 1968, p. 113.

possible justification for this system was the Soviet threat. For twenty years American leadership has predicted huge Soviet arms-building programs and imminent Soviet attacks. These false predictions had evidently deadened many congressmen and Americans to the reality of the Soviet willingness to annihilate itself by attacking the United States.

The proponents in the United States government of installing the ABM-MIRV systems followed the new classic pattern of making a case for their multibillion–dollar system. Obviously, it was assumed by these advocates that most Americans would have forgotten the earlier fiascos of the bomber gap, the missile gap, and the Tallinn Line.

First, key officials projected the Soviet Union as a reckless and dangerous opponent that might strike at any time. For example, in 1969 Senator Henry Jackson (Dem.-Wash.) characterized the Soviet Union as "a dangerous, unpredictable opponent" with a "growing military capability."[52] This common liturgy of the Cold War is so well worn and unchallenged (at least until recently) that the cold warriors of America have only to pay it basic lip service to trigger an almost Pavlovian reaction among some Americans.

In the second stage, American leaders invoked the great strength of this "dangerous, unpredictable opponent" and cited the unbelievable *capability* of the Russians to do whatever they say the Soviet will do. Thus, Secretary Laird claimed that the Soviet Union had deployed more than 230 SS-9 missiles and that they had the *capability* to build 420 by 1975.

In Laird's struggle for more funds for the B-1, the Underwater Long-range Missile System, the ABM system, and others, the Secretary of Defense released classified information on the Soviet SS-9 missile. This new terror weapon could carry approximately 20–25 megatons and was capable of carrying MIRV. But what Secretary Laird did not indicate was that the SS-9 was not much more powerful than the American Operational Titan missile (10 megatons) and that the SS-9 with its roughly 12,000 pounds of thrust was almost insignificant when compared with American Saturn Rocket (1,500,000 pounds of thrust). If the United States had wanted larger rockets for MIRV or higher yield warheads, the technology for them had been available since the early 1960s. The United States had simply decided that the destructive power of a number of low yield weapons spread accurately over the same area would accomplish more destruction than one large warhead. Likewise, American rockets were more accurate than their Soviet counterparts and therefore did not have to deliver as heavy a payload to accomplish the same mission.*

Mr. Laird claimed that these SS-9 missiles would be equipped with "multiple warheads" but failed to distinguish between MIRV and MRV—or put another way, between whether this system was a counter-city MRV and therefore not a first-strike weapon or a counter-force MIRV and therefore capable of a first strike.[53] The director of research at the Pentagon, Dr. John S. Foster, joined his boss and predicted that by 1975 the Soviet Union would have the *capability* with 500 SS-9s to destroy 90 percent of the American ICBM force.[54] (This 90 percent figure

---

* The problem of whether to emphasize missile accuracy or high yield warheads is basically a question of the technology available. Due to the fact that the United States has always led the Soviet Union in missile accuracy, the United States chose to emphasize this characteristic rather than developing high yield warheads for its missiles. The official rationale for this decision is offered below by Secretary McNamara:

> Gross megatonnage is not a reliable indicator of the destructive power of an offensive force. For example, one missile carrying ten 50 kiloton warheads (a yield of ½ megaton) would be just as effective against a large city (2 million people) as a single 10 megaton warhead with 20 times the total yield.

Mr. McNamara continued:

> Even against hard ICBM sites, the ten 50 kiloton warheads would (*given the accuracy we anticipate* [emphasis added]) be more effective than a single 10 megaton warhead. And, of course, it would take 10 times as many ABM interceptors to defend a city against ten 50 kiloton warheads as it would against a single 10 megaton warhead.

See: U.S. Congress, Senate, *Authorization for Military Procurement, 1969,* 90th Cong., 2d sess. (February 2, 1968), p. 114. The above statement by Secretary McNamara goes a long way toward explaining the official reasons why the United States government decided to deploy massive numbers of MIRVd missiles.

is roughly the same figure used during the missile gap for the destruction of American deterrent forces.)

The congressional testimony of the Department of Defense left some disturbing questions unanswered:

(1) The Minuteman missile can be fired sixty seconds after the decision is made to fire it. The Ballistic Missile Early Warning System (BMEWS) and reconnaissance satellites guarantee between 15 and 20 minutes warning time in the event of an attack. If the United States received warning of an attack that would destroy 90 percent of the existing Minuteman force (well over 2,000 incoming warheads), why should not the United States launch some of these Minutemen (leaving empty holes to be attacked) and save the Polaris system as a reserve?

(2) Or, conversely, even if a majority of the Minuteman forces were destroyed, there is no known method by which the Soviet Union could track and destroy the 41 subs carrying over 650 Polaris missiles. This force alone is a more than adequate deterrent to a Soviet attack on any part of the United States.

But such questions did not prevent Secretary Laird from persevering in his attempt to gain the funds he wanted for the ABM and MIRV systems. The tried and true method of accomplishing this goal was to frighten the American people, and the best way to do this was to invoke the fear of a Soviet surprise attack on the United States. That is exactly what Secretary Laird did when he stated that there was no doubt that the Soviets ". . . are going for a first strike capability."[55] To support this position, Mr. Laird pulled out the stops before the Senate Foreign Relations Committee and claimed that:

(1) The Soviet Union was going forward with a new sophisticated ABM system.

(2) The Soviets were outspending the United States on strategic weapons by a 3–1 advantage.

(3) The Soviets were undertaking a crash program to overtake the United States in atomic submarines by 1974.

(4) The Soviet Union was deploying Fractional Orbiting Bombardment system (a counter-city, not counter-force system).

And, for good measure, Mr. Laird assured the committee that the Chinese would test fire an ICBM in the next 18–20 months and would have an imposing 25 ICBMs by 1974–1975.[56]

Along with Laird's decision to "release" secret information on the existence of the SS-9 and the American projections of the future numbers of these missiles, could anyone doubt that the United States was indeed in dire peril of surprise attack by Soviet Russia? The basic difference between Mr. Laird's approach and that of earlier advocates of "American superiority" was the degree of paranoia and hysteria that characterized Mr. Laird's attempt to sell his weapons system to the United States Congress and the American people. If Mr. Laird had ever faltered in his earlier ideas expressed in *America's Strategy Gap*, he had obviously returned to them. He believed that the only way to deal with the Soviet threat was based on "American superiority" and that to even allow "parity" would eventually lead to the "military occupation of the United States."[57]

While this standard Cold War perception of the Soviet Union was once again outlined by the Nixon Administration, simultaneously it was allegedly attempting to negotiate in good faith at the Strategic Arms Limitation Talks (SALT) in Vienna. In spite of strong congressional pressure, the Administration refused to freeze deployment of either the Safeguard system or MIRV system. But, as opposed to the initial deployment of Safeguard, the decision to proceed with the Minuteman III and Poseidon systems represented an immediate and serious threat to the balance of terror and world peace.

The United States decision to proceed with the MIRV system once again raised the specter of America preparing for a first strike against the Soviet Union. Once accurate multiple independently targeted warheads were placed on Minuteman and Poseidon, it would be impossible to tell exactly the number of warheads that the United States could deliver. Before the American deployment of MIRV, the United States had a delivery capability great enough to strike *each* Soviet missile and bomber site roughly three times, with enough left over to destroy all major Soviet cities. After the United States deployed its MIRV missiles, the threat of an American first strike would increase immeasurably.

Further complicating the picture was the basic fact that the early MRV system was fundamentally a counter-city system with limited accuracy. The independently targeted warheads (MIRV) were approaching a counter-force weapons system, and there is no doubt that the planned ARV (Advanced Re-entry Vehicle) with its own propulsion system and preplanned evasive action against possible ABM defense could definitely be used as a first-strike weapon on Soviet missile sites.

The Union of Concerned Scientists of MIT concluded:

> The tremendous effort being expended to improve the accuracy of the guidance system of the Poseidon and Minuteman III missiles suggests that the mission of these weapons is for silo busting, not for deterrence.[58]

Mr. Nixon's contention in early 1970 that no efforts would be made to improve the accuracy of the American MIRV system is hard to believe. That the American military services would stop improving the accuracy of weapons they were testing anyhow seems improbable. But even if this were the case, it would take a high degree of gullibility on the part of Soviet leaders to believe this without firm evidence to the contrary.

The situation was further complicated by the fact that the United States was simultaneously undertaking an extensive project of re-enforcing its Minuteman sites to withstand 900 psi (pounds of pressure per square inch). This increase in psi represented the capability to withstand three times the pressure of the earlier re-enforced silos to withstand 250–300 psi. The new Minuteman sites would require almost a direct hit by a four megaton weapon to be destroyed. Likewise, the command center for the Minuteman (each controlling 10 missiles) were re-enforced to withstand pressure of up to 7,000 psi. This project was begun under the Johnson Administration and evidently continued under Mr. Nixon.[59]

Along with the increased hardening of Minuteman silos, evidence appeared of increases in the American intelligence effort over the Soviet Union. Ever since the downing of the U-2 aircraft in 1960, the United States had relied on the use of satellites for intelligence information concerning the Soviet Union, including the location of Soviet airfields and missile sites. By 1970, the United States had launched 280 military satellites compared to about 160 launched by the Soviet Union.[60]

Likewise, the United States had been engaged in a much more extensive underground nuclear testing program than had the Soviet Union since the signing of the Test Ban Treaty in 1963. The Atomic Energy Commission reported that since the test ban, the United States had conducted 186 "announced tests" compared to 28 for the Soviet Union—six and one-half times more than the number of Soviet tests.[61]

As evidence began to mount on the American capability for a possible first strike against the Soviet Union, it became apparent that the next phase of the Safeguard system (Phase II) would be designed, if it worked, to prevent a second strike by the Soviet Union on American cities. And, as Ralph Lapp pointed out, "Anything that erodes Soviet second-strike capability must be viewed as very provocative."[62]

But the final and most frightening aspect of the MIRV system was the actual increase in the number of warheads the United States would be able to deliver accurately on Soviet targets by missiles alone. In February 1968, Mr. McNamara issued his final "posture statement" on the defense position of the United States. In 1968, Mr. McNamara claimed that the United States had more than a 3–1 lead over the Soviet Union in the ability to deliver thermonuclear warheads, and by 1973 the United States would increase the number of deliverable warheads by five times. Mr. McNamara's 1968 figures did not include the American fighter-bombers in Europe and other locations, or the aircraft on American aircraft carriers. His figures for deliverable warheads in 1968 were as follows:

	UNITED STATES	SOVIET UNION
ICBMs	1,054	720
Submarine-launched Missiles	656	30
Intercontinental Bombers	697	155
Total force loadings, approximate number of *warheads*	4,500	1,000[63]

According to Mr. McNamara, once the MIRV system was complete in 1973, the United States would have:

> 3,000 Minuteman Warheads (three 300 kiloton warheads per Minuteman III)
> 4,960 Poseidon Submarine-launched Missiles (31 submarines, with 16 missiles each at 10 MIRVd warheads per missile)
> 160 Polaris Submarine-launched Missiles
>   54 Titan II

Total warheads 8,174

In addition, by 1973, the United States was scheduled to have 281 B-52 bombers and 253 FB-111 (fighter-bombers).[64] The Nixon Administration continued all of these programs.

By 1970, the Soviet Union had only 50 cities the size of Hiroshima and only 200 cities with a population over 100,000. According to Secretary McNamara the delivery of only 400 single megaton warheads on the Soviet Union would be enough to destroy over one third of the population and over three fourths of Soviet industry.[65] If this is the damage that 400 megatons could do to the Soviet Union, then it seems pointless to speculate as to the

SOVIET POPULATION* AND INDUSTRY DESTROYED

Number of Single Megaton Delivered Warheads	Total Population Fatalities†	Percent	Industrial Capacity Destroyed
100	37,000,000	15	59 percent
200	52,000,000	21	72
400	74,000,000	30	76
800	96,000,000	39	77
1200	109,000,000	44	77
1600	116,000,000	47	77

* An urban population of 116 million is assumed for the year 1972.
† Fatalities are calculated on the basis of "prompt response"—i.e., death within 24 hours.

effect of the delivery of the 30,000 megatons that the United States had stored and ready to deliver. Nonetheless, below is Secretary McNamara's estimate of what the delivery of up to 1,600 warheads would do to the Soviet population and its industrial capacity.[66]

When the above weapons system and projections for the future are analyzed, at least one major question emerges in the mind of either a Soviet or American analyst. If 100 warheads would kill 37 million Soviet citizens within the *first* 24 hours of hostilities, and if 400 warheads would increase this toll to 74 million Russians, why did the United States feel compelled to increase the number of deliverable missile warheads from 1,700 to over 8,000? This type of overkill does not represent a deterrent force, it represents a potential first-strike system, and it would be illogical to assume that the Soviet leaders would believe anything else.

In view of Soviet inferiority and the past history of the arms race, the argument that the Soviet Union had the capability to build comparable ABM-MIRV systems and therefore would build these systems simply does not hold up. That the Soviet Union had the *capability* to build toward a bomber gap or a missile gap has never been denied. The simple fact is that they chose not to maximize production of these systems, but to build only those forces felt essential to deter an attack on the Soviet Union. When the Soviet Union finally did engage in large-scale missile production, it was in response to a threatening American superiority in *all* strategic weapons systems. Likewise, the fact that eventually the Soviet Union could build some type of ABM and MIRV systems is not the question. Since the United States is proceeding with the MIRV program which will be completed (8,000 warheads) by 1973, the real possibility exists that the American system would be finished when the Soviet Union was only in the initial stage of its deployment of a sophisticated MIRV system. Once again the impetus and initiative for a major escalation of the arms race has come from the United States.

If the United States continues with its ABM-MIRV plans there will be another major escalation of the arms race, initially with the Soviet Union and then with China. At the present time the Soviet Union does not have parity with the United States, and it would be foolhardy to believe that they are going to sit idly by while the American nuclear strike force increases five times.

The leaders of the Soviet Union must consider the possibility that the American arms programs are geared for a future surprise attack on the Soviet Union, or at a minimum aimed at nuclear blackmail of Soviet diplomacy throughout the world. Here is the picture of American military programs that, after a close study, a Soviet leader would receive in 1970:

(1) The large number of increasingly accurate American MIRV missiles would constitute a real threat to the Soviet ability to retaliate.

(2) The continued improvement and effort in the American intelligence effort could pinpoint all Soviet military targets for destruction.

(3) The large number of American underground nuclear tests could give the United States an important advantage in nuclear technology.

(4) The hardened American Minuteman missiles could survive any Soviet retaliatory strike and then hold Soviet cities as hostages should the Soviet Union fail to surrender.

(5) The American attempt to build an effective ABM system *might* endanger the certainty that the Soviet Union deterrent force could get through on a second strike.

(6) And, finally, the dramatic increase in the American nuclear delivery advantage might mean that an irrational American President could feel that a first strike was a viable means of destroying the Soviet Union without receiving a retaliatory attack on the United States.

Faced with increasing American superiority, the Soviet Union will be forced to escalate its own arms program. During the 1970s, they will develop and deploy MIRV. Then, just as the leaders of the United States have cited the 1970 Soviet achievement of ICBM parity as proof of their wisdom in the 1960s, they will tell the American public, "I told you so." There has never been a better example of the self-fulfilling prophecy.

Epilogue

As the arms race escalates into the 1970s, I feel that it is my responsibility to attempt an assessment of the possibilities of stopping this modern form of insanity. The best place to start such an assessment is with an inquiry into why the United States feels that it is essential to maintain an absolute superiority in the number of thermonuclear delivery vehicles. From this point, it is then possible to assess the possibilities of *meaningful* arms reduction at the SALT talks in Vienna. Finally, I would like to submit a modest proposal for meaningful arms reduction that appears to me to be realistic in the sense that it would work if tried by the governments involved.

The first question that must be asked, even if inadequately answered, is why in an age of thermonuclear plenty, the United States is attempting to maintain such an absolute nuclear superiority over the Soviet Union (and China). Why the continued myth creation on the part of the United States government? Most of the leaders of both superpowers admit that the complexity and diversity of nuclear delivery systems make a first-strike surprise attack impossible to execute without being destroyed in the process. Therefore, if the goal of American superiority is not simply to deter a Chinese or Soviet attack (as this could be done with nuclear parity or less), what is the reason for the decision to embark upon another apparently needless major escalation of the arms race? Although there are numerous domestic economic reasons for taking this course, the major military reason appears to be a relatively simple, if incorrect, one. The United States is still committed to maintaining the status quo in the noncommunist world. Once it was discovered that this could not be done with nuclear weapons alone, the decision was made to use larger, more conventional, military forces to accomplish this purpose. However, the willingness to intervene all over the world with conventional power meant that U.S. leaders believed that American nuclear power was so absolute that neither the Soviet Union nor China would challenge these military efforts to maintain the American empire. The reasoning here was fairly basic. If the United States always maintained at least four times as much deliverable nuclear power as any of its enemies, it would not only deter an attack on the United States, but it would also give to the United States a free hand militarily throughout the rest of the world. In the age of thermonuclear plenty this is an extremely dangerous policy to pursue; nonetheless, it was the one chosen by the various administrations of the United States government.

But even as the Nixon-Laird team embraced the doctrine of massive nuclear superiority, the Administration was going through the motions of arms limitation talks in Vienna. The American philosophy at Vienna remained the same as it had been under past Administrations—the United States will arm in order to disarm. While the diplomats talked, American MIRVs became operational and the Administration mustered an additional $1.3 billion appropriation through Congress for the expansion of the ABM system. These multibillion-dollar systems were to be the "bargaining chips" at Vienna in negotiations with the Russians.*

However, one potent fact casts serious doubts as to the sincerity and integrity of the American position at Vienna—that is, that in the thermonuclear balance of terror only the strategically "superior" nation can make major concessions without endangering its security. In this case, only the United States with its vastly superior arsenal could afford to reduce its numerical advantage without fear of a surprise Soviet attack. If the leaders of the Soviet Union moved to reduce their already inferior strategic delivery system, this would further increase the possibility of a surprise attack by the superior American forces. For example, if the United States stopped its deployment of MIRV missiles in an attempt to freeze the arms ratio at roughly a 2–1 American advantage, there would still be no way

* *The New York Times,* August 13, 1970.

that the Soviet Union could launch a surprise attack against a dispersed American system. However, were both sides to reduce their delivery systems by one thousand vehicles, the American advantage would shift dangerously from a 2–1 advantage to a 3–1 superiority.

It would seem that there are only three rather remote chances for any immediate, successful effort for a real arms limitation agreement at Vienna/Helsinki. The first would be a fundamental change in the military-political policies of the United States government. The second would be the willingness of the Soviet Union to agree to a treaty that would make Soviet strategic inferiority permanent. Both of these possibilities seem very remote in 1970. A third option for the future of the arms race would be for the United States and the Soviet Union to agree that China is the "enemy" and enter into a joint agreement on strategic arms to contain China. Apparently, the arms race will continue.

In view of this terrifying, predictable course of events, I feel compelled to offer a partial solution to such an abysmal future. Such a solution must recognize the reality of the balance of terror and the existing nature of the modern-nation state.

It is my conviction that in the age of nuclear plenty and in view of the recent history of the nation-state, total disarmament is not possible at this time. Mankind is destined to live with some type of balance of terror for the foreseeable future. Likewise, since modern nation-states have given their citizens scant reasons for trusting their own nation, it would be foolhardy to expect the governments of these nations to trust each other. Therefore, a plan for arms limitation should not demand mutual trust among the United States, the Soviet Union, and eventually China.

In addition, at a time when the weapons of war are capable of completely destroying a nation and its society, any plan for disarmament must not entail any increased risks to the fundamental security of the nations involved. In other words, at no time during the implementation of an arms limitation agreement should any nation be vulnerable to a surprise attack against which it cannot retaliate effectively.

Thus a viable solution to the arms race between the United States and the Soviet Union would not be based on mutual trust, would entail no additional risks to national security, and can be accomplished only by the "superior" nuclear power. It seems to me that the following plan meets these prerequisites. The United States should announce the following plan for strategic arms reduction:

(1) That the United States would immediately freeze the deployment of MIRV-ABM and destroy existing systems.

(2) That the United States, under strict international supervision (including Russian and Chinese), would begin immediate, unilateral destruction of 100 missiles and/or bombers per month for the next twenty-four months.

(3) That the United States would invite the Soviet Union to join this process at 40 Soviet missiles or bombers per month.

(4) That regardless of the Soviet reaction to this proposal the United States would proceed with the destruction of 2,400 delivery vehicles and their nuclear weapons over the next two years.

(5) That, should the Soviet Union join this process, the goal should be the destruction of all strategic delivery systems except ten nuclear submarines with Polaris-type missiles (160 missiles).

(6) That once this state was reached, the two powers would meet to discuss further steps to reduce the possibility of thermonuclear war and the cost of the arms race.

The numbers and exact timing of this proposal could obviously vary and the end result would depend upon the Soviet reaction, technological developments in the interim, and the position taken by the Chinese government.

But, the fact remains that at the end of the twenty-four-month cycle the United States would still have over 1,400 delivery vehicles that could easily deter a Soviet or Chinese attack on American territory. Likewise, if the Soviet Union co-operated, ten nuclear submarines with 16 missiles each would be more than sufficient to mutually deter an attack by either power on the other.

This proposal does not include mutual trust among the powers, nor does it entail any risk to the security of the United States or the Soviet Union. If successfully implemented, the gains would be immeasurable in the reduction of the costs and tensions of the arms race. The threat of thermonuclear war would be reduced and literally a trillion dollars could be saved over the next 15 to 20 years that would have been spent on arms production. Once China had developed a firm degree of confidence in its own form of minimum nuclear deterrence, China could be brought into this arrangement and would probably seek active participation due to the future costs that could be avoided in an arms race with both the Soviet Union and the United States.

Although a proposal such as the one offered above may make sense to some readers, likewise it is obvious that such a plan will not be tried by the only government in the world powerful enough to attempt it—the government of the United States. The combination of the American commitment to empire and the domestic forces working for a continuation of the arms race make it impossible. The commitment to arms limitation is just like so many other aspects of the arms race—it is a myth.

Perhaps Nat Hentoff placed the arms race in its true cosmic perspective when he said: "Our last myth may be that we cannot become the first star to have willfully destroyed itself."

Appendix A

COMPARATIVE WEAPONS SYSTEMS—UNITED STATES AND THE SOVIET UNION 1945–1970

This Appendix is intended to give the reader an overall picture of the comparative strategic military power of the United States and the Soviet Union from 1945 to 1970. All of the information in this Appendix came from unclassified sources. Much of the data listed below came from official documents of the United States government, particularly congressional hearings and special studies. The remainder came from private investigations, mass media periodicals, and books by experts in the field. Almost without exception, the media sources claimed to have obtained their information from an "official source," or a "high government official," or from the official intelligence estimates themselves.[1] [Notes for Appendix A will be found on pages 165–167.]

As can be seen from the text of this study, these public figures corresponded closely to the official intelligence estimates released by the United States government several years after they appeared mysteriously in the press. There does not appear to be any doubt that throughout the twenty-five years under study there were numerous leaks to the press by government and military officials in an attempt to gain support for their position on a given weapons system or military appropriation.

Even a cursory glance at this Appendix will indicate that at no time during the period under study was the United States in danger of strategic inferiority or even parity: the period of "maximum danger" was always put at some point in the future and when this time came, a new future period of "maximum danger" was defined. Likewise it can be easily seen that at no time during the last twenty-five years has the Soviet Union maximized

153

its production of strategic weapons systems, and has only entered into sustained building programs under the extreme pressure of a substantial American superiority in strategic arms. Finally, it is obvious that during this period the Soviet Union never attempted to assume a first-strike posture vis-à-vis the United States; being content to build enough strategic arms to deter an attack by the United States, but never to threaten a first strike on this couutry.

1945–1949: During this period the United States had a monopoly on atomic weapons and the means to deliver them. The American delivery vehicle was the B-29 bomber stationed at overseas bases on the periphery of the Soviet Union.

1949: *The New York Times* (for complete bibliographical information, see footnotes).
The Soviet Union explodes its first atomic weapon in August 1949.

WEAPONS

United States—atomic stockpile in three figures.
Soviet Union—unknown.

DELIVERY MEANS

United States—a quantitative and qualitative lead. Roughly 500 B-29s stationed at overseas bases.
Soviet Union—TU-4 ("Bull") operational. Aircraft equivalent of the United States B-29, incapable of reaching the United States (no in-flight refueling and no Soviet overseas bases).[2]

1951–November 1952: *The New York Times*
United States explodes the first hydrogen bomb.

WEAPONS

United States—stockpile in four figures (also has developed 5-kiloton tactical weapon).[3]
Soviet Union—30–80 atomic bombs.[4]

DELIVERY MEANS

United States—using the B-29 and introducing the B-36 and B-47.
Soviet Union—still using the TU-4 with no overseas bases.[5]

1953: *The New York Times* and *Air Force*
Soviet Union explodes its first hydrogen bomb in August.

WEAPONS

United States—over 1,000 atomic or hydrogen weapons.
Soviet Union—100 to 200.[6]

DELIVERY MEANS

United States—B-36 and B-47 operational.[7]
Soviet Union—over 1,000 TU-4s.[8]

1954: *The New York Times*

WEAPONS

United States—2,000–3,000 weapons stockpile.
Soviet Union—300–400.[9]

DELIVERY MEANS

United States—using B-36, B-47, and the B-52 being phased in.[10]
Soviet Union—TU-4: over 1,000 (still no long-range capability, no in-flight refueling).
TU-16: (Badger) operational, with a range of over 4,000 miles (one-way strike to parts of the United States).[11]
TU-20: (Bear) compares very favorably with United States B-36 production beginning.[12] Range of over 7,000 miles.[13] TU-20 even given credit for matching the B-52 in many important areas of performance.[14] 500 Myasishchev 500 (Bison) comparable to B-52. Range of 6,000 miles. In production.[15]

1955: WEAPONS

United States—stockpile of over 5,000.
Soviet Union—over 500.[16]

DELIVERY MEANS

Both sides with about the same as above, only with an increase in operational aircraft.[17]

1956–1957: In August 1957 the Soviet Union announced the first successful firing of an ICBM.[18]

WEAPONS

United States—stockpile of 7,000–10,000 weapons.
Soviet Union—over 2,000.

1956–1957   (continued)

DELIVERY MEANS

Both systems still growing along the same lines, with the exception of the addition of the B-58 to the United States system.[19]

1957: At the end of 1957 General Thomas Power (SAC commander) claimed that the United States had 2,500 heavy-combat jet aircraft capable of reaching the Soviet Union. These aircraft were spread over 32 bases located in the United States and 27 overseas bases.[20]

1958: WEAPONS

Both sides with sizable stockpiles by this time.

DELIVERY MEANS

United States—250 B-52s and 1,800 B-47s and an unknown number of B-58s. (Hanson Baldwin set the figure at 4,000–5,000 aircraft capable of carrying megaton-range weapons to the Soviet Union.[21]

Soviet Union—Less than 200 Bison and Bear bombers operational.

The figures listed below during the period 1957–1961 represent the various projected estimates during the "missile gap" period.

July 1958: *The Reporter*

	UNITED STATES (ICBM'S)	SOVIET UNION (ICBM'S)
1959	0	100
1960	80	500
1961	70	1,000
1962	130	1,500
1963	130	2,000[22]

January 12, 1959: *The New York Times*

	UNITED STATES (ICBM'S)	SOVIET UNION (ICBM'S)
1960	30	100
1961	70	500
1962	130	1,000
1963	130	1,500
1964	130	2,000[23]

March 9, 1959: *Aviation Week*

> 1959—Soviet Union with 100 ICBMs.
> 1962—Soviet Union with 600 ICBMs.[24]

March 25, 1959: *The New York Times*

> 1959—Today, Soviet Union with 150 long-range bombers.
> 1960—Soviet Union with 100 ICBMs.
> 1962—Soviet Union with 500 ICBMs.[25]

April 1959: *Fortune*

> Earlier estimates of Soviet ICBM strength.
> > 1959—10 ICBMs
> > 1960—100 ICBMs
> > 1961—500 ICBMs
> "Downgraded" estimates of early 1959 of Soviet ICBMs.
> > 1961—60–100 ICBMs (Russian)
> > Mid-1962—or later, 500 Russian ICBMs[26]

September 28, 1959: *U.S. News & World Report*

	UNITED STATES (ICBM'S)	SOVIET UNION (ICBM'S)
1959 (now)	10	10[27]

October 7, 1959: *Washington Post and Times Herald*

	UNITED STATES (ICBM'S)	SOVIET UNION (ICBM'S)
1960	30	100
1961	70	500
1962	130	1,000
1963	130	1,500[28]

February 2, 1960: *The New York Times*

	UNITED STATES (ICBM'S)	SOVIET UNION (ICBM'S)
1961	50	150 (3–1)[29]

February 7, 1960: *The New York Times*

	UNITED STATES (ICBM'S)	SOVIET UNION (ICBM'S)
February 1960	3	10
June 1960	18	38
June 1961	40–50	140–200
1963	200	500[30]

February 18, 1960: *The Reporter*

	UNITED STATES (ICBM'S)	SOVIET UNION (ICBM'S)
1961	50	150
1962	200	600 (3–1)[31]

From March 1960 to December 1960: Interestingly, and inexplicably, during the presidential campaign of 1960, those involved in the "missile gap" controversy refrained from making specific predictions as to the future of the missile gap.

January 1961: *The New York Times*

	UNITED STATES	SOVIET UNION
Long-range bombers	500	about 190

Both sides with only a "handful" of ICBMs and missile-launching submarines.[32]

January 23, 1961: *U. S. News & World Report*

UNITED STATES (EXISTING STRENGTH)	SOVIET UNION
9 Atlas ICBMs	35 ICBMs
32 Polaris IRBMs	500–800 IRBMs (cannot reach the U.S.)
60 Thor IRBMs	
20 Snark missiles	
600 long-range bombers	150
1,100 medium-range bombers	1,500 (cannot reach the U.S.)
400 carrier-based bombers	none
2,000 Air Force fighter-bombers	none capable of reaching the United States

UNITED STATES (PROJECTED STRENGTH)		SOVIET UNION
Mid-1961	50 ICBMs	150–200 ICBMs
	48 Polaris	
Mid-1962	100 ICBMs	500 ICBMs
	144 Polaris	
Mid-1963	300 ICBMs	1,000 ICBMs
	240 Polaris	
Mid-1964	870 ICBMs	1,500 ICBMs[33]
	336 Polaris	

February 1, 1961: *The New York Times*

UNITED STATES (RETALIATORY FORCE IN MISSLES)
  48 Polaris
  60 Thor missiles in Britain—range 1,725 miles
  30 Jupiters in Italy
  15 Jupiters en route to Turkey
  12 Atlas[34]

February 27, 1961: *U.S. News & World Report*

UNITED STATES	SOVIET UNION
124—missile delivered warheads	20–50
3,500—bombers with range to reach enemy's homeland	200–300[35]

July 9, 1961: *The New York Times*

UNITED STATES	SOVIET UNION
100 Atlas	Less than 50 ICBMs[36]
48 Polaris	

November 13, 1961: *Newsweek*

UNITED STATES	SOVIET UNION
45 ICBMs	35–50 ICBMs

These figures supposedly came from the National Intelligence Estimate.[37]

Early 1962: The Institute for Strategic Studies

	WESTERN ALLIANCE	COMMUNIST BLOC
ICBMs	63	50+
MRBMs	186	200
Long-range bombers	600	190
Medium-range bombers	2,200	1,100
Aircraft carriers	58	None
Nuclear submarines	22	2[38]

December 20, 1962: *The New York Times*

UNITED STATES	SOVIET UNION
126 Atlas	75–100 ICBMs[39]
54 Titan	
20 Minutemen	
Over 100 Polaris	

1962: The Institute for Strategic Studies

UNITED STATES	SOVIET UNION
650 B-52's with "hound-dog" air-to-air missiles	70 Bear long-range bombers
1,000 B-47's (in-flight refueling)	1,000 Badgers, medium-range
55 B-58's	
Atlas operational	50–100 ICBMs
Titan operational	
80 Polaris	
	Unknown number of Bisons (B-52) and Bounders (B-58) [40]

January 10, 1963: *The New York Times*

UNITED STATES	SOVIET UNION
200 ICBMs	75–100 ICBMs
144 Polaris (9 subs)	Approximately 60 submarine-launched missiles [41]
45 Jupiter	
60 Thor	

Early 1963: The Institute for Strategic Studies

	WESTERN ALLIANCE	COMMUNIST BLOC
ICBMs (over 2,000-mile range	450–500	75+
MRBMs (700–2,000-mile range)	250	700
Long-range bombers (over 5,000-mile range)	630	200
Medium-range bombers (over 2,000-mile range, including major carrier-based aircraft)	1,630	1,400
Nuclear submarines	32	12
Conventional submarines	212	445 [42]

Early 1964: The Institute for Strategic Studies

	WESTERN ALLIANCE	COMMUNIST BLOC
ICBMs (over 2,500-mile range)	475	100+
Fleet ballistic missiles	192	100

	WESTERN ALLIANCE	COMMUNIST BLOC
IRBMs and MRBMs (600–2,100 mile)	—	800
Long-range bombers (over 5,000-mile range)	630	200
Medium-range land-based bombers (over 2,000 miles excluding carrier air-based aircraft)	780	1,400
Carrier-based bombers (over 2,000-mile range)	600	—
Carriers (including commando and escort carriers)	38	—
Nuclear submarines	33	23[43]

April 15, 1964: *The New York Times*

These are official Pentagon figures released in 1964 to avoid an election year "security gap" debate.

UNITED STATES	SOVIET UNION
540 Long-range bombers	270
750 ICBMs	below 200
192 Polaris	substantially fewer with only a 500-mile range[44]

July 14, 1966: *The New York Times*

UNITED STATES	SOVIET UNION
800 Minutemen	300 Total ICBMs
54 Titan II	—
80 Minutemen II	—
934 Total ICBMs	300 Total ICBMs
400 Polaris with 656 operational by the end of 1966	150 short-range missiles
25,000 stored megatons	12,000 stored megatons

United States still far ahead of the Soviet Union in number of long-range bombers and carrier naval aircraft capable of delivering a nuclear weapon.[45]

Early 1967: The Institute for Strategic Studies

	WESTERN ALLIANCE		COMMUNIST BLOC	
Missile and Air Power				
ICBMs	934	(854)	300	(270)
Fleet ballistic missiles	624	(544)	150	(120+)
IRBMs and MRBMs	—	(—)	750	(750)
Long-range heavy bombers	595	(625)	200	(200)
Medium bombers	222	(430)	1,200	(1,250)[46]

(Figures in parentheses are the ISS estimates for early 1966.)

The chart listed below adequately reflects the Soviet strategic arms build-up starting in 1966. However, even a chart of this nature is to an extent misleading in any attempt to calculate the balance of terror between the United States and the Soviet Union. For example, the United States has over 300 tactical fighter-bombers, the F-4, stationed in Europe. This bomber has a range of 2,300 miles with an in-flight refueling capability, travels more than twice as fast as a B-52, and can carry weapons

COMPARISON OF U.S. AND SOVIET STRATEGIC NUCLEAR WEAPONS SYSTEMS[48]

OFFENSIVE

	LAND-LAUNCHED MISSILES	SUB-LAUNCHED MISSILES	INTERCONTINENTAL BOMBERS
1,400			
1,200	1,350		
1,000	United States 1,054		
800			
600	Soviet	656	
400			536
200		205	
0			150

1966 1967 1968 1969 1966 1967 1968 1969 1966 1967 1968 1969

———————— United States
— — — — — Soviet Union

in the megaton range. These supersonic aircraft can make the trip from Hamburg to Moscow in 40 minutes. The Soviets have no equivalent system. The United States has similar systems in Thailand and other points on the Soviet or Chinese border.[47]

The figures below adequately represent the projections of the weapons systems of the United States and the Soviet Union if both nations decide to place MIRVs on their missiles. However, the reader should be reminded that in 1970, The Minuteman III system was becoming operational and the Poseidon system was due to become operational by December 1970. On the other hand, the Soviet system was not operational and there was no "hard" intelligence available on exactly when the Soviet system would be built.

1970: United States and Soviet Strategic Warheads

	UNITED STATES	SOVIET UNION
Bombers	2,144	600
ICBMs (land based)	1,054	1,350
Missiles (submarine)	656	205
Total	3,854	2,155

United States and Soviet Strategic Warheads (if both sides MIRV their missiles as predicted)

	UNITED STATES	SOVIET UNION
Bombers	2,144	600
ICBMs (land based)	3,000	4,050
Missiles (submarine)	5,120	1,645
Total	10,264	6,295[49]

The above MIRV predictions are based on what the United States plans to do and what American leaders *predicted* the Soviet Union had the *capability* to do. Also, I tend to doubt the accuracy of the claim that the Soviet Union had 600 bombers capable of reaching the United States.

Below is listed a more precise breakdown of the projected American MIRV system. These are the figures given by Secretary McNamara in his final "posture" statement to Congress.

If the United States proceeds with this program, the American warhead lead would shift from 2–1 to 9–1 by about 1973.

United States: Projected deliverable warheads when MIRV program completed.

    3,000 Minuteman warheads (ICBMs)
    4,960 Poseidon warheads (submarine launched)
      160 Polaris warheads (submarine launched)
       54 Titan (ICBMs)
    ─────
    8,174[50]

Appendix A Notes

1. The reader who wants an even more detailed account of the reporting on strategic weapons systems during the arms race should consult Edgar M. Bottome, *The Missile Gap: A Study of the Formulation of Military and Public Policy* (Cranbury, New Jersey: Fairleigh Dickinson University Press, 1970). I am indebted to the publishers of this work for their permission to reprint part of this study in this book.

2. *The New York Times*, October 2, 1949; *ibid.*, November 27, 1947; Samuel Huntington, *The Common Defense: Strategic Programs in National Security* (New York: Columbia University Press, 1961), p. 59; *The New York Times*, October 5, 1951.

3. *The New York Times*, May 7, 1950.

4. *The New York Times*, June 7, 1951.

5. Leonard Bridgeman, ed., *Jane's All the World's Aircraft* (London: Samson Low, Marston & Company Ltd., 1952), p. 18.

6. *The New York Times*, December 10, 1953.

7. "Weapons," *Air Force*, Vol. 40, no. 8 (August 1957), 353.

8. Asher Lee, *The Soviet Air Force* (New York: The John Day Company, 1962), pp. 132–134.

9. *The New York Times*, February 13, 1954.

10. "Weapons," p. 353.

11. Lee, *The Soviet Air Force*, p. 133.

12. "Reds Put Muscle in Strategic Air Arm," *Aviation Week*, Vol. 60, no. 11 (March 5, 1954), 91.

13. *Communist Bloc and the Western Alliances: The Military Balance 1961–1962* (The Institute for Strategic Studies: London), p. 3.

14. "How Good Is Russia's Long-Range Turboprop Bear Bomber?", *Air: Air Intelligence Training Bulletin* (published by the United States Air Force), Vol. 9, no. 9 (September 1957), 39.

15. "Reds Put Muscle in Strategic Air Arm," p. 92.

16. *The New York Times*, February 13, 1955.

17. Lee, *The Soviet Air Force*, p. 234.

18. *The New York Times*, August 27, 1957.

19. "Weapons," p. 353.

20. *The New York Times*, news article quoting General Thomas S. Power, September 27, 1957.

21. Hanson Baldwin, *The Great Arms Race* (New York: Frederick A. Praeger, 1958), p. 39.

22. Thomas R. Phillips, "The Growing Missile Gap," *The Reporter* (January 8, 1959), 20:11. The figures below were attributed to Joseph Alsop as of July 1958. The same figures were reproduced in *The New York Times*.

23. *The New York Times*, "U.S. Raising Goals as Critics Foresee Gap," news article by Richard Witkin, January 12, 1959.

24. "Soviets Study Military Aspects of Space," *Aviation Week* (March 9, 1959), 70:314. Russia reported to be building fifteen ICBMs per month (based on a "conservative" estimate).

25. *The New York Times*, news article by Hanson Baldwin, March 25, 1959.

26. Charles J. V. Murphy, "The Embattled Mr. McElroy," *Fortune* (April 1959), 59:242. These estimates appear to represent the downgraded United States estimates referred to earlier in 1959.

27. "The U.S. is about even with the Soviet Union in Missiles," *U.S. News & World Report* (September 28, 1959), 47:63.

28. *Washington Post and Times Herald*, "After Ike the Deluge," news article by Joseph Alsop, October 7, 1959.

29. *The New York Times*, news article by John W. Finney, February 8, 1960.

30. *The New York Times* (editorial), February 7, 1960.

31. Thomas R. Phillips (General, United States Army, ret.), "The Great Guessing Game," *The Reporter* (February 18, 1960), 22:26. Mr. Phillips reported that the Soviet Union was producing ICBMs at the rate of fifty per month.

32. *The New York Times*, official Pentagon figures released in 1964 on United States and Soviet strategic weapons as of January 1961 (April 16, 1964).

33. "Is the World Balance in Missiles Shifting to U.S.?" *U.S. News & World Report* (January 23, 1961), 59:65–66.

34. *The New York Times*, "Kennedy's Defense Study," news article by Hanson Baldwin, February 1, 1961.

35. "The Truth About the Missile Gap," *U.S. News & World Report* (February 27, 1961), 50:41. "Gap" favors the United States.

36. *The New York Times*, news article by Hanson Baldwin, July 9, 1961.

37. "Was There Ever a Missile Gap or Just an Intelligence Gap?" *Newsweek* (November 13, 1961), 58:23.

38. *The Communist Bloc and the Western Alliance: The Military Balance, 1961–1962* (London: Institute for Strategic Studies, 1962), back cover, p. 25.

39. *The New York Times*, December 20, 1962.

40. *The Military Balance, 1962–1963*, p. 5.

41. *The New York Times*, "The Soviet Need for a Super-Bomb," news article by Hanson W. Baldwin, January 10, 1963.

42. *The Military Balance, 1962–1963*, p. 26.

43. *The Military Balance, 1963–1964*, p. 34.

44. *The New York Times,* the Pentagon released its official figures on comparative United States-Soviet military strength to avoid another "missile gap" debate in the 1964 presidential election (April 15, 1964).

45. *The New York Times,* "U.S. Lead in ICBMs Is Said to Be Reduced by Build-up in Soviet Union," news article by Hanson W. Baldwin, July 14, 1966.

46. *The Military Balance, 1966–1967,* p. 43.

47. Ernest Abers, *et al.* (Union of Concerned Scientists, Cambridge: MIT Press, 1969).

48. *The New York Times,* November 18, 1969.

49. *Ibid.*

50. U.S. Congress, Senate, *Authorization for Military Procurement, Research & Development, Fiscal Year 1969 and Reserve Strength,* 90th Cong., 2d sess., testimony by Secretary of Defense McNamara, pp. 116–117.

Appendix B

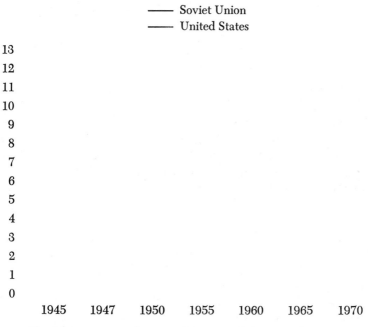

Total Manpower in the Armed Services of the United States
and the Soviet Union—1945–1970

The total manpower figures for the Soviet Union and the United States from 1945 to 1970 break down as follows: *

	UNITED STATES	SOVIET UNION
1945	12,000,000	11,365,000
1948	1,700,000	2,874,000
1951	2,800,000	3,100,000
1955	2,600,000	5,763,000
1960	2,200,000	3,623,000
1963	2,700,000	3,300,000
1966	3,000,000	3,100,000
1968	3,500,000	3,200,000
1970	3,400,000	3,200,000 (approximate figures)

At least two observations should be made on the above figures. First, once the Soviet Union obtained an intercontinental bomber in 1955, the number of men under arms began to be reduced. Second, the rise in the number of Americans under arms starting in 1960 reflected the shift of American strategy from complete reliance on atomic weapons to the Kennedy-McNamara strategy of flexible response.

* These figures are approximate and can be found in: P. M. S. Blackett, *Studies on War* (New York: Hill and Wang, 1962); Raymond Garthoff, *Soviet Military Policy: An Historical Analysis* (New York: Frederick Praeger, 1966); and the various studies done by The Institute for Strategic Studies.

Glossary

This Glossary is intended to help the reader decipher the almost impenetrable amount of jargon that surrounds American military policy. Where there is disagreement over definitions of concepts, the writer has attempted to define a given term as it is used in this book. For this Glossary, the writer has drawn heavily on works by such men as P. M. S. Blackett and Ralph Lapp and from The Institute for Strategic Studies.

It should be noted that the term "range" here refers to a delivery vehicle making a one-way trip to its target, whereas "radius" means a two-way trip.

ABM: Anticontinental Ballistic Missile. A weapons system including detection, tracking, and calculation of the extended trajectory of incoming missiles, and the launching of a guided missile which will destroy the attacking missile. The current American system is called Safeguard.

Airborne Alert: An alert system in which a certain number of long-range bombers are kept in the air constantly, ready to retaliate in case of an enemy surprise attack.

AMSA: Advanced Manned Strategic Aircraft. One of the names given to the Air Force replacement for the B-52. Cost estimates indicated that the production and maintenance of 200 of these aircraft will run at least $10 billion. Renamed the B-1. A supersonic, intercontinental bomber.

ARV: Advanced Re-entry Vehicles. A MIRV system in which each of the re-entry warheads has its own propulsion system. This system is projected for the future and is definitely a potential first-strike system due to its accuracy. This system has already cost $1.3 billion and $600 million is planned for the next five years.

Background Briefing: A briefing given by a government official to the press. The information in this type of briefing is intended for "background" only. The identity of the briefer is supposedly secret and in many cases the information given in the briefing is not supposed to be made public. (This same type of briefing can be given to congressional leaders.)

BMEWS: Ballistic Missile Early Warning System. This consists of three huge radar installations designed to give twenty-minute warning of a missile attack.

Bomarc: United States Air Force surface-to-air (antibomber) missile. The Army's NIKE system was adopted instead. Now obsolete.

Bombers—Soviet Union:

> *TU-4* (named "Bull" by NATO). Early Soviet bomber that was operational about 1948. This aircraft had a range of 2,000 miles and was not capable of reaching the United States.

> *TU-16* (Badger). A medium-range subsonic bomber with a range of approximately 3,000 miles. Operational, 1955.

> *TU-20* (Bear). This was a Soviet intercontinental subsonic bomber with a range of 7,800 miles. Operational, 1956 (turboprop).

> Myasishchev 500 (Bison). Soviet intercontinental bomber comparable to the American B-52. This bomber was operational in 1955, with a range of 6,050 miles. (B-52 has a range of 10,000 miles.)

> *TU-22* (Blinder). This is a supersonic medium-range (2,000 miles) Soviet bomber. There is some doubt as to the present operational existence of this bomber.

Ilyushin 28. Soviet medium-range bomber. This is a twin-jet tactical bomber with a range of 1,500 miles. The Soviet Union placed less than 30 of these in Cuba during the 1962 crisis.

Bombers—United States:

B-29. Medium-range bomber with a range of 2,000 miles. Operational during World War II. Located at overseas bases on the periphery of the Soviet Union, this bomber was the major American delivery vehicle for atomic weapons until the B-36 became operational in 1951–1952.

B-36. Long-range, turbojet, intercontinental bomber with a range of approximately 8,000 miles. Operational 1951–1952.

B-47. Medium-range jet bomber with a range of 3,200 miles without in-flight refueling. This aircraft was stationed at overseas bases and in the United States with an in-flight refueling capability. Operational in 1952. Bases located in Greenland, Iceland, Britain, North Africa, Saudi Arabia, Formosa, Okinawa, Japan.

B-52 A-G. Long-range bomber (10,000 miles) that was operational in various versions from 1955 to 1961. Later versions equipped with air-to-surface missiles.

B-52 H. Long-range bomber (12,000 miles) equipped with air-to-surface missiles.

B-58 (Hustler). Supersonic medium-range bomber (2,000 miles) with in-flight refueling.

B-1. New long-range (10,000 miles) American heavy bomber with supersonic speeds and air-to-surface missiles.

C5A: New American super transport being built by Lockheed Aircraft. Estimated cost overruns on production of this aircraft are running as high as $2 billion. Has a range of 5,000 miles and can carry a cargo of 100 tons, or approximately 500 men.

CBW: Chemical-biological warfare.

CEP: Circular error probability. A measure of missile accuracy. Defined in terms of the radius of a circle within which 50 percent of the missiles impact. The CEP of American ICBMs in 1970 was below one-half mile and predicted to drop to within hundreds of feet of its designated target area.

CIA: Central Intelligence Agency, United States government. Responsible for the over-all assimilation of American intelligence efforts.

Counterforce Doctrine: Essentially a first-strike doctrine aimed at the destruction of the enemy's nuclear capability to prevent effective retaliation. Once this was accomplished, the enemy's cities could be held as hostages by the remaining nuclear power, and the war could be won. (See also, second-strike counterforce.)

Defense: The actual military act of defending against an enemy attack. Contrasted with deterrence, which is the prevention of such an attack.

Deterrence: Convincing a potential aggressor, in advance, that it can and will be made to suffer more by aggression than can be gained by it.

DEW: Distant Early Warning system, to warn of an impending enemy bomber attack.

DIA: Defense Intelligence Agency. The attempt by President Kennedy in 1961–1962 to consolidate the intelligence services of the Army, Navy, and Air Force in an effort to reduce confusion within the American intelligence system.

Divisions (Army): An American division normally runs between 14,000 and 20,000 men, while a Soviet division normally runs between 9,000 and 14,000 men.

Explorer I: First United States satellite. Placed into orbit on January 1, 1958, by a United States Army Jupiter C missile. (Satellite weighed 30.8 pounds.)

F-4 (Phantom): An American fighter-bomber capable of carrying an 8,000–10,000 pound bomb load. It has a range of 2,000 miles. This aircraft has a thermonuclear capability. There are 325 F-4s in Europe capable of reaching the Soviet Union in less than an hour.

F-14: The Navy's replacement for the TFX aircraft. Projected costs on this aircraft indicate that it will cost $25 billion by 1980. The Navy would like to purchase 1,200 of these planes at $10 million each.

FDLS: Fast Deployment Logistic Ships. These vessels would be built for tactical functions only, to be positioned near trouble spots with a full load of combat and support equipment, or poised ready in a United States port. The United States Navy has requested 30 of these ships, each capable of carrying enough equipment for two troop divisions to be brought in, 500 at a time, by the new C5A super transport.

First Strike: The attempted surprise delivery of nuclear warheads on the enemy's nuclear delivery systems in an attempt to destroy the enemy's ability to retaliate.

Flexible Response: An attempt by the Kennedy-McNamara Administration to give the United States nonnuclear, conventional military response to perceived aggression. Called for a substantial build-up of American conventional and counter-insurgency forces.

FOBS: Fractional Orbital Bombardment System. A system under development to place a nuclear warhead into partial orbit before impact. This system could be used to cross the southern ice cap rather than the closer northern one between the United

States and the Soviet Union. At the present time it is primarily a counter-city weapon due to its limited accuracy (CEP).

Force de Frappe: The French medium-range hydrogen bomber force designed to give France an independent deterrent force against the Soviet Union. The fact that the Mirage IV bomber *might* be able to attack Moscow and Leningrad means that this force is much more successful than American leaders have been willing to admit.

GALOSH: Soviet antiballistic missile deployed around Moscow. The Russians built 67 of these and then stopped work on the project. The system was evidently obsolete before they began construction. It was roughly equivalent to the obsolete American Nike-Zeus system.

Ground Alert: An alert system in which a certain number of long-range bombers are kept in constant readiness on the ground. These bombers could be airborne fifteen minutes after warning of an impending enemy attack was received.

Hardened Operational Missile Site: A missile launch site in which missiles are stored in underground silos from which they can be fired, and which are protected against all but a very close strike by nuclear weapons. American Minuteman sites have begun increasing the invulnerability of these sites from 300 pounds per square inch (psi) to 2,000 psi.

ICBM: Intercontinental Ballistic Missile. A surface-to-surface missile with ballistic-type trajectory and a range of 5,000 miles or more.

IRBM: Intermediate-Range Ballistic Missile. A surface-to-surface missile with ballistic-type trajectory and a range of about 1,500–2,000 miles. The Soviet Union placed 12–16 of these in Cuba during the 1962 crisis. Earlier, about 1959, the United States had placed a number of these missiles in Great Britain, Italy, and Turkey.

Jupiter: United States liquid-fueled intermediate-range (1,500 miles) missile once deployed in Italy and Turkey.

Kiloton: Equivalent of 1,000 tons of TNT.

20 Kt. Twenty thousand tons of TNT. Nagasaki bomb—destroys everything within a radius of 1¼ miles with serious damage to an area of 4.6 miles.

40 Kt. Does serious damage within a radius of 1½ miles and destroys an area of 7 square miles.

500 Kilotons. This weapon will destroy an area of over 50 square miles. Minuteman III with approximately three 400-megaton warheads (MIRV).

Massive Retaliation: The doctrine formally announced by John Foster Dulles in January 1954. Under this doctrine, the United States would reserve the right to retaliate at times and places with means of its own choosing. This doctrine was in response to the frustration of the Korean War and was designed to deter any form of aggression, not only an attack on the United States.

Megaton: The equivalent of one million tons of TNT. A thermonuclear or hydrogen device. The United States has 30,000 stored and deliverable megatons, the Russians 20,000.

1 Megaton. One million tons of TNT equivalent. Basic warhead of the Minuteman I. This explosion will destroy an area of over 60 square miles, or destroy everything within a radius of six miles.

10 Megatons. An American B-52 can carry four of these hydrogen weapons. This weapon will seriously damage an area within a 12-mile radius, or over 400 square miles.

20 Megatons. The B-52 could carry several of these weapons. When this weapon is exploded, it will dig a hole a mile across and 800 feet deep. The diameter of the fireball would be 4½ miles and the blast effect would *level* everything in an area of over 200 square miles. If this area were

square, it would represent a square 14 miles on each side. Deadly fall-out would be showered over 5,000 square miles downwind from the explosion.

MICCS: Minuteman Integrated Command and Control System. Firing and targeting computers for Minuteman—taking it out of hands of man. A computer card is slipped into computer at each Minuteman control site in order to fire the missiles. These control centers are located in protective hardened sites capable of withstanding 7,000 psi.

Midas: An American earth satellite designed to give early warning to the United States in case of enemy missile attack. The first operational Midas was launched in the fall of 1961.

Minimum Deterrent: A nuclear striking force to be used against an enemy's cities in the event of nuclear war. A limited strike force designed to deter an enemy attack by threatening the destruction of its population centers, essentially a second-strike doctrine. An essential corollary to this doctrine is the capability to fight a limited war, so that limited aggression can be met with less than an all-out nuclear response.

Minuteman: A hardened, solid-propellant ICBM which serves as one of the principal United States deterrent weapons. Range over 6,500 miles. More than 1,000 Minutemen are now operational.

Minuteman I. This missile carries a warhead of over 1 megaton and has a range of 6,300 miles (operational 1962).

Minuteman II. This missile carries a warhead of 2 megatons and has a range of 9,600 miles (operational 1966).

Minuteman III. This missile carries multiple independently targeted warheads. Normally it will carry three warheads, each with approximately 400 kilotons of explosive power (operational 1970).

MIRV: Multiple Independent Re-entry Vehicle. Multiple warhead carried by either a Minuteman III (3 warheads) or the Poseidon (10 warheads) system. As the CEP of these warheads is reduced from less than one-half mile to several hundred feet, this system increasingly becomes a potential first-strike system. Plans in 1970 called for the production of over 8,000 MIRV warheads. The American MIRV system for the Minuteman and Poseidon were operational in 1970.

Missiles—Soviet:

> *SS-9.* A heavyweight Soviet strategic missile. Rated by United States authorities as capable of throwing a single twenty-five-megaton warhead or three five-megaton MIRVs. In 1970, the MIRV capability of the SS-9 was apparently not operational.

> *SS-11.* A liquid-fueled Soviet strategic missile with a warhead of one megaton.

> *SS-13.* A solid-fueled Soviet strategic missile with a warhead less powerful than the SS-11.

MLF: Multilateral Nuclear Force. An American plan that would place a nuclear delivery system under either the joint command of the European NATO allies or substantially under the control of the United States command. Discarded after initial exploratory talks with European nations.

MOL: Manned Orbiting Laboratory. An Air Force space system that cost over $3 billion before development ceased in 1969.

MRBM: Medium-Range Ballistic Missile. A surface-to-surface missile with ballistic-type trajectory and a range of about 950 miles. The Soviet Union attempted to place 24 of these missiles in Cuba during the 1962 crisis. This missile was not capable of reaching major American SAC bomber bases nor American Minuteman bases.

MRV: Multiple Re-entry Vehicle. A precursor to the independently targeted *MIRV.* The MRV warheads are not independently targeted and therefore are not accurate enough for a first-strike capability; rather, the warheads are all aimed at the same general target and then are sprayed around that target in the manner of a shotgun blast. This is an effective counter-city weapon, but not an effective counter-force weapon. This system was operational for the United States sometime in 1966–1967 and apparently is becoming operational for the Soviet Union in 1970.

MSR: Missile Site Radar. Designed to guide Sprint and Spartan missiles of the American Safeguard ABM system.

National Military Command System: This system was designed to establish alternate command-center provisions for the airborne control of American bomber, Minuteman, and Polaris launchings.

NATO: The North Atlantic Treaty Organization.

Navaho: Early air-breathing missile. Development of this missile was stopped in 1957 after a cost of over $600 million.

Nike Systems: Name given to a number of antibomber and antimissile programs of the United States.

> *Nike-Ajax.* Early United States missile designed for bomber defense (surface to air).

> *Nike-Hercules.* This system replaced Nike-Ajax in 1958. It had a range of 50–75 miles and was effective at altitudes of 100,000 feet. This antibomber missile carried an atomic warhead. The Air Force Bomarc missile system lost out to Nike-Hercules in competition for bomber defense funds.

> *Nike-Zeus.* An early United States Army ABM system. The Spartan part of the Safeguard system is an improved ver-

sion of the Nike-Zeus. This missile carried an atomic warhead and the Army claimed it would be effective in protecting American cities, but both President Kennedy and President Eisenhower refused funding for this system.

Nike-X: Code name given to a system designed to provide a thick defense shield against an attack on United States cities. System is still under development by the United States Army.

Pad: A missile load-bearing surface, constructed or laid on the ground (or underground) upon which a permanent or mobile catapult or launcher can be placed.

Passive Defense: Features of a weapons system that enable it to survive damage resulting from enemy action. Armor plate, strategic location, and hardened underground missile silos are examples of such features. This term can also be used in connection with Civil Defense projects.

Polaris: Navy underwater-to-surface, or surface-to-surface solid-propellant fleet ballistic missiles.

Polaris A-1. This missile became operational in 1960 with a range of 1,380 miles and a payload of 0.7 megaton.

Polaris A-2. This missile became operational in 1962 with a range of 1,700 miles and a payload of 0.7 megaton.

Polaris A-3. This missile became operational in 1964 with a range of 2,850 miles and a payload of 0.7 megaton. There is evidence to indicate that by 1966–1967 this missile was equipped with multiple re-entry vehicles with at least three warheads each.

Poseidon: Navy's subsurface-to-surface MIRV missile. This missile became operational in 1970–1971 with a range of approximately 2,800 miles. It is equipped with MIRV, with each missile carrying between 10 and 14 warheads. Upon completion of the

Poseidon system sometime in 1973, there will be over 4,000 Poseidon warheads.

Pre-Emptive War: This is a war launched by a nation, when it believes that an enemy attack is imminent (i.e., within minutes or hours), in order to avoid having its nuclear forces destroyed by a surprise attack.

Preventive War: The launching of a first-strike nuclear attack by a nation when it feels that war is inevitable at some time in the future, i.e., not imminent. This sort of attack would be based on the nation's belief that a nuclear war today would be more favorable to its national interests than one in the future when its enemy's strength had increased.

Regulus Missile: A first-generation, slow, air-breathing, submarine surface-launched missile. Replaced by the Polaris.

SAC: The Strategic Air Command, commanded by General Thomas Power during the period of the missile gap, and then by General Curtis LeMay. Units of the U.S. Air Force assigned the mission of deterring a strategic attack on the United States. Made up of long-range and medium-range bombers, and ICBMs and IRBMs.

Safeguard: Name given to American ABM system approved by Congress in 1969. This system consists of long-range Spartan missiles (400-mile range) with a megaton-range warhead, and Sprint short-range 25-mile missile (altitude approximately 10,000 feet) with a kiloton-range warhead. The guidance system for Safeguard is MSR (Missile Site Radars). These radars are extremely vulnerable to an enemy attack as they can only withstand one tenth of the overpressure (psi) needed to destroy a Minuteman site. Without the MSR, the Safeguard system is "blind."

SALT: Strategic Arms Limitation Talks. Started in 1969 between the United States and the Soviet Union. During the first two years of these talks the United States approved the Safeguard ABM system and the deployment of operational MIRVs on Minuteman III and Poseidon.

Samos: American intelligence reconnaissance satellite used to determine the location of Soviet strategic weapons systems and other intelligence information.

SCAD: Subsonic Cruise Armed Decoy. A stand-off weapon designed as a penetration aid for the B-1 bomber. SCAD acts as a decoy in the sense that it appears on an enemy's radar screen as a bomber. It does carry a nuclear warhead. A B-52 or the new B-1 bomber could carry up to 30 of these, some with nuclear warheads.

Second-Strike Counterforce: Defined by Secretary of Defense McNamara in a speech at Ann Arbor, Michigan, June 16, 1962 (not the first to define it). This doctrine rules out surprise nuclear attack as a rational act. Instead, if nuclear war is initiated against the United States, American retaliatory power would respond in a controlled fashion after the enemy's first strike. The United States retaliatory forces would attack all Soviet nuclear installations, but not its cities, and then see if war can be stopped. City strikes against the Soviet Union would be used last. The goal is to stabilize the "balance of terror," but the implied superiority needed to follow the doctrine could be seen as a first-strike nuclear force.

Sentinel: United States ABM system announced by the Defense Department in 1967. Modified in 1969 and renamed Safeguard.

Skybolt: Air-to-surface missile that the United States was going to sell to Britain in 1963, but the arrangement was canceled at the Nassau meeting.

SLBM: Submarine-Launched Ballistic Missile. Examples: Polaris and Poseidon.

Snark: An early American missile.

Spartan: A long-range antimissile missile. This missile is part of the Safeguard system and has a range of about 400 miles and is equipped with a megaton-range warhead.

Sprint: A short-range antimissile missile. This missile is part of the Safeguard ABM system and has a range of 15–25 miles and a warhead of approximately 10 kilotons. This missile is designed for altitudes ranging from 5,000 to 100,000 feet.

Sputnik I: The world's first earth satellite, launched by the Soviet Union, October 4, 1957.

Scram: A short-range attack missile that forms part of the weapons system of the G-H type B-52 bomber, the B-58 supersonic bomber, and the FB-111 bomber, and is designed to penetrate heavy terminal bomber defenses.

Strategic Delivery Vehicle: A bomber or missile which is capable of striking the homeland of an enemy with a nuclear warhead.

TFX: Original name given to the F-111 experimental fighter-bomber designed to meet the needs of both the Air Force and the Navy. As of 1970, it has done neither.

Targeting: In missile warfare, plotting the correct trajectory for a designated target.

Thor: Early United States Air Force IRBM, range around 1,750 miles, payload 1,500 pounds. The United States placed these missiles in Great Britain in 1959.

Titan II: A two-stage liquid propellant ICBM which can be silo-launched employing storable propellants, and can be launched in less than a minute. It has greater thrust, range, and payload than any other American ICBM. Range 12,000 miles, 5 megatons. Operational, 1963.

USIA: United States Information Agency.

USIB: United States Intelligence Board. Submits national intelligence estimates to the President or the National Security Council. Membership consists of representatives of the United States Air Force (A-2), Navy (Office of Naval Intelligence), and Army (G-2), the director of intelligence of the Atomic Energy Commission, State Department (Assistant Secretary of State), Federal Bureau of Investigation, National Security Agency, and the director of the Defense Intelligence Agency. The director of the CIA is chairman of the USIB.

ULMS: Undersea Long-Range Missile System. Missiles located in pads at the bottom of oceans or lakes. Secretary Laird requested $44 million for the development of this system for 1970. A major debate concerning this system could take place in the 1970s.

UMT: Universal Military Training. A plan for meeting American manpower needs for the Cold War. Debated during the late 1940s, but it was finally defeated and the United States accepted the Selective Service draft system to meet its military manpower needs.

Weapons System: Entity consisting of an instrument of combat, such as a bomber or missile together with all related equipment, support facilities, and services required to bring the instrument upon its target.

Notes

CHAPTER I

1. This analysis of the period prior to 1953 is very brief. For more detail the reader should consult Gar Alperovitz, *Atomic Diplomacy: Hiroshima to Potsdam* (New York: Vintage Press, 1965); D. F. Fleming, *The Cold War and Its Origins* (New York: Doubleday & Co., 1961), Vol. I; P. M. S. Blackett, *Atomic Weapons and East West Relations* (London: Cambridge University Press, 1956); Dean Acheson, *Present at the Creation* (New York: W. W. Norton & Co., 1969); Ralph E. Lapp, *The New Force: The Story of Atoms and People* (New York: Harper & Bros., 1953); Raymond Garthoff, *Soviet Military Policy: An Historical Analysis* (New York: Frederick Praeger, 1966); Marshall D. Shulman, *Stalin's Foreign Policy Reappraised* (Cambridge, Mass.; Harvard University Press, 1963); and Samuel Huntington, *The Common Defense: Strategic Programs in National Security* (New York: Columbia University Press, 1961).

2. Blackett, *Studies on War* (New York: Hill and Wang, 1962), pp. 214–242; Garthoff, *Soviet Military Policy*, p. 23. See also Appendix B.

3. Lapp, *The New Force*, p. 116.

4. This information was gained by surveying various public sources, primarily *The New York Times*, from 1945 to 1951.

5. Richard C. Hewlett and Oscar E. Anderson, *The New World: 1939–1946: A History of the Atomic Energy Commission* (University Park, Penn.: Penn State University Press, 1962), 1:417.

6. United States Atomic Energy Commission, *In the Matter of J. Robert Oppenheimer*, transcript of Hearing before the Personnel Security Board, April–May 1954, United States Government Printing Office, 1954, p. 33.

7. *The New York Times*, November 27, 1947, quoting Secretary of the Air Force Symington. Even at this early date he was calling for at least 630 heavy bombers near the Soviet Union as part of the "austerity program" imposed on the Air Force. Also, since the United States had several hundred overseas bases at this time, 500 bombers does not sound like a high figure. Huntington, *The Common Defense*, p. 59. Huntington contends that the Strategic Air Command had 18 aircraft wings, or roughly 810 planes (one wing has 45 planes).

8. *The New York Times*, October 2, 1949.

9. *The New York Times*, September 18, 1946, reprint of Secretary Wallace's letter to President Truman of July 23, 1946.

10. *The New York Times,* news article by Hanson Baldwin, "The Defense Hearings," October 27, 1949.

11. Clark R. Mollenhoff, *The Pentagon: Politics, Profits and Plunder* (New York: G. P. Putnam's Sons, 1967), p. 124. At this early stage in the debate, the basic decisions involved in NSC #68 had not been made and the services believed that an increase in one service appropriation meant a decrease in their allocations. (See next chapter.)

12. *The New York Times,* news article by Hanson Baldwin, October 27, 1949.

13. For an excellent study of the Universal Military Training debate, see John W. Swomley, Jr., *The Military Establishment* (Boston: Beacon Press, 1964).

14. *The New York Times,* quoting Secretary of the Air Force Stuart Symington, October 19, 1949.

15. *The New York Times,* news article by Hanson Baldwin, October 26, 1949.

16. *Ibid.,* October 8, 1949. The Navy also had its number of new planes reduced to about 50 per month, as compared to 300 planes a month before Pearl Harbor. The Navy had asked for $1.3 billion for its air arm and the President had cut this request to $687 million. This figure was further reduced to $387 million.

17. *The New York Times,* quoting Admiral W. F. Halsey, October 13, 1949.

18. Shulman, *Stalin's Foreign Policy,* p. 119. This fact seems to have come out by mistake in a television broadcast by Senator Edwin C. Johnson. The official statement that the United States had made the decision to proceed with the development of the H-bomb was not made until January 31, 1950, by President Truman.

19. Lapp, *The New Force,* p. 93.

20. Blackett, *Atomic Weapons and East-West Relations,* pp. 38–48.

21. Dr. Ernest J. Sternglass, Professor of Radiation Physics, University of Pittsburgh, "The Death of All Children," *Esquire,* September, 1969, pp. 1a–1d. Dr. Sternglass' theory that a thermonuclear exchange would genetically destroy all human life has not been definitely proved.

22. Shulman, *Stalin's Foreign Policy,* pp. 28–29.

23. Gabriel A. Almond, *The American People and Foreign Policy* (New York: Frederick Praeger, 1950), p. 104.

24. Huntington, *The Common Defense,* pp. 50–51, quoting Senator Henry Jackson (Dem.-Wash.). Much of the background work on NSC #68 has been done by Huntington, and this author is indebted for this analysis.

25. *Ibid.*

26. *Ibid.,* p. 51, quoting Paul H. Nitze, from "The Need for a National Strategy," address to the Army War College, Carlisle Barracks, Pennsylvania, August 27, 1958. Mr. Nitze was one of the original authors of NSC #68 and was speaking of this paper before the War College.

27. *Ibid.*, p. 51.

28. *Ibid.*, p. 59.

29. James M. Gavin, *War and Peace in the Space Age* (New York: Harper & Brothers, 1958), p. 22.

30. Huntington, *The Common Defense*, p. 54.

31. Walter G. Hermes, *Truce Tent and Fighting Front* (Washington, D.C.: Government Printing Office, 1966), p. 513. It is worth noting that the highest troop commitment in Korea was 300,000 men, whereas by 1968 the United States had over 500,000 men in Vietnam.

32. Seymour Kurtz (ed.) *The New York Times: Encyclopedic Almanac: 1970* (New York: *The New York Times*, 1969), p. 720.

CHAPTER II

1. John W. Spanier, *The Truman-MacArthur Controversy* (Cambridge: Harvard University Press, 1959), p. 259.

2. *The New York Times*, President Eisenhower's State of the Union address (text), February 3, 1953.

3. *Ibid.*

4. *The New York Times*, news article by Hanson Baldwin, October 21, 1953.

5. Samuel Huntington, *The Common Defense: Strategic Programs in National Security* (New York: Columbia University Press, 1961), p. 25. In spite of the awareness of the need for existing military preparedness, the United States continued to plan for industrial mobilization in the event of war.

6. *The New York Times*, January 8, 1954.

7. *The New York Times*, statement by Secretary of State Dulles before the Council on Foreign Relations, January 13, 1954.

8. *The New York Times*, news article by James Reston, January 17, 1954.

9. *U.S. Congressional Record*, 83rd Cong., 2d sess., Vol. 100, pt. 1 (January 6 to February 5, 1954), p. 467; *The New York Times*, speech by Adlai Stevenson to the Southeast Democratic Conference, March 7, 1954.

10. *U.S. Congressional Record*, Vol. 101, pt. 5 (May 5 to May 25, 1955), reprint of speech by Senator Warren Magnuson (Dem.-Wash.), p. 5932. Senator Magnuson's speech also reflects the highly partisan nature of the debate over massive retaliation.

11. John Foster Dulles, "Policy for Security and Peace," *Foreign Affairs*, (April 1954), 32:357.

12. *Ibid.*, pp. 357–358.

13. *Ibid.*, p. 363. When Secretary Dulles referred to a "variety of means and scope for responding to aggression" he must have been referring to alternative nuclear responses, not conventional responses. During this

period there was a steady decline in the combat readiness of the United States Army.

14. *The New York Times*, February 13, 1954. Air Force documents at this time were listing Soviet long-range aircraft at 300–400, but based on Department of Defense official figures this would appear to be an exaggeration by the Air Force. See "How Good Is Russia's Long-Range Turboprop Bear Bomber?", *Air Intelligence Training Bulletin* (published by the United States Air Force, September 1957), 9:39. These Air Force figures would seem to be a precursor to the "bomber gap" that was to develop in 1955.

15. *The New York Times*, February 7, 1951; *ibid.*, March 12, 1951.

16. Ralph E. Lapp, *The New Force* (New York: Harper & Brothers, 1953), pp. 64–67, 133. P. M. S. Blackett, *Atomic Weapons and East-West Relations* (London: Cambridge University Press, 1956), p. 41.

17. *The New York Times*, September 19, 1951. Senator McMahon was chairman of the special Senate committee on atomic energy.

18. Ralph E. Lapp, *The New Force* (London: Cambridge University Press, 1965), quoting Senator Brian McMahon, p. 133.

19. *The New York Times*, February 13, 1949.

20. W. W. Rostow, *The US and the World Arena* (New York: Harper & Brothers, 1967), p. 332.

21. B. H. Liddell Hart, *Deterrence or Defense* (New York: Frederick Praeger, 1960), p. 82.

22. Maxwell D. Taylor (General, United States Army, ret.), *The Uncertain Trumpet* (New York: Harper & Brothers, 1959), pp. 65–66.

23. Dwight D. Eisenhower, *The White House Years: Mandate for Change 1953–1956* (Garden City, New York: Doubleday & Company, 1963), p. 452.

President Eisenhower gave the following figures on manpower and budget reductions.

Manpower	December 1953	October 1954	June 1955
Army	1,500,000	1,400,000	1,000,000
Navy-Marines	1,000,000	920,000	870,000
Air Force	950,000	960,000	970,000

Budget (in billions of dollars)

	Fiscal 1954	Fiscal 1955
Army	12.9	8.8
Navy-Marines	11.2	9.7
Air Force	15.6	16.4

See also, Huntington, *The Common Defense*, p. 75.

24. *Ibid.*, p. 102.

25. When Eisenhower came to office after the Korea build-up in 1952, the United States had 20 Army divisions, 18 regimental combat teams

(roughly the equivalent of 3 divisions), and 3 Marine divisions, *ibid.*, pp. 60–61. When Eisenhower left office, there was a total of 11 combat-ready divisions and of the 11, only 3 were deployed in the United States as a reserve. See Arthur M. Schlesinger, Jr., *A Thousand Days: John F. Kennedy in the White House* (Boston: Houghton Mifflin, 1965), pp. 315–316. Schlesinger goes on to admit that the force for the invasion of Cuba was not readily available following the Bay of Pigs.

26. *The New York Times,* news article by Hanson Baldwin, January 13, 1953.

27. The fact that the United States was not a formal member of CENTO in no way detracts from the fact that it was designed by the United States as a means of achieving its perceived national interests. See John Campbell, *Defense of the Middle East: Problems of American Policy* (New York: Frederick Praeger, 1960), pp. 49–62.

28. *The New York Times,* October 21, 1954.

29. *The New York Times,* quoting Secretary of Defense Charles Wilson, March 30, 1956.

30. Statement by Air Force Chief of Staff, General Hoyt S. Vandenburg, *Aviation Week* (June 11, 1951), 54:11.

31. Huntington, *The Common Defense,* p. 71.

32. Testimony by Secretary of Defense, Neil McElroy, U.S. Congress, Senate, Committee on Appropriations, Department of Defense Appropriations for 1960 (discussing the bomber gap), *Hearings,* 86th Cong., 1st sess. (May 1959), 4:5.

33. Senator Charles Goodell (Rep.-N.Y.), press release quoting General Curtis LeMay, April 3, 1969.

34. Allen Dulles, *The Craft of Intelligence* (New York: Harper & Row, 1963), p. 149.

35. U.S. Congress, House Committee on Appropriations, *Hearings* on Fiscal Year 1960 Defense Budget, 86th Cong., 1st sess., pt. 1 (February 19, 1959), 10:378 testimony by SAC commanding officer, General Thomas Power.

36. *The New York Times,* "Air Manual Hints Soviet Tricked U.S.," April 18, 1960.

37. Raymond Garthoff, *The Soviet Image of Future War* (Washington, D.C.: Public Affairs Press, 1959), pp. 74–75.

38. Marshall D. Shulman, *Stalin's Foreign Policy Reappraised* (Cambridge: Harvard University Press, 1963), quoting Joseph Stalin, p. 185.

39. H. S. Dinerstein, *War and the Soviet Union* (rev. ed.) (New York: Praeger, 1962), pp. 215–217.

CHAPTER III

1. For a closer look at the missile gap, the concerned reader should consult my book, *The Missile Gap: A Study of the Formulation of Military and Public Policy* (Cranbury, New Jersey: Fairleigh Dickinson University

Press, 1970). The author would also like to express his thanks to this publisher for allowing part of this study to be reproduced in this book.

2. Robert Hagan and Bart Bernstein, "Military Value of Missiles in Cuba," *The Bulletin of the Atomic Scientists* (February 1963), 19:11. These figures are confirmed by Senator Stuart Symington (see below, this chapter).

3. Soviet budgetary figures on national defense are notoriously difficult to analyze, if not impossible. However, one of the best efforts at this type of analysis was made by Abraham S. Becker of the Rand Corporation. Becker's analysis showed that the Soviet military budget had been reduced from 1955 to 1959, and then, following a rather drastic increase in 1959, was again reduced in 1960 and possibly 1962. Mr. Becker's figures are given below and are in billions of rubles. The figures represent the "estimate total high" spending in the Soviet Union for defense purposes.

Year	1955	1956	1957	1958	1959	1960	1961	1962
Number of Rubles in Billions	15.00	14.81	14.39	14.63	18.00	17.15	17.0 to 26.1	16.6 to 23.4

See Abraham S. Becker, *Soviet Military Outlays Since 1955* (Santa Monica, Calif.: The Rand Corporation, 1964) (Memorandum RM-3886-PR), p. 91. If Mr. Becker's figures are correct, then these figures offer additional evidence that the Soviet Union was pursuing a policy of "minimum deterrence" during this period.

4. The 25 largest cities in the United States had a combined population of 60.8 million according to the 1960 United States Census.

5. The question legitimately can be asked, Why did the Soviet Union bother with missile development at all? The answer appears to be (1) to avoid a future technological gap in missile development that could not be closed (either with the United States or China); and (2) the increased effectiveness of antibomber surface-to-air missiles raised the possibility that an almost perfect bomber defense *might* be developed by an adversary at some future date.

6. Harry Howe Ransom, *Can American Democracy Survive Cold War?* (Garden City, New York: Doubleday & Company, 1963), p. 209. This report originally appeared in *Aviation Week* (October 21, 1957), pp. 26–27. Also reported in *The New York Times,* November 21 and 24, 1957. In January 1960, Hanson Baldwin identified Soviet missile testing sites as (1) at Kapustin Yar (near Stalingrad/Volgagrad), and (2) near Tyura Tam (near the Aral Sea); see *The New York Times,* January 23, 1960.

7. *The New York Times,* news article on the CIA by Tom Wicker, John W. Finney, Max Frankel, E. W. Kentworthy, and others, April 27, 1966; also reported in Charles J. V. Murphy, "Khrushchev's Paper Bear," *Fortune* (December 1964), 70:225–227.

8. Allen Dulles, quoting Secretary of Defense Gates in 1960, *The Craft of Intelligence* (New York: Harper & Row, 1963), p. 67.

9. *Ibid.,* p. 65.

10. Murphy, "Khrushchev's Paper Bear," pp. 58–59.

11. The possibility remains that President Eisenhower had highly sensitive intelligence sources known to only a few government officials, although the existence of such sources has never been proved. The reports that President Kennedy had intelligence sources (or a source) inside the Kremlin during the 1962 Cuban missile crisis certainly would indicate the possibility that Eisenhower had the same type of source. See the reports on the activities and trial of Oleg V. Penkovsky (former colonel in the Soviet Army) who was accused of passing Russian rocket information to Western intelligence sources. *The New York Times,* May 8, 1963, November 2, 1965, and January 7, 1961; and *The Penkovsky Papers* (New York: Doubleday & Company, 1965). Allegedly, Colonel Penkovsky passed valuable military intelligence information to Western intelligence sources from April 1961 to August 1962. Colonel Penkovsky was arrested on October 22, 1962, tried, and executed as a spy. Edward Crankshaw (who wrote the Foreword to *The Penkovsky Papers*) accepted the authenticity of the "papers" beyond question (p. 4), while the CIA claimed they were a forgery (*The New York Times,* November 2, 1965).

12. Dulles, *The Craft of Intelligence,* p. 164.

13. *Ibid.*

14. Dwight D. Eisenhower, *The White House Years: Waging the Peace* (Garden City, New York: Doubleday & Company, Inc., 1965), p. 221. A writer in *The Boston Globe* claimed that the Gaither Report estimated what the Russians *could* do rather than what they *would* do (capability versus intent). *The Boston Globe,* "Ike Discloses Gaither 'Missile Gap' Report," article by David Wise, September 26, 1965.

15. Eisenhower, *Waging the Peace,* pp. 389–390.

16. See Appendix A for estimates of this downward revision.

17. "Next Generation Seen as Missile Race Key," *Aviation Week,* quoting General Bernard Schriever (January 27, 1958), 68:35. Although at one time the United States programmed about 230 first-generation ICBMs (a small number compared to the final production of second-generation missiles), in reality fewer than 200 were produced, counting both the Titan and Atlas systems. In all probability, both the programmed and produced number of first-generation missiles would have been less if the Eisenhower Administration had not been under such heavy pressure to produce more missiles because of the feared missile gap.

18. The Minuteman attained operational status in 1962, while the Polaris was operational in 1960.

19. U.S. Senate, Committee on Armed Services and the Committee on Aeronautical and Space Sciences, Preparedness Investigating Committee, *Joint Hearings on Missiles, Space and Other Major Defense Matters,* 86th

Cong., 1st sess. (January 29 and 30, 1959), p. 46. (Hereafter referred to as the *Joint Hearings, 1959.*)

20. *Ibid.,* pp. 46, 49. During this same testimony, Secretary McElroy indicated that the reduced budget request for missile development in 1960 was due to the fact that the United States had stopped the development of the first-generation Snark and Regulus missiles.

21. *The New York Times,* official Pentagon figures for January 1961, April 1964, and April 15, 1964. (See Appendix A.)

22. American intelligence sources publicly claimed this limited Soviet missile production program in 1960. See U.S. Congress, Senate, Committee on Armed Services and the Committee on Aeronautical and Space Sciences, Preparedness Investigating Subcommittee, *Joint Hearings on Missiles, Space and Other Major Defense Matters,* 86th Cong., 2d sess. (February–March 1960), p. 142. (Hereafter referred to as *Joint Hearings, 1960.*)

23. *Joint Hearings,* 1959, pp. 26–27.

24. *Joint Hearings,* 1960, p. 442. Note: these two sets of estimates made in 1959 were not made public until 1960.

25. U.S. Congress, Senate, Committee on Appropriations, Department of Defense Appropriations for 1960, *Hearings,* 86th Cong., 1st sess. (May 1959), 4:5.

26. *Joint Hearings,* 1960, p. 442. It was impossible to determine which set of figures had upset Senator Symington when presented by Secretary of Defense McElroy, or if Senator Symington had seen both sets and still disagreed.

27. It was possible that Senator Symington's other information came from the "crash" set of figures, but this seems unlikely.

28. As seen above, this statement in books by Schlesinger, Sorensen, Spanier, Huntington, and in the *Joint Hearings,* 1960.

29. See Appendix A. The one exception to the 1959 "revision" was found in an article by Joseph Alsop (October 7, 1959, in Appendix A). By the end of 1959, the projected number of Soviet missiles for 1962 was reduced to 400 ICBMs. It is noteworthy that the public estimates that appeared accurate lagged from three to five months behind the changes made in official estimates.

30. See below, this chapter.

31. *The New York Times,* text of President Eisenhower's fiscal 1961 budget message, January 19, 1960.

32. U.S. Congress, Committee on Armed Services, Preparedness Investigating Subcommittee, in conjunction with the Committee on Aeronautical and Space Sciences, *Joint Hearings,* text of General Power's speech before the Economic Club of New York, January 19, 1960, 86th Cong., 2d sess. (February 2, 3, 4, 8, 9, and March 16, 1960), p. 4. This speech had been submitted to the Pentagon and State Department for clearance and was approved. It is worth noting that General Power's "95 percent" destruction was the same figure used in 1970 by Secretary Laird.

33. *Joint Hearings,* 1960, pp. 21, 36. General Power did admit, under intense questioning, that the Soviet Union had only one ICBM base operational at that time. *Ibid.,* pp. 25, 49.

34. *Joint Hearings,* 1960, p. 23.

35. The reader should keep in mind that this advantage had existed since the beginning of the missile gap debate. In 1957, according to the United States Air Force, the United States had 2,500 heavy-combat jet aircraft, 27 overseas bases, and 32 bases in the United States. *The New York Times,* quoting SAC commander, General Thomas Power, September 27, 1957.

36. *The New York Times,* "Washington Finds No Proof Moscow Had Capability to Launch ICBM's," by Hanson W. Baldwin, March 25, 1959; *ibid.,* "McElroy Reports U.S. and Russians Lag on Missiles," news article by Jack Raymond, June 28, 1959; Charles J. V. Murphy, "The Embattled Mr. McElroy," *Fortune* (April 1959), 59:242; "Missiles: Ours and Russia's" (this article reported the alleged strain on the Soviet economy), *Newsweek* (July 13, 1959), 54:52.

37. This downward revision also raised the question of whether United States intelligence estimates were based on Soviet "intent" or "capability."

38. In 1964, one author claimed that after the CIA success with the U-2 photo reconnaissance aircraft, the Air Force bought its own U-2 planes and began to fly "spy" missions over the Soviet Union. (See Murphy, "Khrushchev's Paper Bear," p. 224. Two other authors hinted that the Air Force might have had its own U-2 photographs and stated flatly that the Air Force did use its own photo interpreters to come up with different conclusions than the CIA on Russian missile programs. See David Wise and Thomas B. Ross, *The Invisible Government* (New York: Bantam Books, published by arrangement with Random House, Inc., 1964), p. 226. Neither of these reports could be substantiated by official documents. However, there does not appear to be much doubt that the Air Force did have its own photo interpreters analyzing U-2 photographs.

39. Once this was done, the number of intelligence figures was reduced considerably. (The "crash" estimates had been dropped in early 1960.) However, SAC did not accept the lower figures, so two sets of possible figures were still in existence.

40. See Appendix A.

41. During this period there were reports of "leaks" of intelligence information. See the *Joint Hearings,* 1960, and the reports of the alleged McNamara "background briefing" of February 1961.

42. Schlesinger, *A Thousand Days,* p. 317; McGeorge Bundy, "The President and the Peace," *Foreign Affairs* (April 1964), 42:354.

43. Stewart Alsop, "The Alternative to Total War" (quoting Secretary of Defense McNamara), *Saturday Evening Post* (December 1, 1962), 235:18.

44. Myron Rush and Arnold I. Horelick, *Strategic Power and Soviet Foreign Policy* (Chicago: University of Chicago Press, 1966). This was one of the major themes developed in this book.

45. In the process of explaining the missile gap, Senator Symington attempted to justify his own role in its development and also implied that he was not certain it had really disappeared. U.S. Congress, Senate, Armed Services Committee, *Hearings, Military Procurement Authorization for Fiscal Year 1963*, 87th Cong., 2d sess. (January–February, 1962), 10:49–50; Senator Stuart Symington, "Where the Missile Gap Went," *The Reporter* (February 15, 1962), 26:21–22.

46. U.S. Congress, Senate, Armed Services Committee, *Hearings on Procurement for 1963*, 87th Cong., pp. 49–50.

47. *Ibid.*

48. It was not possible to determine which set of figures or whose estimates Senator Symington based his percentages on, although it is safe to speculate that he used one of the higher sets of intelligence figures available (probably either the "crash" figures or those of the Air Force, if they were different).

49. For those who did not accept the downward revisions, the projected 1,500 Soviet ICBMs by 1962 remained a possible reality.

50. U.S. Congress, House, Appropriations Committee, Department of Defense Appropriations Subcommittee, *Hearings for Fiscal 1963*, testimony by General Frederick H. Smith, Jr., Vice-Chief of Staff, U.S. Air Force, 87th Cong., 2d sess., pt. 2 (February 1962), p. 489.

51. Some of the major aspects of these three factors have been dealt with elsewhere in this study and will not be repeated here.

52. Senator Henry M. Jackson (Dem.-Wash.), "Organizing for National Survival," *Foreign Affairs* (April 1960), 38:446.

53. *Ibid.*, pp. 455–456.

54. Bernard K. Gordon, "The Military Budget: Congressional Phase," *Journal of Politics* (November 1961), 23:692.

55. Also *Air University Quarterly* could be counted on for support of the Air Force position.

56. Also *Military Review* represented the point of view of the Army, while the *U.S. Naval Institute Proceedings* represented the Navy's. See Huntington, "The Military Lobby: Its Impact on Congress, Nation," *Congressional Quarterly Review* (March 24, 1961), 14:466.

57. *Ibid.*, pp. 40–52. A congressional committee investigated the connection between the military and industry in a series of special hearings in 1959. See U.S. Congress, House, Committee on Armed Services, Subcommittee for Special Investigation, *Hearings, Employment of Retired Military and Civilian Personnel by Defense Industries*, 86th Cong., 1st sess., Vol. 8 (July, August, September, 1959). The so-called *Hébert Hearings*.

58. See Fred J. Cook, *The Warfare State* (New York: The Macmillan Company, 1962), pp. 12–15; Victor Perlo, *Militarism and Industry: Arms*

Profiteering in the Missile Age (New York: International Publishers, 1963), pp. 161–170. Mr. Perlo attempted to prove there was (and is) a direct political and financial connection between many of the key personalities in the missile gap controversy and the business community. (Senator Stuart Symington, p. 161; Senator Henry Jackson, p. 161; Robert C. Sprague, co-chairman of the Gaither Report, p. 170.) This book is obviously not about the "military-industrial complex" *per se.* The reader interested in this aspect of the arms race should consult Sidney Lens, *The Military-Industrial Complex* (Philadelphia: Pilgrim Press and The National Catholic Reporter, 1970).

59. For example, see the series of five articles by Joseph Alsop in *The New York Herald Tribune,* starting January 24, 1960. Just prior to this series by Mr. Alsop claiming American strategic inferiority, President Eisenhower had disclosed that the United States Atlas ICBM was operational and that the United States had 2,100 strategic bombers, *The New York Times,* text of President Eisenhower's news conference, January 14, 1960. These 2,100 bombers gave the United States at least a 3–1 advantage over the Soviet Union.

60. For example, see Henry Kissinger, *The Necessity for Choice.* Earlier Kissinger had been one of the major authors of the 1959 Rockefeller Report that accepted the missile gap. In 1964 and 1968 Kissinger was Nelson Rockefeller's major foreign and defense policy adviser. In 1970, he was Nixon's most important defense policy adviser. For the Rockefeller Report see *International Security: The Military Aspect* (Garden City: Doubleday, 1958).

61. *Joint Hearings,* 1960 (Senate), testimony by General Maxwell D. Taylor (U.S. Army, ret.), pp. 190–191; Samuel P. Huntington, *The Common Defense: Strategic Programs in National Politics* (New York: Columbia University Press, 1961), pp. 446–456. Mr. Huntington used the figures: Air Force, 47 percent; Army, 22 percent; and Navy, 29 percent.

62. This was the year of the Soviet ICBM and Sputnik. It was also the year of a recession in the United States.

63. It also appeared that the Alsop brothers, who had done a great deal to create the impression of the missile gap in their writings, escaped any serious damage to their reputations as reporters.

64. *The New York Times,* reprint of the figures submitted by the House Republican Policy Committee on January 25, 1961, and February 9, 1961. In *The New York Times* of April 16, 1965, roughly these same figures were used by the Pentagon as their estimate as of January 1961. See *The New York Times,* April 16, 1964. These figures ignored the various American IRBMs, medium-range bombers, and carrier-based aircraft—all capable of hitting a Soviet target. The Russians had no capability in any of these three categories that could reach the United States. Also, Appendix A indicates that 1961 saw a profusion of estimated missile strengths, yet none of these figures for this year indicates a "missile gap" favoring the Soviet Union, with the possible exception of very early 1961 estimates.

65. *The New York Times,* news article by Jack Raymond, "Kennedy Defense Study Finds No Evidence of 'Missile Gap,'" February 7, 1961; *ibid.,* statement repeated, February 9, 1961; several years later, former President Eisenhower wrote that after his successor assumed office "word conveniently leaked out of the Pentagon that the 'missile gap' had been closed." Eisenhower, *Waging the Peace,* p. 390; also in Schlesinger, *A Thousand Days,* p. 499.

66. *The New York Times,* February 8, 1961.

67. Harold W. Chase and Allen L. Lerman (eds.), *Kennedy and the Press: The News Conferences,* texts of all President Kennedy's news conferences (New York: Thomas Y. Crowell Company, 1965), pp. 19–20.

68. *The New York Times,* "Missile Gap Report Denied by McNamara," February 17, 1961.

69. "Defense: The Missile Gap Flap," *Time* (February 17, 1961), 77:12; "The Ammo Was Political," *Newsweek* (February 20, 1961), 57:24; "The Truth About the Missile Gap," *U.S. News & World Report* (February 27, 1961), 50:41.

70. "The Truth About the Missile Gap," p. 41. See Appendix A, February 27, 1961, for the weapons chart listed.

71. Claude Witze (senior ed.), "Airpower and the News," *Air Force* (March 1961), 44:39.

72. *The New York Times,* text of President Kennedy's news conference, March 2, 1961; *ibid.,* March 9, 1961.

73. From March 8, 1961, to October 11, 1961, President Kennedy held a total of 11 news conferences and the question of the missile gap was not raised in any of them. When a major question of national defense was raised on October 11, 1961, it dealt with the military credibility of the United States to deter aggression during the Berlin crisis rather than directly with the missile gap.

74. *The New York Times,* October 22, 1961.

75. Chase and Lerman, *Kennedy and the Press,* text of news conference by President Kennedy, November 14, 1961.

76. Alsop, "The Alternative to Total War," p. 18.

77. *Developments in Military Technology and Their Impact on United States Strategy and Foreign Policy, Study #8* (prepared at the request of the Committee on Foreign Relations, United States Senate) (Washington, D.C.: Washington Center for Foreign Policy Research, The Johns Hopkins University, 1959), p. 58. Referred to hereafter as *The Johns Hopkins Report,* 1959.

78. For a detailed analysis of this new doctrine see *The New York Times,* text of a major address by Secretary of Defense Robert McNamara at Ann Arbor, Michigan, June 17, 1962; and U.S. Congress, House, Committee on Armed Services, *Hearings on Military Posture,* 88th Cong., 1st sess., Vol. 2 (January 30, 1963).

79. Schlesinger, *A Thousand Days,* p. 245.

80. Numerous writers have expounded this belief and it would seem to be based on sound reasoning. See B. H. Liddell Hart, *Deterrence or Defense* (New York: Frederick A. Praeger, 1958); F. O. Miksche, *The Failure of Atomic Strategy* (New York: Frederick A. Praeger, 1958). Glenn M. Snyder, *Deterrence and Defense: Toward a Theory of National Security* (Princeton, New Jersey: Princeton University Press, 1961).

81. See Horelick and Rush, *Strategic Power and Soviet Foreign Policy*. The authors develop this point as one of the major themes of their book.

82. Donald S. Zagoria, "China's Crisis of Foreign Policy," *The New York Times Magazine*, May 1, 1966.

83. *The New York Times*, March 26, 1962; and *The Communist Bloc and the Western Alliance: The Military Balance 1962–1963* (London: The Institute for Strategic Studies), p. 5.

84. For an example of this kind of "confrontation" thinking see Barry Goldwater, *Why Not Victory?*

CHAPTER IV

1. Arthur M. Schlesinger, Jr., *A Thousand Days: John F. Kennedy in the White House* (Boston: Houghton Mifflin, 1965), p. 500.

2. Robert S. McNamara, *The Essence of Security: Reflections in Office* (New York: Harper and Row, 1968), p. 80.

3. Schlesinger, *A Thousand Days*, p. 318.

4. Clark R. Mollenhoff, *The Pentagon: Politics, Profits and Plunder* (New York: G. P. Putnam's Sons, 1967), p. 242.

5. Stewart Alsop, interview with President John F. Kennedy, *The Saturday Evening Post* (March 31, 1962), 235:14. The reader should also be reminded that President Kennedy learned that the missile gap was a myth within a month of assuming office (see previous chapter).

6. Schlesinger, *A Thousand Days*, p. 318.

7. McNamara, *The Essence of Security*. In his Introduction, Secretary McNamara referred to massive retaliation as "useless."

8. Mollenhoff, *The Pentagon*, pp. 232–235. This was the same committee under Lyndon Johnson that had done more than any other congressional committee to establish the missile gap.

9. *Ibid.*, p. 236. An American division runs approximately 15,000 men, but it can vary from 12,000 to 20,000, as stated previously. A Soviet division runs from 9,000 to 12,000 men. At this time, the Soviet Union was credited with 175 combat divisions (of which 60 percent were considered combat ready) and an army of approximately 2.5 million men. The United States Army had 1,045,000 men.

10. Schlesinger, *A Thousand Days*, pp. 315–316.

11. *Ibid.*

12. McNamara, *The Essence of Security*, p. 82. McNamara claimed that

he had raised the number of "combat assigned divisions" by 66 percent during his term of office.

13. Stewart Alsop, "The Alternative to Total War," in an interview with Secretary of Defense McNamara, *The Saturday Evening Post* (December 1, 1962), 235:19.

14. U.S. Congress, House of Representatives, *Hearings on Military Posture*, 88th Cong., 1st sess., House Doc. No. 4 (January 1963), p. 288. Testimony by Secretary of Defense Robert S. McNamara.

15. *Ibid.*, p. 300. The doctrine of flexible response had definite implications for the role of the United States in NATO (see below in this chapter).

16. McNamara, *The Essence of Security*, p. 97.

17. Alsop, "The Alternative to Total War," p. 16. Official Department of Defense estimates as of 1961 placed the comparative United States-Soviet Union strategic delivery systems in the following manner.

United States	Soviet Union
16 Atlas ICBMs	35 T-3 ICBMs (8,000-mile range)
32 Polaris missiles	None comparable
600 Long-range bombers	200 Long-range bombers

The New York Times, Official Department of Defense figures for 1961, released April 16, 1965. The reader should keep in mind that in 1961 the United States had over 1,200 medium-range bombers that could also reach Soviet territory.

18. U.S. Congress, House of Representatives, *Hearings on Military Posture*, p. 309.

19. Klaus Knorr, "Passive Air Defense for the United States," in *Military Policy and National Security*, William W. Kaufman (ed.) (Princeton: Princeton University Press, 1956), p. 101.

20. David Horowitz, *The Free World Colossus* (New York: Hill & Wang, 1965), p. 367.

21. I. F. Stone, *The New York Review*, series on the military-industrial complex (March 27, 1969), p. 10.

22. Horowitz, *The Free World Colossus*, p. 372.

23. McNamara, *The Essence of Security*, p. 73.

24. *The New York Times*, January 10, 1963; *ibid.*, April 15, 1964.

25. McNamara, *The Essence of Security*, p. 90.

26. J. S. Butz, Jr. (technical ed.), "How Far Is the Red Air Force Ahead?" *Air Force and Space Digest* (September 1961), p. 52.

27. *Jane's All the World's Aircraft, 1963–1964* (New York: McGraw Hill, 1964), pp. 307–309. By 1968 this publication had ceased to mention the Bounder. Some American students of the Soviet Air Force claimed that this bomber was operational as early as 1959; see Ashe Lee, *The Soviet Air Force* (New York: The John Day Company, 1962), p. 138. In 1970,

the Soviet Union still did not have an operational supersonic long-range bomber.

28. *The New York Times,* November 6, 1961. At the same time the Secretary of Defense was attacked for these actions by Senator Henry Jackson (Dem.-Wash.). The reader should keep in mind that Boeing headquarters is located in Seattle, Washington.

29. McNamara, *The Essence of Security,* p. 92.

30. *The New York Times,* April 15, 1964.

31. Noam Chomsky, *American Power and the New Mandarins* (New York: Pantheon, 1969), p. 126.

32. Schlesinger, *A Thousand Days,* pp. 539–548.

33. Seymour Kurtz (ed.), *The New York Times, Encyclopedic Almanac 1970* (New York: *The New York Times,* 1969), pp. 718–719.

34. D. F. Fleming, *The Cold War and Its Origins* (Garden City: Doubleday and Company, 1961), 2:947–948. In spite of Fleming's highly critical analysis of American foreign political and diplomatic policy throughout this large study, he never comes to grips with the fact that the United States maintained strategic nuclear superiority throughout the postwar period. He seems to accept the missile gap as a reality, but it should be remembered that he wrote his study during the height of the missile-gap period.

35. Schlesinger, *A Thousand Days,* p. 345.

36. Some of the best evidence to support this conclusion on the 1961 Berlin crisis can be found in Raymond Garthoff, *Soviet Military Policy* (New York: Praeger, 1966), pp. 115–120; and Myron Rush and Arnold I. Horelick, *Strategic Power and Soviet Foreign Policy* (Chicago: University of Chicago Press, 1966), pp. 108–115.

37. Garthoff, *Soviet Military Policy,* p. 116.

38. Horowitz, *The Free World Colossus,* p. 208, quoting Richard Nixon.

39. Schlesinger, *A Thousand Days,* pp. 252–259.

40. Reported by Fletcher Knebel, "Washington in Crises," *Look,* December 18, 1962.

41. Schlesinger, *A Thousand Days,* p. 315.

42. See Garthoff, *Soviet Military Policy,* p. 120; Schlesinger, *A Thousand Days,* p. 796; and Rush and Horelick, *Strategic Power and Soviet Foreign Policy,* p. 127.

43. *The Communist Bloc and the Western Alliance: The Military Balance, 1962–1963* (London: The Institute for Strategic Studies, 1963), p. 5; *The New York Times,* December 20, 1962; *ibid.,* January 10, 1963.

44. The best examples of this type of thinking can be found in Thomas S. Power (General, United States Air Force, ret.), *Design for Survival* (New York: Coward-McCann, Inc., 1964), p. 21; or Alsop, "The Alternative to Total War," p. 15.

45. There are numerous sources that accept, at least in part, this interpretation. See Allen Dulles, *The Craft of Intelligence* (New York: Harper

& Row, 1963), p. 165; Thomas Wolfe, *Soviet Strategy at the Crossroads* (Cambridge: Harvard University Press, 1964), pp. 23, 33.

46. Garthoff, *Soviet Strategy in the Nuclear Age* (revised) (New York: Praeger, 1962), p. 190. This report indicated that in 1956 the Soviet Union had over 4,000 modern interceptor aircraft for the defense of the Soviet Union.

47. *The New York Times*, October 23, 1962, text of President Kennedy's special address on the Cuban missile crisis.

48. Garthoff, *Soviet Military Policy*, p. 193.

49. Samuel P. Huntington, *The Common Defense: Strategic Programs in National Politics* (New York: Columbia University Press, 1961), p. 120.

50. Garthoff, *Soviet Military Policy*, p. 201.

51. Horelick and Rush, *Strategic Power and Soviet Foreign Policy*, reprint of statement by Premier Khrushchev from *Pravda*, January 17, 1963, p. 177.

52. Jerome Frank, *Sanity and Survival* (New York: Vintage, 1967), quoting a report by the Federation of American Scientists, p. 16.

53. Schlesinger, *A Thousand Days*, pp. 910–912. Among the most prominent early opponents of the Test Ban Treaty were General Thomas D. White (former Air Chief); Admiral Lewis Strauss; Admiral Arthur Radford; General Curtis LeMay; General Thomas Power; Edward Teller (the "father of the H-bomb"); Senator Thomas Dodd (Dem.-Conn.); and Senator Everett Dirksen (Rep.-Ill.).

54. *Ibid.*, p. 910.

55. *Ibid.*, p. 912.

56. *Ibid.*, p. 913.

57. I. F. Stone, "The Test Ban Comedy," *The New York Review* (May 7, 1970), p. 14.

58. *I. F. Stone's Weekly*, September 22, 1969; see also, Stone, "The Test Ban Comedy," p. 21.

59. Alsop, "The Alternative to Total War," p. 17.

60. U.S. Congress, House of Representatives, *Hearings on Military Posture*, p. 430, testimony by Secretary McNamara.

61. *Ibid.*, p. 300.

62. B. H. Liddell Hart, *Deterrent or Defense* (New York: Praeger, 1960), p. 138.

63. Richard J. Barnet and Marcus G. Raskin, *After 20 Years: The Decline of NATO and the Search for a New Policy* (New York: Vintage, 1966), p. 89. This is an excellent study of the development of NATO.

64. McNamara, *The Essence of Security*, p. 43.

65. *The Military Balance, 1968–1969* (London: The Institute for Strategic Studies, 1969), pp. 52–53.

66. McNamara, *The Essence of Security*, pp. 80–81.

67. *Ibid.*, p. 86. The reality of a lack of conventional options and the failure of the Kennedy Administration to develop such an option must have

been realized by Secretary McNamara. Before he left office, he had increased the number of tactical nuclear weapons in Europe by over 100 percent. In 1966, Mr. McNamara claimed that the United States had 7,000 tactical nuclear weapons in Europe (see *The New York Times,* September 24, 1966).

68. *The New York Times,* news article by Henry Tanner, "Rusk Says Pacific Is Flank of NATO," December 16, 1966. Many Europeans rejected the implications of this statement at the time, and the United States government has not mentioned this doctrine since in public.

69. *The New York Times,* Secretary McNamara's Ann Arbor speech, June 17, 1962.

70. Alastair Buchan, "The Future of Western Deterrent Power: A View From the U.K.," *The Bulletin of the Atomic Scientists,* 7:277. In the same issue were articles on the same subject by Raymond Aron (France) and Klaus Knorr (United States).

71. Karl E. Keyer, *The Boston Globe,* November 14, 1968, reprint of a 1968 article in the *New Left Review.* The article covered a report by Richard Neustadt in 1964 on the attitudes of the Labor party toward the MLF.

72. Barnet and Raskin, *After 20 Years,* p. 52.

73. Denis Healey, "What Could Britain Do?" *The New Republic* (December 22, 1962), p. 10.

74. James Warburg, *Germany: Key to Peace* (Cambridge: Harvard University Press, 1953), p. 189; and Marshall Shulman, *Stalin's Foreign Policy Reappraised* (Cambridge: Harvard University Press, 1963), p. 185.

CHAPTER V

1. The Seldon resolution (HR 560) passed the House on September 20, 1965, by a 312–52 roll-call vote. Due to the importance of this shift of attitude on the part of the House of Representatives and its substantial approval by the State Department with minor reservations, part of the resoluton is included here. The resolution stated that "the intervention of international Communism, directly or indirectly, however disguised, in any American state, conflicts with the established policy of the American Republics for the protection of the sovereignty of the peoples of such states and the political independence of their governments. . . ." It expressed the sense of the House that "In any such situation *any one* [emphasis added] or more of the high contracting parties to the Inter-American Treaty of Reciprocal Assistance may . . . take steps to forestall or combat intervention, domination, control, and colonization, in whatever form, by the subversive forces known as international Communism and its agencies in the Western Hemisphere." From *Congressional Quarterly Almanac* (Washington, D.C.: Congressional Quarterly Service, 1965),

21:518. Even a cursory reading of the 1947 Rio Treaty would indicate that both the spirit and letter of this resolution were in direct violation to this treaty.

2. *Public Papers of Lyndon Johnson*, 1966, Vol. II, Public Papers Press of the Presidents (Washington, D.C.: Government Printing Office), p. 1287.

3. *The New York Times*, text of a press conference by Secretary Rusk, October 23, 1967.

4. *The New York Times*, quoting Secretary Rusk, May 25, 1966. It is interesting to note that as of 1966 the United States had not yet made the switch from Russia as "enemy" to China as "enemy"; both were lumped together in spite of their obvious differences toward national "wars of liberation."

5. W. W. Rostow, "The Test: Are We the Tougher?" *The New York Times Magazine* (June 7, 1964), pp. 112–113.

6. Robert McNamara, *The Essence of Security: Reflections in Office* (New York: Harper & Row, 1968), p. 145.

7. *Ibid.*

8. *Ibid.*, pp. 52, 57.

9. *Ibid.*, p. 58.

10. *The New York Times*, November 4, 1969. Some estimates on the total cost of building and maintaining the B-1 over a five-year period have gone as high as $20 billion.

11. *The New York Times*, January 6, 1969. I. F. Stone, *The New York Review*, "The War Machine Under Nixon" (June 2, 1969), p. 10. This writer is indebted to the continuous, excellent analyses of military affairs by I. F. Stone over the years.

12. U.S. Senate, *Hearings*, Department of Defense Appropriations for Fiscal 1969, 90th Cong., 2d sess., Part II, p. 868. At the time of this hearing, the United States Navy was engaged in a major effort to gain additional antisubmarine warfare funds from Congress.

13. *The New York Times*, February 7, 1960.

14. *The Communist Bloc and the Western Alliance: The Military Balance, 1962–1963* (London: The Institute for Strategic Studies, 1963), p. 5; *The New York Times*, December 20, 1962.

15. *The New York Times*, January 10, 1963; *ibid.*, April 15, 1964. Most of these figures represent official Department of Defense figures released in April 1964. It should be noted that by 1964, the B-47 medium-range bomber was being phased out, but that the United States still had fighter-bombers in Europe and on its aircraft carriers that could carry thermonuclear weapons and could reach the Soviet Union.

16. *Ibid.*, July 14, 1966.

17. U.S. Congress, Senate, *Authorization for Military Procurement, Research & Development, Fiscal Year 1969 and Reserve Strength*, 90th Cong., 2d sess., February 2, 1968, testimony by Secretary of Defense McNamara, p. 116.

18. *The Military Balance, 1968–1969*, p. 52.

19. *The New York Times,* May 12, 1969; *The Boston Globe,* news article by George Wilson, January 20, 1969.

20. *The New York Times,* October 29, 1961.

21. *Ibid.,* July 17, 1962.

22. *Ibid.,* November 8, 17, 1963.

23. Marshal V. D. Sokolovsky (ed.), *Military Strategy: Soviet Doctrine and Concepts* (New York: Praeger, 1963), from the Introduction by Raymond Garthoff, p. xix.

24. Raymond Garthoff, *Soviet Military Policy* (New York: Praeger, 1966), p. 57.

25. *Ibid.,* pp. 193–194. It is worth noting here that recently Soviet Marshal I. Krylov challenged this doctrine and stated: "Victory in war, if the imperialists succeed in starting it, will be on the side of world socialism." In the past, statements of this kind by Soviet leaders have reflected insecurity and inferiority, and if this is the case, then the possibility arises that once again the United States has succeeded in frightening the leaders of the Soviet Union. Marshal Krylov's statement appeared in *The New York Times,* September 12, 1969.

26. William Zimmerman, *Soviet Perspectives on International Relations, 1956–1967* (Princeton: Princeton University Press, 1969), pp. 229–230. This quote came from G. Gerasimov, "The First Strike Theory," *International Affairs,* No. 3 (March 1965), pp. 35–39.

27. *Ibid.,* p. 217. This quote came from N. Talenskii, "June 22: Lessons of History," *International Relations,* No. 6 (June 1966), p. 46.

28. Clark Mollenhoff, *The Pentagon: Politics, Profits and Plunder* (New York: G. P. Putnam and Sons, 1967), p. 272.

29. *The New York Times,* March 25, April 18, 1963.

30. *Ibid.,* August 14, 1963.

31. *Ibid.,* news article by Hanson Baldwin, August 15, 1963.

32. Mollenhoff, *The Pentagon,* p. 292.

33. *The New York Times,* Mr. Nixon's "Security Gap" speech, October 25, 1968.

34. *The New York Times,* February 2, 1968.

35. *The Military Balance, 1966–1967,* p. 43.

36. A detailed discussion of the TFX goes far beyond the scope of this study. Suffice it to say that this aircraft has been designated the F-111 and has yet to be successfully tested over a sustained period. It was designed and approved by Secretary McNamara in order to meet the Air Force (and Navy) demand for a new bomber and for tactical air support. Thus far it has been unable to accomplish either of these missions. The interested reader should see R. J. Art, *TFX Decision: McNamara and the Military* (Boston: Little, Brown, 1969).

37. *I. F. Stone's Weekly* (July 14, 1969), p. 4.

38. Abers, *et al., MIRV* (Cambridge: Union of Concerned Scientists, June, 1969); Ralph E. Lapp, "Can SALT Stop MIRV?" *The New York Times Magazine* (February 1, 1970), p. 40.

39. Lapp, "Can SALT Stop MIRV?" p. 14; *The Boston Globe*, news article by Richard H. Stewart, April 14, 1970; *The Boston Globe*, "Letter to the Editor" from S. A. Forter, director of Polaris and Poseidon Guidance, MIT Draper Laboratory, February 25, 1970. Mr. Forter claimed that the United States already has "an operational MIRV capability." Finally, this planned deployment of MIRV was in *The New York Times*, October 28, 1969.

40. Until August 1970 the United States government was very careful in its press releases and stated only that the Soviet Union has tested a "multiple warhead," but it never said that the Soviet Union has tested an *independently targeted warhead*. This includes the Soviet tests up through the series in April 1970. This same point is also contended by Richard H. Stewart in a news article in *The Boston Globe*, April 14, 1970; and by *I. F. Stone's Weekly* (July 14, 1969), p. 4. Evidently, in August 1970, the Soviet Union conducted its first test of an independently targeted warhead. Secretary of Defense Laird claimed that the Soviet Union tested such a weapon and stated that it would be operational by 1972. Mr. Laird contended that this was "a very realistic projection," *The New York Times*, August 27, 1970. In view of past projections of Soviet behavior by the Department of Defense, I would contend that Laird's prediction is open to some doubt as to its accuracy. Before the Soviet MIRV test, Laird had strongly implied that the Soviet Union had MIRV because they possessed a high-thrust missile (the SS-9) to carry such warheads; but this line of reasoning was patent nonsense. MIRV is mainly a question of technology, not thrust. The earlier Atlas and certainly the Titan could launch MIRV if the MIRV technology had been available to put independently targeted warheads on these missiles.

41. Zimmerman, *Soviet Perspectives on International Relations, 1956–1957* (Princeton: Princeton University Press, 1969), pp. 232–234. The Shelepin quote is taken from *Pravda*, June 3, 1966.

42. *The Military Balance, 1968–1969*, p. 52.

43. Abers, *et al.*, *MIRV*; Secretary of Defense Clark Clifford in his posture statement to Congress before leaving office stated that the Soviet Galosh system (around Moscow) "resembles in certain important respects the Nike-Zeus system which we abandoned years ago because of its limited effectiveness." See *I. F. Stone's Weekly* (February 24, 1969).

44. *The New York Times*, October 28, 1969; Lapp, "Can SALT Stop MIRV?" p. 15.

45. Laird, *A House Divided: America's Strategy Gap* (Chicago: Henry Regnery Company, 1962). Nixon and Laird did not disappoint their supporters. On the first round of escalation of the arms race by the new Administration, the Air Force received MIRV, the B-1, and the C5A transport; the Army got Safeguard; and the Navy got Poseidon.

46. *Ibid.*, p. 41.

47. *The New York Times*, Nixon's "Security Gap" speech, October 25, 1968. In this speech, Mr. Nixon said that the Soviet Union had achieved

superiority over the United States in ICBMs, manned bombers, and nuclear submarines.

48. *Washington Newsletter* (Washington, D.C.: Friends Committee on National Legislation, June 1969), quoting Assistant Secretary of Defense Robert Moot, p. 1.

49. *The New York Times,* February 8, 1970; *ibid.,* May 1, 1970.

50. Abers, *et al., MIRV.*

51. *The New York Times,* February 8, 1970.

52. *The New York Times,* July 19, 1969.

53. *Ibid.,* quoting congressional testimony by Secretary of Defense Laird, January 8, 1970.

54. *Ibid.,* May 12, 1969.

55. *The Boston Globe,* quoting congressional testimony by Secretary Laird, June 18, 1969.

56. *The New York Times,* reprint of Secretary Laird's testimony before the Senate Foreign Relations Committee, February 2, 1969. In the spring of 1970, the Chinese placed an earth satellite in orbit, indicating the reality that eventually they will have a limited ICBM capability.

57. Laird, *America's Strategy Gap,* p. 51.

58. Abers, *et al., MIRV.*

59. Donald C. Winston, "Superhard Silos Seen ABM Replacement," *Aviation Week and Space Technology* (May 13, 1968), 88:32.

60. Abers, *et al., MIRV.* Estimates on the costs of this type of intelligence effort run from $2 to $4 billion a year.

61. *I. F. Stone's Weekly,* report of phone conversation with the Atomic Energy Commission, September 22, 1969.

62. Lapp, "The Fear of First Strike," *The New Republic* (June 28, 1969).

63. U.S. Congress, Senate, *Authorization for Military Procurement,* 90th Cong., 2d sess., Feb. 2, 1968, testimony by Secretary of Defense McNamara, p. 116.

64. *Ibid.,* pp. 126–127.

65. McNamara, *The Essence of Security,* p. 54.

66. U.S. Congress, Senate, *Authorization for Military Procurement,* 90th Cong., 2d sess., Feb. 2, 1968, testimony by Secretary of Defense McNamara, p. 118.

Index

ABM-MIRV debate: xvi–xvii, 55, 118–19, 125–46
Advanced Manned Strategic Aircraft (AMSA): 117, 171
Advanced Re-entry Vehicles (ARV): 142, 171
After 20 Years: The Decline of NATO and the Search for a New Policy in Europe: 104
Airborne alert: 51, 73, 171
Aircraft carriers: 6, 8, 10, 12, 52, 68, 73, 115–16, 119, 122, 143, 159, 161, 204
Air Force and Space Digest: 59, 84
Air Force Association: 59
Airlift capacity: 99–100, 115
Air power: 7, 17, 20, 115
Algeria: 31
Alsop, Joseph: 61
Antibomber system. *See* Tallinn Line
Anticontinental ballistic missiles (ABM): xiii, xvi–xvii, 13, 30, 39, 84–86, 97, 105, 115, 118–19, 123–46, 148, 150, 171
Anti-submarine warfare (ASW): 119
Arms race: xiii–xiv, xvi–xviii, 1, 4, 34, 37, 40, 42, 63, 72, 75, 80–87, 93, 96–97, 111, 114, 118–19, 122–24, 126, 129–31, 133, 135–37, 145, 147, 149, 150–51
Army Magazine: 59
Aron, Raymond: 107
Association of the United States Army: 59
Atlas missile: 47, 64, 73, 83, 120, 158–60, 193, 197, 200, 206

Atomic airplane: 84, 86
Atomic cannon: 13, 25, 30
Atomic Energy Commission: 13, 34, 143

Background briefing: 64–65, 172
Baghdad Pact. *See* Central Treaty Organization
Balance of power concept: xiii, 15, 19
Balance of terror: xiii–xiv, xviii, 1, 12–13, 15, 91–95, 118, 124, 136, 141, 148–49, 162
Baldwin, Hanson: 32, 156
Ballistic Missile Early Warning System (BMEWS): 140, 172
Barnet, Richard: 100, 104
Becker, Abraham S.: 192
Berlin: 86–88, 198; blockade, 6, 88
Blackett, P.M.S.: 2
Boeing Aircraft: 60, 133, 201
Bolivia: xv
Bomarc missile: 60, 172
Bomber gap: xvii, 16, 35–38, 43, 49, 84–86, 138, 145
Bombers, Soviet Union: 1, 9, 24, 35, 41–42, 64, 73, 83, 90, 92, 119–22, 129, 132, 143, 154–56, 158–63, 170, 172–73, 200, 207; Ilyushin 28, 90, 172; Mach 2 (Bounder), 84–85, 160, 200; Myasishchev 500 (Bison), 4, 35–36, 38, 49, 120, 155–56, 160, 172; TU-4 (Bull), 3, 154–55, 172; TU-16 (Badger), 120, 155, 160, 172; TU-20 (Bear), 120, 155–56, 160, 172; TU-22 (Blinder), 172

209

Bombers, United States: 3, 6, 47,
    64, 66–67, 73, 83, 85, 90,
    120–22, 132, 143–44, 154–56,
    158–63, 173, 187, 197, 200; B-1,
    13, 70, 115–18, 128–29, 138,
    173, 204, 206; B-29, 2–3, 5, 7,
    154, 173; B-36, 1, 5–11, 13–14,
    154–55, 173; B-47, 9–10, 51,
    120, 154–56, 160, 173, 204;
    B-50A, 13; B-52, 9–10, 12, 36,
    51, 83, 85, 117, 120, 122, 129,
    144, 155–56, 160, 162, 173;
    B-58, 83, 85, 120, 156, 160, 173;
    B-70, 51, 74, 84–85, 117, 127
Braun, Werner von: 61
Buchan, Alistair: 107
Bundy, McGeorge: 89
Byrnes, James F.: 3

C-5A: 99–100, 103, 115–16, 173,
    206
Cambodia: 80, 116
Carrier aircraft: 25, 51–52, 73,
    120, 143, 158, 160–61
Castro, Fidel: xv, 75, 88–89, 92,
    113
Central Intelligence Agency
    (CIA): xv, 45–48, 54, 89, 128,
    174, 195
Central Treaty Organization
    (CENTO): 33, 191
Chemical-biological warfare
    (CBW): 174
China: xv, 6, 19, 31, 72, 75,
    112–16, 135–37, 146, 147,
    149–51; and Russia, 40, 69,
    71–72, 149
Chomsky, Noam: 86
Chrysler Corporation: 60
Circular error probability (CEP):
    174
Civil defense: 82
Clifford, Clark: 206
Collective security: xiv, 19, 22,
    31–34

Commentary: 60
Congo: 103
Constitutional questions: 22, 32
Containment: 3, 19
Counterforce doctrine: 10, 23–24,
    41, 59, 142, 174
Credibility: 23–24, 40, 70–71
Crossbow missile: 118
Cuba: xv, 75, 80, 86, 88–96, 104,
    113; Bay of Pigs, xv, 30, 88–89,
    111; missile crisis, 69, 71–72,
    88, 90–96, 97, 193

Defense: 39–40, 70, 91, 174, 202
Defense Intelligence Agency
    (DIA): 40, 53, 128, 174
DeGaulle, Charles: 29, 98, 104,
    108
Delivery systems: 1, 4, 9, 11, 16,
    23–24, 36, 42, 44, 67–68, 70,
    80–81, 83, 91–92, 94–95, 124,
    129, 147–48, 150, 154–58
Deterrence: 4, 16, 21, 24, 29, 41,
    51, 62, 68, 70–71, 73, 83, 106,
    108, 113, 145–46, 147–48, 151,
    174
Deterrent gap: 66–67, 72, 91
Dirksen, Everett: 202
Disarmament: Soviet Union, 1,
    169; United States, xvi, 1, 5, 14,
    169. See also Strategic Arms
    Limitation Talks
Distant Early Warning System
    (DEWS): 174
Divisions (Army): 16, 19, 26–27,
    30, 69, 70, 78–79, 99, 101, 174,
    190–91, 199, 200
Dodd, Thomas: 202
Dominican Republic: xv, 76, 80,
    105, 111, 114–15
Douglas Aircraft: 60
Draft system: 6
Dulles, Allen: 44, 52
Dulles, John Foster: xv, 18–19,
    21–25, 30–34, 112

Economy: Soviet Union, 42, 52; United States, xiv, 66
Eisenhower, Dwight D.: 17, 18, 20–21, 34–35, 46–47, 51, 54, 60, 62, 68, 76, 78, 88–89, 112, 125, 190, 193, 197, 198
European Defense Command: 32
Explorer I satellite: 175

F-4 (Phantom): 175
F-14: 174
F-111. *See* TFX
Fall-out, radioactive: 12, 96
Fast deployment logistic ships (FDLS): 115–16, 175
First strike: 41, 65, 73, 81–82, 128, 129, 131, 134, 136, 139–40, 142–43, 145–46, 147, 154, 175
Fleming, D.F.: 87, 201
Flexible response: xv, 77–80, 86, 99, 170, 175, 200
Force de frappe: 106, 108, 176
Foreign Affairs: 22
Foreign policy, Soviet Union: xvii–xviii, 37–38, 72
Foreign policy, United States: xiv, xvi, 1–3, 18, 31–34, 47, 69, 75, 77, 80, 98, 103, 111–14, 131, 136–37, 149
Foster, Dr. John S.: 139
Fractional Orbital Bombardment System (FOBS): 140, 175–76
France: 103–4, 106, 108–9

Gaither Report: 46, 193
Galosh system: 132, 176, 206
Garthoff, Raymond: 2, 38
Gates, Thomas: 43, 52–53
Gavin, Gen. James: 17
Gerasimov, G.: 124
Germany: 26–27, 31–33, 40, 103–4, 106, 109; North German Plain, 27, 101. *See also* Berlin
Gilpatrick, Roswell: 65
Goldwater, Barry: 66, 85

Great Britain: 40, 93–94, 104, 106–9
Greece: xv, 103
Ground alert: 67, 73, 176
Guatemala: 88–89

Hardened Operational Missile Site: 134, 142, 146, 176
Healey, Denis: 108
Hentoff, Nat: 151
Ho Chi Minh: xv, 75, 113
Hound Dog missile: 118, 160
A House Divided: America's Strategy Gap: 133, 141
Humanitarian considerations: 8, 9–10, 28–29
Hungarian revolution: 19, 24, 75, 78
Huntington, Samuel: 30
Hydrogen weapons. *See* Thermonuclear weapons

Indochina: 23, 31, 34, 75, 116. *See also* Cambodia; Laos; Vietnam
In-flight refueling: 4, 10, 13, 36, 51, 67, 119, 120, 154–55, 162
Intelligence, United States: 41–57, 85, 87, 89, 128–29, 142–43, 146, 153, 193, 194, 195, 196, 207
Intercontinental ballistic missiles (ICBM): xvii, 10, 12, 38, 39–45, 47–48, 50–53, 55–58, 64, 67–68, 72–73, 83, 91, 106, 120–22, 124, 126–27, 129, 132, 137, 139, 141, 143, 146, 155–64, 176, 193, 195, 200, 207
Intermediate-range ballistic missiles (IRBM): 12–13, 40, 51–52, 60, 68, 71, 90–91, 158, 161–62, 176
Interservice rivalry: xix, 6–10, 20, 30, 35, 45, 58–59
Iraq: xv, 33, 75

Jackson, Henry: 63, 133, 138, 201
Jane's All the World's Aircraft:
  84–85
Johnson, Lyndon B.: 63, 77–79, 87,
  108, 109, 111–12, 118, 126–27,
  134, 199
Johnson doctrine: 112
Jupiter missile: 13, 60, 73, 92–94,
  121, 159–60, 177

Kassem, Gen. Abdul Karim el: xv,
  75
Kennedy, Edward M.: xvii
Kennedy, John F.: xv, 53–54,
  62–66, 68–69, 74–80, 84–93,
  96–97, 111–12, 125, 128, 193,
  198, 199
Khrushchev, Nikita: 38, 42, 48,
  72–73, 87–96, 123–25
Kiloton: 11, 29, 102, 128, 139, 154,
  177
Kissinger, Henry: 29, 113, 197
Knorr, Klaus: 107
Korean War: 1, 13–14, 16–20
Krylov, Marshall I.: 205

Laird, Melvin: xvi–xvii, 133–34,
  136, 138–41, 148, 194, 206
Laos: xv, 80, 116
Lapp, Ralph: 143
Lebanon: 78, 103
LeMay, Gen. Curtis: 36, 85, 182,
  202
Limited war: 3, 16, 19–20, 23–25,
  68–71, 75–76, 78–79, 100
Lockheed Aircraft: 103

McElroy, Neil: 47–50, 194
McMahon, Brian: 26
McNamara, Robert S.: xv, 54,
  64–66, 68, 74–75, 77, 79–83,
  85–86, 90, 97–102, 105, 108–9,
  114, 116–17, 127–28, 137, 139,
  143–45, 163, 198, 199, 203, 205
Malinovsky, Marshall: 123, 125

Manhattan Project: 3
Manned Orbiting Laboratory
  (MOL): 179
Manpower: 2–5, 6, 10, 16–17, 22,
  27–28, 30, 69, 70, 76, 78, 87–88,
  99, 101–3, 169–70, 189, 190–91,
  199–200
Mao Tse-tung: 6, 40, 72
Massive retaliation: xiv–xv, 10–12,
  19–25, 30–32, 68, 77, 80, 98,
  177, 199
Medium range ballistic missiles
  (MRBM): 40, 71, 90–91,
  159–62, 179
Megaton: xiii, 11–12, 72, 119,
  138–39, 142, 144, 177–78
Midas satellite: 178
Middle East: 94
Military-industrial complex: 37, 54,
  59–60, 76, 117, 129, 196–97
Military policy, Soviet Union:
  xviii, 36–38, 41–42, 48, 57–58,
  94–95, 145
Military policy, United States:
  xiv, 6–7, 11–12, 14, 20–22, 39,
  43, 58–59, 64, 66–67, 75–78, 80,
  109, 111, 114, 147–49
Military spending: xvi, 7, 14–15,
  20, 35, 37, 40, 45, 58–59, 61–62,
  66, 69, 76, 78, 81, 86, 88, 99,
  103, 112, 140, 148, 188, 190;
  Soviet Union, 124, 140, 192
Minimum deterrent: 42–43, 59,
  80–81, 178
Minuteman Integrated Command
  and Control System (MICCS):
  178
Minuteman missiles: 47, 68, 74, 83,
  116, 117–18, 120–22, 127, 129,
  134–36, 140–42, 146, 159, 161,
  164, 178, 193; Minuteman I,
  122, 178; Minuteman II, 11,
  121–22, 161, 178; Minuteman
  III, 122, 128, 130, 137, 141–42,
  144, 163, 178

Missile gap: xvii, 16, 35–36, 37, 39–72, 74, 83, 86–87, 116, 123, 127, 138, 140, 145, 156–58, 191, 193, 195, 196, 197, 198, 199, 201
Missile Site Radar (MSR): 180
Missiles, Soviet Union: SS-9, xvii, 16, 39, 123, 135, 138–39, 141, 179, 206; SS-11, 179; SS-13, 179
Moot, Robert: 134
Multilateral nuclear force (MLF): 106–9, 179
Multiple Independent Re-entry Vehicle (MIRV): xvi–xvii, 13, 39, 115–16, 118–19, 122, 123, 125, 127–28, 130–46, 148, 150, 163–64, 179, 206
Multiple Re-entry Vehicle (MRV): 84, 121–22, 126–30, 131, 133, 139, 142, 180
Mutual deterrence: 95
Myths: xvi, xix, 14, 39–40, 54, 61, 64, 66, 74, 86, 99, 102, 109, 134, 137, 147, 151, 199

The Nation: 60
Nationalism: 104
National Military Command System: 180
National security: xiii, xvi, 13–14, 20–21, 52, 59, 62
National Security Council Paper #68 (NSC #68): 1, 14–16, 18, 188
Navaho missile: 180
Navy League: 59
Navy: The Magazine of Sea Power: 59
The New Republic: 60
The New York Times: 60, 64
News media: xix, 50, 53, 60–61, 65
Newsweek: 60
Nicaragua: 89
Nike systems: 30, 60, 180–81; Nike-Ajax, 125, 180; Nike-

Hercules, 60, 125, 180; Nike-X, 13, 30, 126, 181; Nike-Zeus, 30, 84, 125, 132, 180, 206
Nixon, Richard M.: xvii, 63, 77, 84, 89, 109, 118, 126–27, 133, 136–37, 142, 148, 206
North Atlantic Treaty Organization (NATO): 26–33, 40, 69–71, 97–109, 111, 180; forces, 19, 26–28, 32, 70, 76, 99–101; Lisbon Conference, 27–28, 33
Nuclear weapons: xiv, 1–6, 8, 10, 13, 68, 70, 75, 98, 105–6, 109, 148, 154–64; tactical, 25–26, 28–30, 32–33, 70, 98, 102, 110, 203
Nuclear Weapons and Foreign Policy: 29

Pad: 181
Partisan politics: 40, 50, 58, 62–66, 93, 127
Passive Defense: 181
"Peaceful coexistence": 38, 95
Pearl Harbor psychosis: 41
Penkovsky, Col. Oleg V.: 193
Polaris missile: 9–10, 12, 47–48, 64, 68, 73, 74, 83, 107, 113, 117–18, 121–22, 124, 126, 129–30, 132, 135, 140, 144, 150, 158–61, 164, 181, 193, 200; Polaris A-1, 1, 181; Polaris A-2, 10, 181; Polaris A-3, 10, 84, 121, 127, 129, 181
Political-military commitments: 69, 75
Poseidon missile: 12, 116, 118, 127, 130, 137, 141–42, 144, 163–64, 181, 206
Power, Gen. Thomas S.: 51–52, 117, 156, 182, 194, 202
Pravda: 95
Pre-emptive war: 182
Preventive war: 182

Radford, Adm. Arthur W.: 8, 202
Rascal missile: 118
Raskin, Marcus: 100, 104
Regulus missile: 9, 12, 47, 182, 194
Revolutionary movements: 112–16
Rostow, Walt W.: 86, 113
Rusk, Dean: 105, 112–13
Russell, Richard: 119

Safeguard: 13, 30, 116, 118, 134–37, 141, 143, 182, 206
Samos satellite: 183
Saturn rocket: 138
Schlesinger, Arthur, Jr.: 74, 87, 89, 117
Scram missile (SRAM): 118, 184
Second strike counterforce: 12, 65, 68, 77, 80–83, 106, 146, 183
Security gap: xvii, 63, 127, 133, 161, 206
Seldon resolution: 111–12, 203
Sentinel: 13, 30, 115–16, 118, 127, 132, 183
Shelepin, A.N.: 131
Skybolt missile: 106–7, 118, 183
Smith, Rear Adm. Levin: 135
Snark missile: 158, 184, 194
Southeast Asia Treaty Organization (SEATO): 33–34
Soviet Perspectives on International Relations, 1956–1967: 131
Spain: 103
Spartan missile: 184
Sprint missile: 184
Sputnik I: 38, 39, 43, 184
Stalin, Joseph: 38, 95
Stevenson, Adlai: 17
Stockpiles, nuclear: 24, 25–26, 34, 72–73, 96–97, 119–22, 144–45, 154–64
Stone, I.F.: 83, 129–30
Strategic Air Command (SAC): 9–10, 13, 16, 51–52, 73, 106, 182

Strategic Arms Limitation Talks (SALT): 131, 141, 147–49, 182
Strategic bases: 2–3, 5, 9, 43–44, 46, 52, 67, 71, 73, 90, 101, 120, 154, 156, 159, 187, 195
Strategic delivery vehicle: 184
Strauss, Adm. Lewis: 202
Submarine-launched ballistic missile (SLBM): 12, 121, 129, 143, 183
Subsonic Cruise Armed Decoy (SCAD): 183
Suslov, Mikhail: 124
Symington, Stuart: 8, 46–49, 54–57, 63, 187, 194, 196

Tactical nuclear war: 21–22
Tactical nuclear weapons. See Nuclear weapons
Talenskii, Gen. N.: 125
Tallinn Line: 115, 126, 128–29, 132, 138
Targeting: 184; indivisible, 105, 108–9
Taylor, Gen. Maxwell: 78–79, 86
Teller, Edward: 61, 126, 202
Test Ban Treaty: 96, 126, 143, 202
TFX: 115–16, 129, 131, 144, 184, 205
Thermonuclear weapons: 1, 6, 10–14, 34, 75, 143, 147, 154–55, 204
Thor missile: 60, 73, 93–94, 121, 158–60, 184
Thurmond, Strom: 125
Time: 60
Titan missile: 73, 83, 120–21, 138, 159–61, 164, 193, 206; Titan II, 144, 161, 184
Trudeau, Pierre: 105
Truman, Harry S.: xv, 14, 17
"Two and half war" doctrine: 75–76

U-2 reconnaissance: 43–46, 71, 81, 90, 142, 195
The Uncertain Trumpet: 78
Underground nuclear testing: 97, 143, 146
Underseas long-range missile system (ULMS): 39, 136, 138, 185
United States Information Agency (USIA): 185
United States Intelligence Board (USIB): 185
U.S. News & World Report: 60
United States Strike Command: 79–80
Universal Military Training (UMT): 6–8, 185

Vietnam: xv, xviii, 7, 45, 75–76, 79–80, 86–87, 94, 99, 111, 113–15, 125, 129, 131, 189

Wallace, Henry: 5–6
Warsaw Pact: 31, 33, 98–101
Weapons systems: 6–7, 11–12, 37, 39–40, 64, 91, 112, 115–19, 123, 131, 133, 142, 145, 153–64, 185
Western Electric: 60, 125
Western Europe: 4, 26–29, 32–33, 70–71, 77, 88, 98, 100–9
White, Gen. Thomas D.: 202
Wilson, Charles E.: 34
Wilson, Harold: 108

Zimmerman, William: 131